D1559913

MORE THAN MEDICINE

More Than Medicine

A History of the Feminist Women's Health Movement

Jennifer Nelson

NEW YORK UNIVERSITY PRESS

New York and London

NEW YORK UNIVERSITY PRESS
New York and London
www.nyupress.org

References to Internet websites (URLs) were accurate at the time of writing. Neither the author nor New York University Press is responsible for URLs that may have expired or changed since the manuscript was prepared.

Library of Congress Cataloging-in-Publication Data
Nelson, Jennifer, 1967– , author.
More than medicine: a history of the feminist women's health movement / Jennifer Nelson.
p. ; cm. Includes bibliographical references and index.
ISBN 978-0-8147-6277-6 (cloth : alk. paper) — ISBN 978-0-8147-7066-5 (pb : alk. paper)
I. Title.
[DNLM: 1. Women's Health—history—United States. 2. Women's Rights—history—
United States. 3. History, 20th Century—United States. 4. History, 21st Century—
United States. 5. Reproductive Rights—history—United States. WA 11 AA1]
RA564.85
613'.04244—dc23   2014027536

New York University Press books are printed on acid-free paper, and their binding materials are chosen for strength and durability. We strive to use environmentally responsible suppliers and materials to the greatest extent possible in publishing our books.

Manufactured in the United States of America

10 9 8 7 6 5 4 3 2 1

Also available as an ebook

To Jerold Nelson and Nola Sterling

CONTENTS

ACKNOWLEDGMENTS

After finishing my first book, I wondered if I would ever write another. Juggling a young son, single parenthood, and a new job as an assistant professor of women's and gender studies made the task seem daunting. But I kept at it; "slow and steady wins the race," a graduate school mentor once told me. In the end, a book is a labor of love and gets written because it needs to be written. That was the case with this book because in many ways it completes my first book. I had left so much unwritten.

This book could not have been written without a full-year sabbatical supported by the University of Redlands. Redlands also generously granted travel funds to help complete research during that year. I had been working little by little on a series of articles, but the year away from courses and administrative duties as director of the Women's and Gender Studies Program finally allowed me the time to understand the scope of this larger project and how I might complete it as a book.

Several colleagues at the University of Redlands have been consistently supportive by sharing ideas, escaping for coffee or drinks (while sharing ideas), and reading chapters of this book in article form. The three colleagues (and dear friends) who top this list are Dorene Isenberg, Kathleen Feeley, and Priya Jha. Other friends and colleagues at the University of Redlands have motivated me through inspiration: these include Leela MadhavaRau, Kelly Hankin, Karen Derris, Leslie Brody, Emily Culpepper, and Kathy Ogren.

Beatrix Hoffman, another good friend and graduate student comrade at Rutgers, read and commented on several chapters while they were still in article form. Beatrix has also been an inspiration since our graduate school years. I thank her for her intelligence and insight into medical and health care history and politics.

Rickie Solinger has also provided motivation and support over the years. She was one of the readers of the manuscript draft and later revealed that to me. Her critical and constructive comments on the earlier drafts certainly made this book stronger. I also thank the anonymous second reader for her careful comments.

I had the very good fortune to be invited to the summer 2013 conference in Münster, Germany, titled "Refocusing the Modern American Family." I want to thank the organizers of that conference for inviting me and allowing me to present a portion of this book. That conference also afforded me the opportunity to meet Johanna Schoen, who very kindly agreed to take time out of her very busy schedule to read the manuscript in its entirety. Her careful feedback most certainly improved the book, while all errors still remain my own, of course.

I also presented portions of this book at the Sallie Bingham Center for Women's History and Culture while visiting Duke University on a Mary Lily Research Grant. Archivist Laura Micham provided invaluable assistance with the Feminist Women's Health Center Records. Smith College granted me a Margaret Storrs Griers Research Grant, which facilitated travel to and use of the Sophia Smith Collection.

Several activists granted me interviews for this book. I won't name all of them here, but I need to explicitly thank Loretta Ross, scholar and activist for reproductive justice. Loretta's social justice activism and powerful advocacy for women with the least access to reproductive control over their lives has been a true inspiration. She also read the manuscript in its entirety before publication, for which I am also truly grateful.

I also want to thank Denise Spencer for her unfailing administrative support. Her humor and personal strength are terrific bonuses. I couldn't direct the Women's and Gender Studies Program without her.

My students at Redlands have also helped me link teaching to research pursuits. Their curiosity about feminist activism encourages me to believe that feminism is alive and well with young women and men. They want to know more about the activists who preceded them, so we need to keep writing for them. Some of them, Abe Weil and Sami Poindexter, have gone on to graduate school themselves and will soon be writing their own books. A couple more, Sabrina Johnkoff and Rachel Thomas, are well on their way to becoming scholars as well.

My son, Nicholas Pierre, was only three years old when my first book was published. When he was little he would take the book out and find his name in the dedication. At fourteen, he may not care quite as much about getting a mention, but, Nicholas, you should know that your good humor, intelligence, musical ability, and charming shenanigans make every day a joy. I look forward to seeing you flourish as a young man.

Finally, thank you to my partner (and now husband), Thomas Cahraman, for everything you do every day. You make life so much better.

Introduction

The Constitution of the World Health Organization declared in 1948, "Health is a state of complete physical, mental and social well-being and not merely the absence of disease or infirmity."[1] Yet, this idea was not predominant in the United States immediately after World War II. Social movement activists in the United States, including those involved in the civil rights, New Left, and feminist movements, gradually transformed the meaning of health care beyond the medical treatment of individual bodies. This book tells a part of that story. Activists involved in the civil rights, New Left, and feminist movements redefined health to encompass traditional notions of medicine—the curative properties of medicine and the medical technologies utilized by medical practitioners—as well as less conventional ideas about "healthy" social and political environments that promote bodies free of disease as well as whole humans who are able to work productively, raise healthy, educated children, and fashion communities free of violence and social inequalities. Civil rights activists like Dr. H. Jack Geiger, for example, argued that the cure for hunger was both plentiful and nutritious food and the eradication of poverty through community action. He recalled,

> [I]n addition to the medical care we provided, we had food and other models of activism. We repaired housing. We dug protected wells and sanitary privies. We urged people to start vegetable gardens, and a thousand families raised their hands, and that gave us a better idea. With a grant from a foundation as a start-up, we rented 600 acres of good land, land that was sitting empty nearby in the Delta [Mississippi], and organized what we called the North Bolivar County Cooperative Farm, in which the members of those thousand families pooled their labor to grow vegetables instead of cotton, and worked for shares in the crops. We invented a new occupation: nutritional sharecropping.[2]

Geiger and other activists created the collective farm and associated medical clinic to address what they believed were the social and economic bases of both ill health and generational poverty.

Later in the 1960s and early 1970s, feminists generated a women's health movement that shifted the struggle to revolutionize health care to a focus on ending the sex discrimination and gender stereotypes perpetuated in mainstream medical contexts. Like civil rights and New Left movement activists, they transformed the meaning of health and health care, associating them with a revolutionized social landscape in which women had power to control their own life choices. Many feminists argued that women's second-class social status was powerfully reinforced by both legal and medical institutions (and the male legislators and physicians who populated those institutions) that narrowly restricted women's ability to make their own choices about reproductive health care. Thus, feminists made the campaign for legal abortion central to the Women's Liberation movement. They maintained that in order for women to shape their own life paths, including making the choice to enter into sexual relationships without necessarily marrying and starting a family, they would need reproductive autonomy, which required both easily accessible and affordable contraception and legal abortion. Yet, feminists quickly expanded their campaign beyond legal abortion, emphasizing that the medical context in which women acquired health care was also fundamental to women's overall health and social status. During the early years of the movement and as it evolved, women of color feminists pressed the movement to make eradication of socioeconomic barriers to health and reproductive autonomy more central to a feminist political agenda.

Historians of the women's health movement usually begin the story with the Women's Liberation movement of the late 1960s and 1970s.[3] I have chosen to ground my telling of the history of how the women's health movement helped transform ideas about health and health care in the earlier civil rights and New Left movements, which laid the groundwork for feminist women's health activism. Ideas about revolutionizing health care in order to transform social hierarchy were very much a part of both civil rights and New Left activism, and many of the women who became involved in the feminist movement first worked with these prior movements. Of course, many histories of the Women's Liberation movement acknowledge the roots of feminism in the civil rights and New

Left movements, so in that sense my telling is not original.[4] My original contribution is to trace how ideas of revolutionary health care that flourished in the 1960s continued to be developed by Women's Liberation feminists and women of color feminists through the 1990s.

Scholars of U.S. feminism have long been complicating the historical narrative in order to better represent the way race and class affected experiences of sex, gender, and reproduction and transformed political demands forged by feminist activists. This book fits into this burgeoning historiographical tradition, which includes my first book, *Women of Color and the Reproductive Rights Movement* (2003). Since the publication of that book, there has been an explosion of historiography that deepens our understanding of how race and class experiences shaped feminist organizing around health and reproduction and affected women's experiences of reproduction and sexuality.[5]

A broader focus on regional diversity has also expanded our historical understanding of feminist movements of the late twentieth century.[6] With chapters on the women's health movement in both Seattle and Atlanta, this book helps to develop our understanding of the movement beyond what had been a rather narrow focus on the movement in New York City, Boston, and other parts of the northeast of the United States. There is no doubt that women's health activists across the country communicated with each other. They shared texts and, as Michelle Murphy points out in her book, "local stratified histories . . . were joined by road trips on interstate highway systems, telephone networks, mimeographed or photocopied pamphlets, manifestos, and periodicals transmitted through mail."[7] As Murphy's description of these networks suggests, we need to better understand feminist activism outside of major urban centers in the United States, on the West Coast, and in the Northeast, and we need to know more about feminist activism in southern states. I also see a need for deeper understandings of the connections and interactions between United States feminists and feminists fighting for gender and sex equality outside of the United States.[8] These parts of the story will need to await another book and future scholars. In this book I will demonstrate that attention to the relationship between socially embedded inequalities and campaigns for better health has deep roots in social movements in the United States, particularly in the movement for civil rights, the New Left social justice campaigns, and feminism.

Civil Rights and Human Rights

While voting and political rights took center stage in the public civil rights movement, much of what poor African Americans wanted and needed on a daily basis had more to do with basic survival—a prerequisite for political enfranchisement. Movement organizers responded to demands for basic needs made by everyday people living with Jim Crow. The Student Non-Violent Coordinating Committee (SNCC) sponsored community projects and freedom schools to attend to basic needs (like demands for food and clothing) among blacks and to build support for the movement. During Freedom Summer (also known as the Freedom Project), in 1964, the Council of Federated Organizations, a coalition of civil rights groups, appealed to medical professionals to support civil rights workers with medical assistance. The Medical Committee for Human Rights (MCHR), an interracial group of physicians, dentists, nurses, and medical students, responded to this call and sent more than one hundred volunteers to Mississippi for Freedom Summer. Some of these volunteers stayed in Mississippi after the voting rights drive ended in reaction to the dearth of medical care available to poor African Americans.[9]

Dr. Geiger was one of the physicians who stayed in Mississippi to address entrenched medical problems among African Americans (many of whom were not civil rights workers) linked to long-standing racial and class inequities. These inequities were sustained by legal Jim Crow segregation and political disfranchisement as well as interconnected systems of economic deprivation enforced by physical violence, which was sanctioned by a powerful white supremacist social and political hierarchy. Geiger recognized that the accrual of legal civil rights would not guarantee the provision of life necessities for African Americans. While important, legal rights alone would do little to dismantle white supremacy. Alondra Nelson, historian of the Black Panther Party and its work to fight medical discrimination, calls the "gap between civil rights and social benefits" a "citizenship contradiction." She explains in her book that the Black Panther survival programs founded in the 1970s were an "effort to provide resources to poor blacks who formally held civil rights, but who by virtue of their degraded social status and social value lacked social and economic citizenship."[10] MCHR, Geiger, and other civil rights activists who created the first Community Health Center demonstration projects in Boston and Mound Bayou, Mississippi, understood that legal rights were hollow guarantees without economic and social transformation that included the empowerment of the poor to help forge solutions to their own problems.

Geiger, MCHR activists, and many feminists, both international and those in the United States, and particularly many women of color feminists, have understood that health rests on the "social determinants of health—housing, and food, and income and education, and employment, and exposure to environmental danger—and their consequences."[11] Thus, while medicine and technical intervention to cure disease is important, it is also fundamental to transform social formations and hierarchies that disempower certain groups on the basis of race, class, sex, sexual orientation, and/or gender so that all humans have access to the means to live healthy lives. All of the activists I write about in this book recognized that social transformation also required the involvement of individuals and communities in their own health promotion. Geiger wrote of this fundamental lesson learned from his work creating Community Health Centers designed to address complex causes of sickness and health in poor communities. "[C]ommunities of the poor," he explained, "all too often described only in terms of pathology, are in fact rich in potential and amply supplied with bright and creative people. . . . [and] health services which have sanction from the larger society and salience to the communities they serve, have the capacity to attack the root causes of ill health."[12] In other words, Geiger believed the solutions to public health problems often existed within communities themselves.

In 2012 Eli Adashi, Geiger, and Michael Fine wrote an article that appeared in the *New England Journal of Medicine* in which they argued that Community Health Centers will continue to play an important role in the successful implementation of the Affordable Care Act (ACA). The ACA will probably insure thirty-two million more Americans with primary care needs. Many of these people will need more than primary medical care, however. Fortunately, the legacy of the civil rights commitment to addressing problems of social inequality is still embedded in Community Health Center (CHC) delivery of health care. The authors note that "CHCs pride themselves equally on providing community-accountable and culturally competent care aimed at reducing health disparities associated with poverty, race, language, and culture. Indeed, CHCs offer translation, interpretation, and transportation services as well as assistance to patients eligible to apply for Medicaid or the Children's Health Insurance Program (CHIP)."[13] Yet, there is concern that the underwriting of the CHCs by the federal government may also narrow health delivery to medical care (combating disease) with reduced emphasis on social transformation.

Women's Liberation

As CHCs were established across the country to address social inequality as a primary cause of ill health in the 1960s and early '70s, women, both patients and organizers, noticed that many practitioners at free clinics (both federally funded in the CHC network and independent clinics) still failed to treat women's health problems seriously or to listen to women when they asked questions about their bodies. Private physicians and hospital staff could be even worse. Women's health activist Barbara Ehrenreich explains that women were often told by doctors that their concerns were "trivial," and those concerns were dismissed. In 1973, in the widely distributed Women's Liberation pamphlet *Complaints and Disorders*, Ehrenreich and Deirdre English wrote that they understood "medical sexism as a social force helping to shape the options and social roles of all women."[14] One of the ways women's "social roles" were shaped was through definitions of the female body as inherently sick if middle class or sickening to others if working class. In both cases women's bodies were managed, although upper-class women were defined as weak and perpetually infirm whereas working-class and poor women's bodies were represented as vectors of disease.[15]

In response to their personal experiences with medical sexism, women involved in a burgeoning Women's Liberation movement began building clinics—literally with their own hands and tools—devoted to women only and began to define health care delivery for themselves in ways that challenged sexed and gendered hierarchical power relationships, which in turn impacted both medical delivery and health. As historian Judith Houck points out, "At issue . . . was the question of professional authority, not between professional groups, but between health care professionals and laypersons without specialized training."[16] These women began what is now termed the "feminist women's health movement," which continues to be a vibrant part of feminist activism to this day.

Illegal abortion stood as one of the primary challenges confronting early Women's Liberation activists involved with the women's health movement at the end of the 1960s and beginning of the 1970s. Women who acquired abortions in the "illegal era" reported a variety of experiences, from hospital abortions doled out by panels of physicians to illegal but relatively safe procedures performed by physicians and other practitioners to dangerous self-abortions and abortions that led to complications and even death. As abortion gradually became legal and more readily available in the states and, after *Roe v. Wade* in 1973, legal nationally, feminists felt they had achieved a large step towards sexual equality.[17] Yet, they still wanted to ensure that abortions were accessible and provided in safe and caring environments, particularly since the Supreme Court decision directed that abortion needed to be provided by physicians. Many feminists did not trust physicians to provide abortions in a feminist setting. As Ehrenreich and English wrote in 1973 in the context of a feminist narration of the development of a medical profession that marginalized women's traditional healing practices, "women's dependence on doctors . . . may have increased since 1900. Doctors moved in on each sexual or reproductive right as soon as it was liberated: they now control abortion and almost all reliable means of contraception."[18]

Feminists also fought to relieve the stigma associated with abortion. Abortion has been the single most debated and controversial health care necessity demanded by feminists. It has also remained a stigmatized procedure—even among women who have abortions. Feminists involved in campaigns to legalize abortion and those active in the women's health movement in the early years of abortion legality wanted women to understand that abortion was a legitimate choice and also that those who made the choice should not feel ashamed. In order to relieve the stigma, they discussed abortion in consciousness-raising groups and held speakouts where they publicly told stories of their abortions.[19] Campaigners against legal abortion, referred to as the "Pro-Life movement," fought to make abortion both illegal and shameful as they emphasized the importance of fetal "life" separate from the lives and bodies of women. Women who had abortions, they argued, were either victims or careless, promiscuous, and responsible for killing their children. Recently the Pro-Life movement has developed a new strategy that blames women for damaging the health of the fetus through drug use or rejection of court-ordered medical interventions such as cesareans.[20]

Women of Color and Human Rights

While feminists involved in the women's health movement and abortion rights campaigns acknowledged that class and race framed health disparities, and often had an impact on who could access a safe abortion or who was subjected to population control measures like sterilization, their emphasis often rested on discriminations associated with sex, sexual identity, and gender. As Michelle Murphy astutely noted in her book, white women in the movement often focused on sharing knowledge about an "already 'healthy'" body, whereas black feminists "repeatedly characterized the collective biopolitical conditions of black women using the words of the civil rights activist Fannie Lou Hamer . . . 'sick and tired of being sick and tired.'"[21] Women of color involved in early feminist organizing pointed out that race and class profoundly shaped which issues were prioritized in any political mobilization around health, reproduction, and the medicalized body. Issues of sterilization abuse, other medical abuses, poverty, and welfare rights were particularly relevant to women of color and often marginalized by white feminists who focused on abortion legality. Women of color feminists fought for legal abortion as well, and improved access to abortion that included state and federal funding, but, at the same time, they insisted that abortion and reproductive rights be understood as fundamentally linked to a campaign for intersecting social justice demands.[22] For example, Beatrix Hoffman, historian of the history of health care rationing in the United States, writes that the National Welfare Rights Organization, an organization comprised of mostly black female welfare recipients, formed a Health Rights Committee in 1970 and demanded, "Just as all people have welfare rights, we believe they also have health rights." They claimed that health care should be provided on the basis of need as a fundamental right rather than on the basis of income. They also demanded that physicians not refuse Medicaid patients or tolerate experimentation on the poor; they wanted hospitals to include community members on their boards.[23] Many white feminists responded positively to criticisms made by women of color, although not without difficult conversations that often left women of color exhausted and frustrated. The feminist campaigns to protect legal abortion often kept abortion on the front burner of battles for reproductive rights and health care reform.

By the 1990s, women of color feminists in the United States, with historical links to the civil rights movement, New Left social justice campaigns, the welfare rights movement, and the Women's Liberation movement, framed their struggle for reproductive justice for all women as a movement broadly associated with human rights. Loretta Ross, reproductive justice activist and historian of the movement, explained, "[W]omen of color activists demand 'reproductive justice,' which requires the protection of women's human rights to achieve the physical, mental, spiritual, political, economic and social well-being of women and girls."[24] The demands of the reproductive justice movement are not demands for legal "rights" alone. Rather, demands hinge on associations between health promotion and the satisfaction of basic human needs. Ross, Sarah J. Brownlee, Dázon Dixon Diallo, and Luz Rodriguez, members of the SisterSong Collective, a women of color reproductive justice organization, clarified that "rights are born out of needs; rights are legal articulations of claims to meet human needs and protect human freedoms."[25] They further explained why a human rights framework is appropriate to help meet women of color's particular political demands: "The United States lacks a sufficient legal framework that guarantees women of color safe and reliable access to health care; emphasis on individual civil and political rights neglects economic, social and cultural human rights." They went on to point out that human rights ensure that legal rights are accessible: "The human rights framework challenges the United States to demand that economic, social and cultural human rights receive the same level of priority and applicability as that given to civil and political rights."[26]

A human rights discourse moves the conversation beyond the dichotomy of the "right to choose" abortion or carry a pregnancy to term versus the absence of that choice to an understanding that real choices require economic, cultural, and social environments that ensure a real range of options. If a woman has the right to choose an abortion but she cannot afford it and federal Medicaid will not pay for it, does she really have a choice? Her choice might be reduced to self-abortion, going without other necessities to pay for an abortion, or carrying an unwanted pregnancy to term. What happened to her right to choose an abortion? Abortion is legal, but it is not accessible to many women. Women of color involved in the reproductive justice movement insist that government has an obligation to ensure an "environment in which policies, laws, and practices enable women to realize their reproductive rights."[27] A human rights frame insists on providing the "means" for meaningful choices—and real access to rights guaranteed by law.

While women of color activists have allied with the Pro-Choice movement, scholars of the reproductive justice movement point out that reproductive justice is not a "subset of the pro-choice movement." Reproductive rights scholar Kimala Price asserts, "It is a movement in its own right; the difference is that intersectional politics are at the center of its political mission and vision. Intersectional politics informs its political agenda."[28] Rather than building a movement around demands for personal reproductive control, reproductive justice activists' inclusive demands foster a coalitional politics across common interests. Maintaining abortion legality, ensuring abortion access, protecting and strengthening women's access to various forms of birth control, educating and protecting women from reproductive abuses and population control, as well as fighting for an environment in which women can bear and raise healthy wanted children are at the center of the coalitional struggles of the reproductive justice movement. Other issues of importance are ensuring the reproductive rights of incarcerated women, ending gender and sexual violence broadly defined, and promoting sexuality education. Price also points out that reproductive justice organizations have organized with social justice movements not associated with reproductive politics or health care promotion; for example, in California, reproductive justice activists partnered with immigrant and civil rights organizations to defeat initiatives that would restrict access to voting.[29]

Chapter Outline

In the remainder of this book, the first chapter traces the emergence of the Neighborhood Health Center movement from the civil rights and New Left movements. Health care was fundamentally linked to the eradication of poverty and the social inequalities that sustained poverty.

Neighborhood Health Centers built by these campaigns for broad health promotion that advocated economic, social, and legal equalities paved the way for today's Community Health Centers, which are likely to provide important preventive health services as the Affordable Care Act is implemented in coming years. The health care movement that came out of the civil rights movement, however, also linked preventive care to addressing the lack of power held by the poor to craft solutions to their own problems. They believed that community health care could be used to mobilize people to fight against economic and social inequalities that produced cyclical poverty and ill health linked to factors such as lack of access to healthy food, clean drinking water, or adequate housing. Although not the first Americans to insist that the roots of ill health were not linked to disease per se, but rather to deep social inequities associated with race and class, those who built the first Neighborhood Health Centers and other community clinics were certainly successful in redefining health and health promotion in national conversations. Yet, while they made race and class central to these conversations, they did not emphasize inequities associated with sex, sexual identity, or gender.

In chapter 2 I recount the Seattle Women's Liberation movement effort—organized by feminists in the University of Washington YWCA—to ensure that women living in Seattle, and traveling to Seattle from other parts of Washington State, surrounding states, and Canada would receive abortions in a safe and caring context. Washington State voters legalized abortion by referendum in 1970, making it one of a handful of states in the country with legal abortion before *Roe v. Wade*. Although nonresidents of the state could not legally acquire an abortion, many women still traveled for the procedure and needed assistance once they arrived in a strange city. University of Washington YWCA feminists organized the Abortion Birth Control Referral Service (ABCRS) to evaluate physicians willing to perform abortions and provide referrals to out-of-state abortion patients, women from rural parts of the state, and Seattle women who wanted an abortion but didn't know whom to contact to obtain one.

Archival sources for this chapter include patient feedback forms provided by ABCRS to women to assess their abortion experiences. Volunteers at ABCRS used the feedback collected on the forms to appraise the performance of doctors, hospitals, and clinics providing abortions.

Yet, these feedback forms also provide a glimpse into abortion patients' feelings about their abortions. Women were provided with a space on the form to discuss their attitude towards abortion and whether it changed after the procedure. These rich responses resonate with Andrea Smith's findings that Native American women's responses to questions about their position on abortion do not fit neatly into a "pro-life" or "pro-choice" category. Smith's article focuses on the attitudes of Native American women and other women of color.[30] Yet, the ABCRS feedback suggests to me that many women's positions on abortion did not fit into discreet categories. The feedback forms collected by ABCRS did not indicate the racial or ethnic identities of the patients, but given the racial and ethnic demographics of Seattle, it is likely that the majority of women were white. It is imperative that we listen to women's actual "voices" to understand how they felt rather than presume that attitudes towards abortion are neatly dichotomized.

Abortion provision in a safe and caring context was only one of the issues Seattle feminists addressed. University of Washington YWCA feminists also created a feminist women's health clinic—named Aradia after the goddess of the healing arts—to increase women's reproductive and sexual autonomy. In chapter 3 I tell how Women's Liberation activists founded Aradia and ran the women's health center to provide contraceptive care, preventive care such as cancer screening, and information about sex, sexuality, and relationships. Seattle feminists were cognizant of differences among women, particularly on the basis of race and class, that contributed to different health and reproductive care priorities. In order to increase women of color's access to reproductive health care, · YWCA feminists founded a Third World Women's Resource Center and an affiliated clinic. They also coordinated a "Feminism and Racism Rap Group" at Aradia to discuss racism in the Women's Liberation movement. These efforts contradict popular notions that white middle-class feminists focused exclusively on their own political demands without considering the different needs of women of color or poor women. Many white feminists were concerned about race and wanted to address their own racist impulses.

In chapter 4 I turn to the Atlanta Feminist Women's Health Center, which opened in 1977. Like Aradia feminists, founders of the Atlanta Feminist Women's Health Center (FWHC) hoped to provide feminist and woman-controlled health services in a compassionate atmosphere. They provided forums in which women could learn about their bodies and discuss the relationship among body knowledge, sexuality, and health. Yet, unlike Aradia feminists in the first half of the 1970s, Atlanta feminists quickly encountered opposition from the anti-abortion movement. The Atlanta FWHC, like its predecessor the Los Angeles FWHC, provided abortions in addition to comprehensive gynecological services. (Aradia did not provide abortions until the 1980s.) Despite their attention to self-knowledge and collaborations among women to promote understanding of the body and sexuality, health centers associated with the Federation of FWHCs, such as the Atlanta clinic, also instituted a more structured system of providing medical care that included fixed fees and medical hierarchy.

Atlanta FWHC faced significant challenges from the anti-abortion movement just two years after opening their doors. A close look at anti-abortion movement confrontations in Atlanta helps us to better understand why feminists often made abortion central to their politics in the 1980s. It also sheds light on the strategies used by the anti-abortion movement: legislative and direct action tactics. Both legislative techniques and direct action campaigns took a significant toll on the Atlanta FWHC, making abortion provision more expensive and thus absorbing scarce resources that could have been spent on other women's health problems. Threats of clinic bombings, harassment, and arson also had a psychologically draining effect on clinic workers. Still, Atlanta FWHC continued to provide abortions and other health services throughout the most intense periods of anti-abortion protest, including during the 1988 Democratic National Convention. HIV testing, in particular, was an important service offered by Atlanta FWHC. In 1987 they expanded their HIV work with the Women with AIDS Partnership Project, which targeted African American and poor women for testing, education, and health services since these groups of women were most vulnerable to HIV transmission and had less access to comprehensive health services.

The Atlanta FWHC struggled with a perception that they largely served the interests of white women, despite their attention to HIV/AIDS and its impact on women of color. Many women of color believed that the Atlanta FWHC and other majority-white feminist organizations displayed subtle forms of racial bias and even racism. In chapter

5, I spotlight the work of Loretta Ross within the National Organization of Women (NOW) in order to explore conversations about race and racism within majority-white feminist organizations focused on reproductive politics and abortion rights. As the director of Women of Color Programs, Ross worked to build coalitions between NOW and women of color organizations. She met with mixed success but eventually left NOW to work with Byllye Avery and the National Black Women's Health Project. Ross believed that NOW continued to marginalize women of color, so, like other women of color activists interested in issues of women's health and reproductive politics, she shifted her focus to independent women of color organizing.

Chapter 6, the concluding chapter of this book, details the creation of a reproductive justice movement among women of color. Critical of the dominant abortion rights discourse about reproductive "choice," they used human rights as their frame for building a movement that focused on transforming the broad social and economic context that they believed was fundamental to achieving reproductive justice for all women. Distancing themselves from a medical model of health care activism, women of color feminists like Loretta Ross, Dázon Dixon Diallo, and Luz Rodriguez argued that fundamental needs—ending poverty, gaining access to jobs and quality housing, and acquiring education—all needed to be met in order to guarantee reproductive justice. Since poor women and women of color had the most trouble satisfying these most basic needs, they suffered compromised reproductive health and control over their reproductive choices. Thus, like the civil rights activists who insisted that economics and access to food were essential to health, women of color activists also insisted that when people are hungry, health care is food, jobs, and community empowerment. Demands to satisfy basic needs cannot be separated from reproductive politics, because a right to reproductive control is hollow without a right to live free of hunger, racism, and violence and without the dignity that facilitates real choices for one's own future and community.

1

"Medicine May Be the Way We Got in the Door"

Social Justice and Community Health in the Mid-1960s

The women's health movement of the 1970s emerged from an earlier movement focused on the use of health care to end poverty in the United States. Health care reform activists of the 1960s, some of whom joined the feminist health reform movement in the 1970s, forged what they believed would be a comprehensive and community-based solution to poverty eradication. Although the implementation of their solutions was never quite as sweeping as some activists wanted, they successfully garnered substantial federal dollars for their programs. These activists intended to use Neighborhood Health Centers (NHCs) to eradicate poverty and to restructure the social hierarchies that ensured certain groups' "generational poverty" by providing health care, linked social services, and economic supports necessary to ensure individual and community health. As Dr. Harry P. Elam, codirector of Mile Square Health Center in Chicago, asserted, "In the ghetto, you cannot separate the delivery of family medical care from housing problems, underemployment, culture, traditions, and mores. Although this concept is not part of traditional medicine, it is the new focus needed in working with the poor today."[1]

One of the key concepts behind the NHCs was that real health could only be achieved if medical care addressed the socioeconomic roots of ill health. This idea influenced medical delivery and training in subsequent decades. H. Jack Geiger, one of the founders of the movement, noted the extent to which changed definitions of health and health care influenced young medical students and doctors by 1972, less than a decade after the creation of the first NHCs: "Substantial numbers of physicians were trying to learn something about the economics of medical care . . . and trying to bring new kinds of medical care services into being instead of perpetuating the old." He argued that these young physicians understood that there was "something wrong with the social order . . . to the extent it makes large numbers of people sick by condemning them to miserable housing, hunger, joblessness, social and biological and environmental stress."[2] Feminist activists of the 1970s employed a similar concept of comprehensive health care that addressed medical care as well as its social context; they developed a broad critique of gender oppression and sex inequality promoted by medical institutions.

This chapter tells the story of the evolution of the NHCs and these new understandings of health care and what it meant to be healthy. NHCs were founded during a grassroots initiative that partly grew out of the civil rights and New Left movement calls for greater "participatory democracy" among those without access to social power or economic resources. NHCs flourished in the 1960s with support from the Johnson administration's War on Poverty spending linked to the Office of Economic Opportunity (OEO). The successes of the NHCs helped perpetuate the notion that real health required broad socioeconomic solutions that targeted and empowered residents of local neighborhoods and communities. NHC planners chose to locate health centers within neighborhoods because residents of neighborhoods faced similar health and socioeconomic problems. Residents also often shared extended family, ethnic or racial ties, and other social connections that could facilitate finding solutions to these problems. Neighborhood affiliation, perhaps most importantly, also encouraged consumers of health care to feel that the health center belonged to them, particularly if they worked there or sat on a community board for the center. Rather than foster feelings of inferiority or exclusion—as many hospitals had done in the past—NHC organizers wanted to empower community residents to make decisions about their own medical care, theorizing that involvement would encourage people to access health resources more readily.

Ideas about community empowerment in the 1960s originated with the civil rights movement, particularly in organizations such as the Student Non-Violent Coordinating Committee (SNCC), which was led by the seasoned civil rights activist Ella Baker. Baker believed that people should become empowered by being their own leaders.[3] The notion of empowerment also resonated strongly with New Left activists—many of whom had also been involved with SNCC—in organizations such as Students for a Democratic Society (SDS). SDS participants and other New Left activists promoted the idea that people did not need powerful leaders; instead, communities would lead themselves.[4] This perspective, coupled with growing popular-media attention to pockets of persistent poverty in the United States (despite national economic growth), led activists to believe that solutions to poverty depended upon the participation of the powerless in finding structural solutions to persistent and complex community deprivations.[5]

Community leadership and empowerment as central ingredients in the fight to alleviate poverty also had roots in academia. Lloyd Ohlin and Richard Cloward, academics associated with Columbia University and the University of Chicago and funded by an organization called the Gray Areas Project, a cover for the Ford Foundation, applied notions of community empowerment in the new urban northern "ghettos." In 1962, the Gray Areas Project funded Mobilization for Youth on the Lower East Side of New York. In Mobilization for Youth they implemented the concept that community involvement in the process of ending poverty would empower the poor to gain control over their own lives.[6] Ohlin and another sociologist, Richard Boone, developed the idea of community empowerment further in President Kennedy's Committee on Juvenile Delinquency. The idea was eventually repackaged as "community action" as it became central to President Kennedy's staff on the Council of Economic Advisers, a group influenced by the "Keynesian Revolution" and appointed to grapple with the poverty issue. Community action was meant to offer coordinated social services (in one location) within poor neighborhoods to make those services more accessible to people who needed them and also to connect the services and the service providers to the communities. Community action also required that social services be responsive to the needs of the poor as articulated by the poor themselves, not by bureaucrats or social workers living outside of poor communities.[7] As Alice O'Connor writes in her comprehensive treatment of the history of government involvement in antipoverty policy, community action promoted "the notion that the federal government would act as a catalyst for change and local community 'empowerment.'"[8]

Antipoverty programs initiated by the Kennedy administration gained renewed traction under President Johnson with his War on Poverty, although he had reservations about community action. Others in his administration, particularly Richard Boone, along with Sanford

Kravitz, Frederick O'R. Hayes, and Jack Conway of the United Auto Workers,[9] were strong advocates of the idea that the poor needed to be empowered politically as community leaders to *end* poverty. More practically, "maximum feasible participation" among communities targeted for antipoverty federal dollars could also help ensure that southern organizations would not set up all-white antipoverty programs. Sargent Shriver, appointed by Johnson to head the new antipoverty program, institutionalized in 1964 by the Economic Opportunity Act as the Office of Economic Opportunity (OEO), adopted ideas associated with community action but made the idea more palatable to conservatives by marketing it as a way to end a "culture of poverty" and give the poor a "hand up, not a hand out." Tension between the politically radical notion of ending poverty through the empowerment of the urban and mostly black poor and ending a culture of poverty by training the poor in middle-class values continued to haunt antipoverty programs funded by the OEO.[10]

Despite this tension, ideas about empowerment that informed the nationwide system of National Health Centers were often idealistic and grounded in a faith in revolutionary change that found expression in the civil rights movement, New Left organizations like SDS, as well as the anti–Vietnam War and student movements, and the progressive wing of the antipoverty movement linked to the War on Poverty that first coined the phrase "maximum feasible participation."[11] Many of those involved in creating and running the NHCs believed that a comprehensive system of community-based health care delivery had the potential to help end poverty and racial inequality in the nation. Although their achievements fell short of these goals, their efforts are worth recounting and considering as we continue to debate how best to reform health care in the twenty-first century in a society still deeply divided by income, race, ethnicity, and sex.

While NHCs existed across the nation, this chapter focuses on the Tufts-Delta Health Center in Mound Bayou, Mississippi, the first rural comprehensive NHC funded by the Office of Economic Opportunity (OEO).[12] I spotlight the health center in the Delta for several reasons. First, there is a large body of primary evidence on this particular center that has not been closely examined by historians focused on the War on Poverty or health care reform. The Tufts-Delta Health Center in Mound Bayou illustrates how the NHC model worked to "overcome the serious obstacles that have made it difficult for poor people to obtain high quality, personal health care," an explicit goal of those who designed and implemented the program.[13] Second, the Tufts-Delta Health Center stands as an important instance of a successful experiment in health care reform. While all NHCs were not as successful, the model for a transformed system of health and health care delivery worked well in Mound Bayou. Third, the Tufts-Delta Health Center provides an excellent example of grassroots support for health care reform. These grassroots efforts were essential to the health center movement's successes and a core element of the NHC reformers' vision for a new health delivery system. Finally, the Tufts-Delta Health Center sources shed light on how women in the community were fundamental to the health center as both health care providers and patients. Women and children as patients and women as practitioners were significantly impacted by the success of the health center in Mound Bayou.

The Tufts-Delta Health Center had counterparts across the country and supporters of community medicine worked towards health care reform in a variety of forums not necessarily associated with federally funded NHCs. To demonstrate the broad reach of these ideas, I also devote part of this chapter to an examination of a series of early 1970s reform efforts in New York City that were less successful than the federally funded NHCs but illustrate the widespread existence of these ideas. The next chapter on the women's health movement is also illustrative of the broad impact of ideas about social medicine and the potential for transformed health care delivery systems to affect changes in relations of power.

Civil Rights Movement Roots of Health Reform

The civil rights movement of the 1950s also addressed health care, but focused primarily on hospital desegregation, including guaranteeing access to hospitals for black patients and equal medical education for black physicians. Hospitals finally began to desegregate in the southern states after the Fourth Circuit Court of Appeals ruled in 1964 in *Simkins v. Cone* that hospitals that had received federal funds authorized by the Hill-Burton Hospital Construction Act needed to desegregate or return their funds. The Supreme Court affirmed the lower court ruling, which invalidated a "separate-but-equal" provision in the original Hill-Burton

Act from 1946 that permitted segregated medical facilities. Hill-Burton had provided substantial funds for hospital construction nationwide after World War II but also ensured that hospitals in the South would continue to exclude African Americans or segregate them in inferior wards.[14] The *Simkins v. Cone* ruling came on the eve of congressional passage of the Civil Rights Act of 1964, which included the Title VI provision authorizing the Department of Health, Education, and Welfare to withhold public funds from institutions that discriminated on the basis of race.[15] The *Simkins* ruling, the Civil Rights Act of 1964, and the creation of Medicare in 1965 gave the federal government the legal and financial muscle it needed to begin to push for desegregation of medical institutions in the South.[16] Segregated medical care had long contributed to poor health among African Americans in the South. Desegregation was an important first step towards improving health among blacks in these regions. At the same time, hospitals found ways around desegregation by converting to private rooms and refusing hospital privileges to black doctors.[17]

While Congress worked to strengthen the Civil Rights Act to provide the federal government with a mandate to enforce new laws against segregation, grassroots movement activists worked simultaneously to transform a culturally segregated southern society. Jim Crow culture was slow to change even after federal law swept away de jure segregation. Many whites and even blacks in the South were so accustomed to a segregated society that they were loath to break customary barriers between the races that reinforced inequality often as powerfully as did legal barriers.

The Freedom Project, organized for summer 1964 by civil rights groups in Mississippi such as the Student Non-Violent Coordinating Committee (SNCC), was as much an attack on southern Jim Crow culture as it was a drive for voter registration. The project brought hundreds of college students to Mississippi to help register black voters and to lend their support in the often overwhelming and exhausting effort of sustaining southern blacks to keep up the fight against embedded traditions of segregation and racial inequality.[18] Over the course of the summer, white northern college students spread out across Mississippi to teach in freedom schools, register black voters, and lend a hand in local voter registration and community projects sponsored by SNCC and the Congress for Racial Equality (CORE).[19]

Accompanying the college students were groups of professionals, including lawyers, law students, ministers, and physicians who also traveled south but often for shorter terms—sometimes just for a week or two—to lend their professional skills and services to the movement. One group of New York physicians traveled to Mississippi for the 1964 Freedom Project with the Medical Committee for Human Rights (MCHR) to provide first aid and basic medical care for civil rights workers. Some of these physicians also felt it was imperative to help end discriminatory health practices in Mississippi. This perspective formed the basis for extending their medical contributions beyond a single freedom summer.[20]

The mid-1960s was a pivotal time in the civil rights movement as organizations sought strategies to energize activists increasingly skeptical about the movement's continued progress. The 1964 Summer Project was a formidable effort that succeeded in channeling new energy into the movement and also drew national attention to continued southern resistance to civil equality. Organizers gambled correctly that by bringing elite and white northern college students to Mississippi, they would attract new national attention to the fight for racial justice. The deaths of two white middle-class volunteers, Andrew Goodman and Michael Schwerner, and one black Mississippi civil rights worker, James Chaney, brought home the high cost of that gamble; but the deaths of the volunteers also focused the attention of the nation on Mississippi and the movement for racial equality. Beyond the deaths of these three young men, 1964 was a summer of severe violence, including lynchings, beatings, bombings, and the burning of buildings. Yet, activists also began to see a transformation in the political orientation of the movement. With the passage of the Civil Rights Act of 1964 and the Voting Rights Act of 1965, many people around the nation believed the movement had achieved its goals. Of course, blacks in Mississippi knew that racial justice was still not a reality as white Mississippians mounted fierce resistance to the new federal laws. Organizations like SNCC became increasingly frustrated with the promise of integration and nonviolence and, as a result, began to focus on Black Power and Black Nationalism.[21] The turn to Black Power also renewed interest in building black community control over local institutions. Demands for community control originating from civil rights and Black Power activists would be influential on NHC programs funded by the federal government.

According to historian John Dittmer, individuals with two differ-ent sets of goals contributed to MCHR work in Mississippi during the summer of 1964. Their health care work and objectives were compatible but not identical. One group focused on the narrower goal of providing medical and immediate emergency care to the civil rights workers. The other group came to Mississippi with the broader and long-term goal of eradicating and replacing the southern segregated and discriminatory health care system with an egalitarian one. The second group, led by physician activist H. Jack Geiger, who, at the time, was the Mississippi field coordinator for MCHR, extended their stay in Mississippi and in other southern states after other northern civil rights activists returned home. By the fall of 1964, MCHR activists in Mississippi had established projects to provide health care to poor African Americans and had made plans to extend the program nationally. This group of MCHR activists played a pivotal role in the transformation of health care access for the poor in the South and elsewhere in the country in the 1960s.[22]

As the goals of the civil rights movement shifted away from gaining the vote and ending legal segregation in the South, MCHR physicians like Geiger channeled War on Poverty funds into medical clinics in both the North and the South to help empower poor African Americans—and poor Americans in general—to become involved in their own health care improvement and delivery.[23] Experience in the civil rights movement convinced Geiger that any real changes to health care deliv-ery needed to fundamentally involve those who would benefit from the services. Thus, a few members of MCHR, founded to provide limited emergency aid to civil rights workers, expanded their goals when Presi-dent Johnson's War on Poverty offered financial support for the trans-formation of health care delivery to the poor.

The most successful Neighborhood Health Centers brought local residents and patients into the planning and implementation of the institutions from the very beginning. NHCs also employed residents, who often lacked a college education or even basic skills, to take paid positions as day care workers, in after-school programs, as employment counselors, in outreach programs, or as health aides. Thus, residential staff could gain skills and professional experience and even advanced degrees through the NHCs (some of whom partnered with local com-munity colleges) that would help them to direct or manage programs within the NHCs or use their skills to find professional employment elsewhere. The goals of the NHCs surpassed the simple distribution of medical care in commodity form—to be exchanged within a market-place that at best lowered the cost for the poor. Instead, the NHCs were designed to empower the least powerful members of society and to radi-cally transform a deeply anti-egalitarian culture that had embedded in-equalities within institutions such as clinics and hospitals.[24]

The Mound Bayou Community Health Center: Community Medicine Enacted

Although there is not one individual responsible for the creation of Neighborhood Health Centers, Dr. H. Jack Geiger was pivotal to the creation of a nationwide system of NHCs. He promoted a vision of medicine as not only a tool for individual health care but also a tool for community transformation.[25] He also believed that health care could be used to promote empowerment if members of the community were given an "assured role in the design and control of their own health services."[26]

Geiger imported the seeds for the community medical center that was built in Mound Bayou, Mississippi, from Pholela, South Africa, where he had traveled in the 1950s while in medical school on a Rock-efeller Foundation grant to investigate a health center also funded by the Rockefeller Foundation.[27] Physicians Sydney and Emily Kark had created the Pholela Health Center in 1940 to serve a Zulu "tribal re-serve" that suffered from desperate poverty. The emphasis at the clinic was not merely on individual health but on promotion of health for the entire community. Kark and other health care providers at the Pholela Health Center were principally attentive to environmental factors, in-cluding sanitation, as major contributors to the community's ill health. They also focused on nutrition and basic preventive care. Everyone in the community was considered a patient regardless of his or her ability to pay for health services elsewhere. This model was so effective that Kark exported it to other South African health centers, including one at Lamontville, a housing project outside of the city of Durban. Kark and his colleagues targeted communities with "high birth rates, high death rates, a heavy burden of both infections and chronic disease, low levels of employment, low literacy, substandard housing and nutrition, and limited medical care resources."[28]

In June 1964, as a participant in the Mississippi Freedom Project, Geiger connected his experiences with the health centers in South Africa to the desperate poverty he found in the southern United States. Geiger traveled to Mississippi in 1964 as a member of MCHR, taking time off from his new position on the faculty of the Harvard School of Public Health. During his month-long stint as a doctor-activist in Mississippi, Geiger found that African Americans lived in communities that were as poor and unhealthful as those he had seen in the tribal reserves of South Africa. He wrote that he "took a long, close look at the poverty, misery, and deprivation—and, inevitably, illness—in the sharecropper shacks and small-town black slums of the Deep South." He recognized that he didn't have to go to Africa to find poverty, as "there was a third world in the United States."[29] Geiger and several other physicians from MCHR, together with the Delta Ministry, a Mississippi civil rights organization, committed to staying in Mississippi once the Freedom Project had ended to continue providing health services for poor African Americans.[30] Several nurses also came south for the Freedom Project and remained in Mississippi to provide health care services with MCHR and the Delta Ministry. One of these, Phyllis Cunningham, discovered that local people were often more comfortable interacting with a nurse than with a doctor. Cunningham provided pregnancy-prevention classes, helped organize for better sanitation facilities and regular garbage pick-up, and helped provide vaccinations.[31]

At a November 1964 meeting, after several months of experience in ad hoc health care provision among the poor black residents of the state, Jack Geiger, Count Gibson, and other MCHR and Delta Ministry physicians brainstormed about the best way to institutionalize better health services for poor African Americans in Mississippi.[32] Geiger argued that a community health center modeled on the one he visited in South Africa in Pholela was the best way to make a long-term commitment to solving comprehensive health problems associated with poverty among African American Delta residents.[33] He also argued that the health center should be controlled by the local blacks who would use it. Gibson, fellow activist and chair of Preventive Medicine at Tufts University Medical School, and John Hatch, professor and civil rights volunteer in Mississippi, decided to partner with Geiger. Gibson offered Tufts Medical School as a sponsor for the project and proffered Geiger a full professorship at Tufts so he could oversee the health center project. Hatch was the only African American of the three. He was born in Kentucky and, as he explained in an interview, had grown up in Arkansas on "the banks of the Mississippi River" and often earned money "working in the fields picking cotton."[34] Hatch trained as a social worker at Atlanta University and joined the faculty as an assistant professor of preventive medicine at Tufts Medical School.[35]

Geiger, Gibson, and Hatch approached the Office of Economic Opportunity (OEO) at the end of 1964 with their idea to implement one Neighborhood Health Center each in an urban and in a rural location, both of which would be administered by the Tufts Medical School. The first grant from OEO—funded with Community Action Program (CAP) dollars—paid for the two comprehensive centers. The Tufts professors, the Delta Ministry, and the handful of doctors and nurses from MCHR still in Mississippi after the Freedom Project ended benefited from growing support for health care reform within Johnson's War on Poverty agencies.[36]

Important contextual factors made the mid-1960s a good time to promote radical health reform. For example, Johnson's landslide victory in 1964 provided the final momentum needed to amend the Social Security Act to support health insurance for those over the age of sixty-five in the form of Medicare and health benefits for families on public assistance with Medicaid. The Watts riots, which occurred in August of 1965, also bolstered arguments that community failure along with poverty contributed to urban violence and ill health in large cities. Many pundits and policy makers began to call for community solutions to poverty and the social ills that accompanied it.[37]

Due to these gathering pressures to improve health care for the poor, the OEO developed the NHC program presented to them by Geiger and the others at Tufts. The details of the program emerged from negotiations for funding. The first two health centers were planned for Columbia Point, a housing project in Boston, which provided living space for six thousand people in twenty-six high-rise buildings, and in Mound Bayou, Mississippi, a small African American town in Bolivar County, which covered a 500-square-mile rural area. Applications to the OEO for health centers in the South Bronx, Los Angeles, Chicago, and Denver quickly followed on the heels of the Tufts projects. OEO funded all of these health centers as demonstration projects in 1965.[38]

Quickly, the NHC program funded comprehensive health service grants across the country with significant congressional support fostered by Senator Edward Kennedy of Massachusetts, who had been impressed by the demonstration project at Columbia Point. Amendments to Economic Opportunity Act legislation authorized in 1966 and 1967 established the OEO Comprehensive Health Services Program to fund a national network of more than 150 health centers. Between 1965 and 1971, OEO spent $308 million and the Department of Health, Education, and Welfare (HEW) spent $110 million on the health center program, which served nearly one million people.[39] The Economic Opportunity Act legislation from 1966 stipulated that the program should make health services "readily accessible to low-income residents . . . furnished in a manner most responsive to their needs and with their participation and wherever possible . . . combined with, or included within, arrangements for providing employment, education, social, or other assistance needed by the families and individuals served." By 1971, three-quarters of the centers were in urban areas, filling a gaping hole in urban health care as medical practitioners followed the wealth to the suburbs. Rural centers included a project on an Indian reservation in Minnesota and others near migratory labor camps in California.[40]

The health centers served the poor for free and the "near poor" on a sliding scale, with about one-half of the employees of the centers coming from the patient population.[41] Although Geiger and others initially conceived of the NHC as free health care institutions designed to provide no-cost services to everyone within a community regardless of income, a 1967 congressional amendment to the Economic Opportunity Act linked NHC full-pay eligibility standards to Medicaid eligibility standards. Patients with incomes above the Medicaid standard could use the NHCs on a sliding scale.[42] One economist who studied the NHCs argued that the most successful programs offered health services to everyone within a geographic area in which the vast majority of residents qualified for free medical care. In those cases there was little stigma for using the program.[43]

Planners of the NHC programs also intended to provide continuity of health services for poor patients accustomed to fragmented emergency room or outpatient public health department care. As one evaluator of the NHC program explained, NHCs responded to "fragmented care that was the only care available to many poor persons" in the form of "chest x-rays, immunizations, VD control . . . the fragments in the outpatient departments with their multiple specialty clinics, the fragments of provider continuity, the fragments with regard to the availability of services at selected times during the day or week, fragments with regard to the family, i.e., clinics that served only children, adults, [or] women" as was provided by most health departments and hospitals nationwide. Rather, the NHCs promised "comprehensive care in the concept of the neighborhood health center . . . implemented by providing single-system access to a full array of primary health care for families." Most health centers housed a general practitioner, a pediatrician, and an obstetrician under one roof. The reasoning behind this design was to prevent patients from shuttling among disconnected clinics or specialty medical departments without any rational coordination of care.[44] Specialists not housed at the NHCs were available by referral. Comprehensive services at health centers often included drug treatment, mental health services, food assistance, and dental care.[45] Legal aid and job placement services were also common.[46]

The two fundamental goals of most health centers were to provide medical care to poor Americans and to involve those using the facilities in the creation and management of those same health care programs.[47] The OEO required health centers receiving funding to link to a local organization in order to bring community residents into the health centers as more than patients. These organizations took a variety of forms: "county medical societies, medical schools, state departments of public health, private group practices, hospitals, and a variety of community organizations."[48] The centers were most often administered by community hospitals, medical schools, and health corporations, but they were also run by health departments and nonprofit groups on occasion.[49] Consumers of health center services were sometimes the force behind the creation of particular centers.[50] Private and community foundations also supported NHCs that had not garnered OEO support. The Student Health Organization (SHO), a national organization of politically progressive medical students, created free clinics grounded in the counterculture movement and the student-populated New Left movement. Nationalist organizations such as the Black Panthers, the Young Lords, and the Brown Berets also provided linked health and community services that emphasized the relationship between health and broad social justice inequalities. The Black Panthers, in particular, with strong institutional ties to federal War on Poverty programs, criticized government-sponsored health centers for not doing enough to involve and empower the communities they served.[51] In the next decade feminist organizations would foster their own related health reform movement that would support health clinics across the nation dedicated to providing services to women.[52]

OEO guidelines for federally funded NHCs required that at minimum 50 percent of membership on NHC "advisory boards" be comprised of local individuals or one-third of a full-fledged "governing board."[53] By 1971 residents were approximately 50 percent of the staff at the centers.[54] Some NHCs pursued community hiring vigorously; the South Bronx NHC composed a staff almost entirely of community residents.[55]

The community board requirement and practice of hiring from within communities generated the most controversy for the Neighborhood Health Centers. Physicians and other professionals sometimes worried that local residents and consumers would demand unrealistic services or try to make medical decisions as part of an NHC community board. Although there is no evidence that community boards tried to influence medical decisions, they often made nonmedical recommendations. For example, one majority-black community board required physicians and nurses to live in the same neighborhood as the health center. They successfully recruited white physicians to move into the community and work at the health center. Another majority-Latino community required staff, including physicians, to learn Spanish in a six-month period. They only hired staff willing to commit themselves to this task. Community groups often argued for particular hours of service that made sense for a neighborhood or made geographical recommendations to project directors. Often residents demanded that medical staff be more sensitive to the community.[56]

Residents also often became involved in NHCs as community health aide workers responsible for outreach to poor families unaccustomed to using preventive medical services. Some of these aides trained to provide basic home health services for patients unable to travel to an NHC. Professional development for these community workers also became part of most NHCs.[57] Thomas Bryan, director of OEO's Office of Health Affairs, which administered the NHC program, explained that "[i]f the professionals can continue the dialogue, they generally discover that the consumers and providers become more sophisticated and a better working relationship will evolve." Dr. Joyce Lashof, codirector of Mile Square Community Health Center in Chicago and director of community medicine at Presbyterian St. Luke's Hospital, also supported community input. She argued, "You absolutely must be able to come through with solutions to honest demands made by the poor . . . you must also be completely honest about what you can and can't do, giving the people all of the alternatives and choices available to them." Thus, a real collaboration would ideally evolve between community members and administrators and physicians delivering the services. Training for both community workers and employees from outside of the community made collaboration easier. Both had to learn to bridge differences and negotiate priorities.[58]

According to Geiger, any real community collaboration required an evolutionary process that did not always succeed. Community control did not just happen because medical administrators said they wanted it. Geiger observed that many NHCs first established anodyne community boards without any real authority and usually comprised of the most vocal or visible community leaders. He recounted that one community board member in Boston accused administrators of failing to foster any real collaboration. This man shouted out at a meeting, "I understand your idea of this partnership! I'll provide the illnesses and you'll run the services, just like always."[59] Over time the community board sometimes agitated for more concrete influence over the NHC policy. Geiger argued that this agitation often caused conflict between professional administrators and community leaders with different priorities for the health center. Understandably, health professionals were not accustomed to negotiating their programs and budget choices with nonprofessional community members. Through negotiation of this conflict, actual collaboration sometimes occurred between community boards and medical administrators. If a community board established bona fide shared power with administrators through conflict and negotiation, they also had to build real ties of communication with community residents. Again, this took sustained commitment and time.[60] Hatch warned that community involvement should not be assumed because residents joined community boards. He asserted, "Simply to place poor people on boards-of-health programs and expect them to compete with the traditional health care industry was foolhardy." He continued, noting that residents "frequently lacked certain technical knowledge and resources, as well as the accepted language with which to gain even more."[61]

Geiger noted that the Columbia Point Health Center tried to build community support—and failed—with a series of living-room meetings about health care and related needs. But after about forty to fifty such meetings, the community organizing stopped. Without sustained efforts, connection with the community and its needs never solidified. Other accounts suggest that violence and crime in the housing project also made community organizing difficult.[62]

In Mound Bayou, by contrast, community action staff spent an entire year meeting with local residents "in their homes, in churches, in schools, and on the plantations in the area. This staff literally knocked on the door of every house in northern Bolivar County inhabited by a black family." They found that community members wanted more than health care; they needed basic services, jobs, better housing and education, and food. Residents expressed these needs over the course of two years of community organizing as staff integrated residents into the process of creating the health center at the foundation.[63]

Before they ever commenced knocking on doors and meeting with residents to define the health problems that residents most wanted to solve, in 1965, Tufts-Delta Health Center founders carefully chose to locate the rural center in the Delta community of Mound Bayou, an all-black community of twelve thousand residents. Freedman Isaiah T. Montgomery had founded the town in 1887. Since its founding, Mound Bayou had been unique in the Mississippi Delta. Emmett J. Stringer, a leader with the National Association of Colored People (NAACP) at the time of the 1954 *Brown v. Board of Education* Supreme Court decision, recalled that growing up in Mound Bayou had a very positive influence on his development as a "race man." He said, "Having seen black mayors and bankers and policemen and superintendents of schools, I knew what was possible, probable, and desirable."[64]

Yet, Bolivar County had long been one of the poorest counties in the nation. The infant mortality rate of the county was astoundingly high in the 1960s, as about sixty per one thousand infants died before their first year. (As a point of comparison, that is about the same rate as Burundi, Uzbekistan, and Nepal; the U.S. rate is currently 6.8 per thousand.) Because the county was ensconced in the Delta region of Mississippi, sharecropping and cotton production had employed most of the residents of Bolivar County. But as cotton production mechanized, sharecropping families found themselves without any means to earn even a meager livelihood to replace that provided by cotton. The residents of Mound Bayou lived on a median annual income of less than one thousand dollars per family per year and unemployment was over 50 percent. By all accounts they also suffered from a severe lack of health care as well as poor sanitation, including unprotected water supplies—70 percent of the population was without a clean water supply. Mound Bayou residents suffered from a lack of adequate shelter as well—some 90 percent of dwellings were unfit for human habitation.[65]

During the initial stages of planning for the center, Hatch explained that he first met with community leaders to defuse opposition to the project, particularly among local medical practitioners who were fearful that the health center would displace their practices. To ensure community involvement at the very beginning of the project, staff immediately incorporated local people into the organization by recruiting residents of Mound Bayou and Bolivar County to go door to door to community homes, churches, and schools to discuss community health needs. They also established a relationship with a local bank, explaining that "the center's million-dollar annual funding and cash flow would be deposited in whichever bank opened a branch in a Black community, hired residents as tellers instead of janitors, and engaged in fair mortgage loan practices."[66]

From these efforts, ten local health associations organized into the North Bolivar Health Council and eventually became the advisory committee and then governing board for the health center. The North Bolivar County Health Council was comprised entirely of African American community residents, all of whom were also patients at the health center. The Health Council defined priority health needs to be addressed by the neighborhood health center. Priority health requirements ranged from improving access to drinking water in a community where people had to walk three miles for clean water to health care for children and the elderly.[67] Community members subsequently used political experience gained with the health center to enter local politics—six local organizers that Hatch had recruited to find out about community needs went on to become mayors of majority-black towns in Bolivar County.[68]

Community members involved in the Tufts-Delta Health Center in Mound Bayou expanded the traditional idea of health care by pointing out that food, jobs, and housing were fundamental requirements for good health. For Geiger and other organizers of the project, it was essential to the success of the clinic that local people identify health needs for themselves. That these were not always traditional health care needs was not a problem. The clinic founders believed that they needed to respond to health priorities set by the people themselves. By 1969, seven thousand black residents of Bolivar County were involved in implementing the services sponsored by the health center; these were services the community members had created for themselves.[69] Geiger and Hatch also recruited black professionals from the North to work at the health center. These included ten doctors and ten nurses. Social workers, a psychologist, a nutritionist, and a pharmacist also counted among professionals recruited for the clinic.[70]

By attending to what local people needed and wanted, the community clinic improved upon more traditional medical provision in the rural South. Geiger wrote that the Mound Bayou clinic provided "the essentials of community-oriented primary care: family health care teams; community organization and health education; the training of local workers as family health aides, environmental sanitarians and health [educators]."[71] Health care was much more than seeing a doctor for these community activists. It meant building a strong economic and social base for the community as a whole.[72] A community vegetable garden became a 500-acre farm cooperative founded by twelve hundred families in the region. "The first farm co-op of people who don't own farms," Geiger commented, recognizing that the vast majority of Delta residents lived on some of the most fertile land in the country but did not produce food for their own consumption. The sharecropping system, shaped by deeply embedded and historical race and class hierarchies, fostered malnutrition in rural areas where local blacks had almost no control over what was grown on the land they inhabited.[73] In just over seven months the co-op grew more than one million pounds of food and effectively ended hunger in the area. As Geiger explained, the most important lesson to impart from the Mound Bayou experiment to health care providers is that "your [health care providers'] priorities may not be those of the people you are concerned with. . . . People who are concerned with survival are going to be worried about that before they are concerned with tuberculosis. They are going to be concerned with housing, jobs, food, their kids, and some other things."[74]

Survival had become a problem for Mound Bayou residents, particularly since mechanization of the cotton crop in the mid-1960s had left thousands of families with no income. A 1967 investigation of the health of Delta residents by a team of six physicians discovered widespread malnutrition among children. They reported that children were dying from hunger and malnutrition. Geiger wrote prescriptions for food to make the point that traditional public health measures such as vaccinations or treatment for tuberculosis would not cure a fundamental need for basic socioeconomic measures like food and income.[75] Geiger explained,

We decided that we had to do something more than keep treating individual cases, and that the first problem we had to address was the lack of food. And so, in the absence of any other resources, whenever we saw a child suffering this combination of infection and malnutrition, we wrote prescriptions for food: RX, so much milk, so much meat, so many vegetables, so many eggs.[76]

By the 1950s and 1960s, as the cotton harvest mechanized and white plantation owners saw no economic incentive to provide medical care to blacks who lived on their land, many rural African Americans went completely without health services. Often they were also without basic transportation to get to a hospital even if one existed in their area.[77] Few white physicians worked in rural black areas, and those who did often neglected poor blacks. Hospitals that did serve African Americans often turned poor patients away if they could not pay. Health insurance was largely unavailable to blacks because of discrimination by national insurance companies like Metropolitan Life.[78] As Dr. L. C. Dorsey, civil rights activist and director of the Delta Health Center in the 1980s, explained, "Doctors on plantations found conditions so unpleasant they didn't want to treat African Americans. Health care for poor people and poor black people was dependent on home remedies."[79] Richard Hall, a reporter writing about the Tufts-Delta Health Center for *Life Magazine*, observed that "blacks in the farm country outside Mound Bayou were accustomed to suffering the pain of their illnesses until it became unbearable. Only then would they seek out a doctor. Even if the doctor was black, he would frequently demand payment on the spot; and if he was white, he would often only talk to them across a desk, asking questions."[80]

There were other social factors stemming from within black communities that also prevented Delta residents from accessing institutionalized health care even when it was available. Many African Americans expressed a strong personal preference for local black midwives over white physicians. This preference can be traced to the legacy of African American health care practices under slavery, which included traditions of lay midwifery among African American women. These traditions continued into the Jim Crow period as black lay midwives still provided the greater part of health care for their communities. The preference for midwifery eroded, however, in the first half of the twentieth century through a complex interaction between public health policymakers and physicians who barred local black midwives from medical practice through a system of regulation and forced "retirement."[81] African Americans in the Delta were also frequently distrustful of white health care providers because of medical abuses—particularly after the Tuskegee (Alabama) experiment (1932–1972) and the high incidence of involuntary sterilizations were revealed in the 1970s. Distrust of the medical establishment needed to be addressed before African Americans would use mainstream health services in large numbers. As Dorsey recalled of the 1970s, "Black people were suffering from the aftershocks of the Tuskegee experiment. . . . I thought it would be real easy to tell people, 'you got free health care,' but many of them were suspicious."[82]

The Tufts-Delta Health Center example suggests that African Americans needed to become agents in the provision of their own health care in order for health care institutions serving poor blacks in the South to succeed and thrive. Community control over the health center fostered a strong sense of personal and community empowerment by providing the opportunity for local blacks to command the expansion of an entire nexus of interrelated health care services that embraced reproductive health, sanitation, housing, education, and jobs. Empowerment was linked to the creation of services by and for the community, rather than the imposition of services on the community by outsiders. Local blacks also capitalized on their involvement with the health center and with professionals who could help residents pursue opportunities well beyond the area served by the health center. An office of education associated with the health center helped local students apply to college and professional schools and helped find information on scholarships. Health center staff also offered high school equivalency and college preparatory classes at night; these courses were accredited by the local junior college. Many of those who attended and/or worked at the health center went on to further their education elsewhere. Staff could also get college credit by working at the health center if they attended the local junior college. Others trained for professional jobs at the health center, such as librarian or medical technician or assistant. A few local employees went on to attend nursing or medical school or to receive training in social work, psychology, pharmacy, or education. The health center fostered an environment that encouraged the pursuit of opportunities that had been markedly absent from black Delta residents' lives up to that point.[83]

Other health centers in the country also brought community members into the medical field by training local residents for jobs. The Mile Square clinic in Chicago employed 271 people, three-fourths of whom were local community members. Many of these local employees, as at the Tufts-Delta Health Center, were outreach workers hired to accompany a public health nurse on home visits. These visits were meant to attract "people into the center who have difficulty understanding the importance of health care." Training for community members cost money, of course, but architects of the community health centers believed that community involvement as well as jobs that provided a living wage fostered community health.[84] In addition to explaining the need for health care to a local population often suspicious of health care professionals, outreach workers followed up on missed appointments, helped people understand the importance of nutrition to good health, and aided people with problems associated with their welfare payments, housing, or jobs.[85] An OEO-supported health center in King City, California, that served both local residents and migrant farm workers trained locals to perform x-rays and provide physical therapy as well as make home visits in Spanish.[86] One example from the Martin Luther King Health Center in New York City, another OEO-supported NHC, illustrates the importance of these home visits. A five-year-old boy had appeared at the clinic six times in three months. A home visit revealed that his "apartment lacked heat, and the winter cold was leaking through a broken window. The family was also short on food and badly needed more clothing." The outreach worker helped the family access welfare benefits that allowed them to heat the apartment and acquire clothing and food. The five-year-old could only get well after these linked socioeconomic problems were addressed.[87]

L. C. Dorsey's interaction with the Tufts-Delta Health Center characterizes the way community involvement in medical services could help transform black people's lives beyond simple health care provision. Dorsey was born on a plantation to sharecropper parents (just a generation removed from slavery) in Washington County, Mississippi. She grew up in neighboring LeFleur County without access to education or job experience except in the fields. As a teenager, Dorsey was a social activist—a self-described civil rights field worker—with the Council of Federated Organizations (COFO), the Student Non-Violent Coordinating Committee (SNCC), and the Southern Christian Leadership Conference (SCLC). From her involvement in the civil rights movement, Dorsey heard about the Tufts-Delta Health Center and was intrigued because she wanted to become engaged with a project that would be sustainable. She explained that she was hired to be a part of community health outreach with the center. Dorsey said that Hatch, at that time director of Community Health Action at the health center, wanted to give young people the chance to grow in the organization, so he hired people with little or no work experience. After a stint as an outreach worker, Dorsey applied to direct the community farm associated with the clinic. Again, she noted she had no direct experience but was given an opportunity to develop her skills on the job. She also utilized Delta Health Center resources to complete her high school degree at the local junior college. Dorsey made clear that her work with the health center helped build her confidence to the point that she eventually completed an undergraduate degree and attended SUNY–Stony Brook for her master's in social work. Ultimately she completed a Ph.D. at Howard University and returned to the center to become its executive director in 1988.[88]

Women's Health as Community Health

Most of the Delta Health Center patients were women, children, and elderly men. Because there was so little paid labor in the South, many young men migrated north to find jobs. As a result of out-migration, the average age of Mound Bayou residents was only about fifteen, and the average age of men in the community was about fifty. Thus, women and their children were very much at the center of the Tufts-Delta Health Center as both patients and workers.[89] With so many women in the community, obstetrics and gynecology were essential specialties at the health center. Two white nurse midwives, one a nun, Sister Mary Stella Simpson and Asa Johansen, both of whom joined the clinic when it opened its doors, worked in this area. The first black female obstetrician/gynecologist to practice in Mississippi, Dr. Helen Barnes, also joined the center in 1968. When she arrived at Mound Bayou, Barnes set up a program for prenatal care, delivery, and contraceptive services, which was supported after 1970 with federal funds accessed through Title X, a program created by President Nixon to promote family planning among poor Americans.[90] Born in Mississippi, Barnes left the state to earn her medical degree from Howard University in Washington, D.C. After completing her degree in 1958, she returned to the Mississippi Delta to serve as one of the few black general practitioners in Greenwood, Mississippi. After returning north to complete specialty training in ob/gyn at Kings County Hospital in Brooklyn, New York, she joined the Tufts-Delta Health Center.[91]

Like Geiger, Barnes discovered that she could not address ob/gyn or infant health without addressing the larger environmental and economic problems that faced the community. She recalled that "[w]e had pediatrics and surgery, but I also found out that it's all right to practice medicine and deal with sanitation and feed people—write a prescription for evaporated milk." Like general health care, ob/gyn and child health services could not be limited to a narrow conception of medical practice. The practice of medicine necessarily expanded to embrace the environmental and economic problems of the Mississippi Delta community. Barnes continued, "I delivered babies every day and night and the nurse midwives would go out to do home visits—take care of the babies. [They would] look and see if they had screens and if they didn't have running water they would dig a well."[92] Thelma Walker, another local woman who became the nursing administrator of the center, added,

> If a nurse in the field finds a home without a water supply—out go the sanitarians and engineers with the well digger invented right here at the center and they dig a well in half a day. If there are rats coming through the floor, we exterminate them. A leaking roof? A privy falling down? Out go workers from the center—and these are local people—to patch the roof, build a new privy or take healthy adults tools from the tool bank we've scrounged together so they can make their own repairs.[93]

Although there was no women's health movement in the late 1960s in the Mississippi Delta, there is abundant evidence that African American women responded positively to contraceptives when they were made available. Dr. Barnes distributed large numbers of contraceptives as part of a "community health improvement program" supported by federal Title X funds. Barnes explained that for many poor black women this was the first time they had been introduced to any kind of family planning. For the most part, she said, black women responded positively to the idea that they could limit their fertility using contraceptive measures. She recalled that women also came to her to be sterilized when they felt they no longer wanted to bear children. Her experience confirms other evidence that African American women wanted to control their fertility as long as they could do so voluntarily.[94]

At the same time, in the late 1960s and early 1970s, many African Americans, including black nationalists, but also other women of color involved in the burgeoning feminist movement, viewed federally sponsored birth control programs as genocidal. Federally funded family planning programs were often associated with ideas of population reduction and population control rather than with notions of creating healthy communities. Black women were particularly adamant that birth control and abortion services needed to be accompanied by other health services that allowed black families to bear and raise the healthy children they wanted. Any emphasis on population reduction as a solution to black poverty made many African Americans very suspicious.[95] As Barnes noted when I asked her why blacks were suspicious of white health care providers, "You can get kicked in the shins only so many times before you decide that you won't trust people anymore."[96] To gain the trust of the populations she worked with, Barnes explained, we "set up a clinic in a community and found more people came to the clinic year after year after year because we were proving to the community that we were going to stay and do what we said."[97]

A collection of letters written by Sister Mary Stella Simpson, one of the nurse-midwives at the health center, serves as a particularly cogent example of how women's health, in particular, needed to be understood in conjunction with larger community development needs. Simpson arrived in Mississippi in 1966 from Evansville, Indiana, to work at the newly opened Tufts-Delta Health Center. As a native of rural Arkansas, Simpson said she "was very familiar with the kind of poverty . . . found in Mound Bayou." Her letters paint a vivid picture of health conditions in the Mississippi Delta during this decade.[98]

One letter reveals the extent to which African Americans in the Mississippi Delta lacked even basic necessities such as adequate shelter, food, and clothing, as well as health care and access to education. Simpson recognized these as fundamental problems that could not be separated from her primary task of providing ob/gyn care to poor women:

> Today was my first day for [obstetrical/gynecological] home visits. . . . On the very first one I had to come back to town to get milk for a baby. He had finished his last bottle. It had gotten really cold, and the 14 people in that family all congregate in one room around a small wood burning stove. . . . The children were all barefoot, therefore could not go to school. The parents have no way of getting shoes for them since they have no income. . . . A year old baby was very ill with diarrhea—had it for a week. So I had to drive the mother with all [her] six children to the clinic. The baby had to be hospitalized.[99]

Another letter addresses the extraordinarily poor housing occupied by Delta blacks. Again, inadequate housing could not be separated from this particular woman's need for prenatal health care: "I went into a shack out in the country on one [prenatal] visit today and found the ceiling was made of cardboard boxes and the roof leaked badly. What a sight! I did the prenatal exam as if this situation was a daily occurrence. 'We'll fix it when it stops raining,' says the husband as he sweeps the water through the cracks in the floor."[100]

Through her letters written home to her convent sisters, Simpson provided a detailed overview of the persistent and basic health problems confronted by poor African Americans who were served by the Tufts-Delta Health Center. Within days of her arrival in the Mississippi Delta, Simpson learned that ob/gyn care was not enough to improve the lives of the women and children she treated. As Geiger, Barnes, and Dorsey had already noted, Simpson found she needed to supply a nexus of health-related provisions such as sanitation, screens on windows to keep out mosquitoes, other basic housing improvements, clothing, nutritional information, and food. Without these vital necessities, the provision of any medical care was pointless.

Persistent problems recorded by Simpson were lack of food, inadequate housing, and inadequate clothing. In one letter she wrote, "The last place I visited was the worst ever. The dogs and cats go and come through the walls. It has a high front porch and an old washtub turned upside down for a step. I was scared stiff to put my weight on it, but it held. The mother and daughter were wearing rags held together by safety pins and had bare feet."[101] The lack of basic necessities was so profound that health center doctors, nurses, and nurse-midwives spent much of their time helping to find food and clothing, repairing screens on windows, pressuring landowners to provide better housing, and connecting patients with welfare entitlements such as food stamps.

Women also lacked basic health education, which compromised the health of their children. Although the health center midwives and physicians, including Sister Simpson, encouraged breast-feeding, few women practiced it at first. Physicians at Taborian, the local Mound Bayou hospital, discouraged women from breast-feeding their children because it was viewed as inconvenient (for the hospital that had to support women who breast fed, not the mothers). This left women with no option but to use formula, which required sterilizing bottles and finding clean water. Many homes on the white-owned plantations and farms in the region were without running water or a well. Some families used water from the bayou until it dried up in the summer. Some families were also without the means to boil water, and women often didn't know that a bottle could not be rinsed and reused. Because of the unsanitary conditions, diarrhea was a constant problem with small children and a major cause of high infant mortality.[102] In 1960 the infant mortality rate in the Mississippi Delta was more than sixty deaths per thousand live births, more than twice as high as the rate for white infants.[103] This number was high compared to the national rate in 1960, which was about forty-five deaths per thousand live births for African Americans and just over twenty for whites.[104] Although both white and black infant mortality rates had been declining nationally since the mid-1930s, the rate of decline for whites was 3.2 percent annually, while the rate of decline for black infants was only 2.6 percent.[105]

The women in Mound Bayou and Bolivar County were very enthusiastic about breast-feeding when they were given some coaching as to how to get started. Because good mothering is something that is learned and not instinctual or natural, new mothers often need to be shown how to breast-feed their babies.[106] In the past it had been grandmothers and granny midwives who passed on this knowledge. Without these traditional health care providers, however, women in Mound Bayou and surrounding areas were often reliant on indifferent physicians and hospital staff until the community health center was founded. Sister Simpson recorded the enthusiasm for breast-feeding she witnessed among the new mothers:

> We are starting to see results! Breast-feeding is beginning to catch on. We hope to have 100 percent of our mothers feeding this way before the year ends. The mothers enjoy our classes, too. . . . We seem never to get away from the sessions. . . . They ask questions for hours! One of the mothers delivered her baby only a few days before the next class. She didn't want to miss it, so we went to her home and had class there![107]

For many of these patients, a home visit by a nurse midwife was their first encounter with a health care practitioner. Many women had received no prenatal care, had never had any sort of medical care as children, and bore their children without any medical support. Simpson also confirmed reports that some doctors and hospitals in the area that did provide care for poor African Americans were neglectful or inadequate for the population. In one case a mother took her eleven-month-old baby who would not eat to two different doctors before Simpson helped her to get her child into a hospital that would feed the child intravenously. Another eighteen-year-old patient was due to deliver her baby any day and was experiencing preeclampsia. She had extremely high blood pressure and protein in her urine but had never been seen by a doctor.[108] Simpson also cared for a child whose hand had been badly burned and had healed into a fist—the child would remain handicapped for the rest of his life—because a neighborhood doctor had neglected to treat him properly.[109] Sister Simpson noted that prenatal care was seldom the only care given on a home visit: "If the prenatal exam was the only thing we did on such visits, they wouldn't take so long. But when you see a little one with impetigo all over his face, you doctor him, which often takes a couple of hours."[110] As Barnes pointed out, "Medicine may be the way we got in the door, but medicine is not the number one priority. There are other priorities; food is number one and then a way to make a living."[111]

The clinic quickly transformed the health of the population in the area served by the Tufts-Delta Health Center. When the health center was first established, clinic services and training for community staff occurred in an abandoned church parsonage and in an old movie theater in town. After about a year, a new building was built for the health center. By 1969, the clinic was able to provide hospital equipment to patients in their homes when there was not enough space to accommodate patient needs at Taborian Hospital. Prenatal and postnatal care both improved dramatically over the first three years of the clinic's existence. Thelma Walker reported that ob/gyn care had grown from almost nothing in the community to a majority of pregnant patients attending the clinic before the fifth month of their pregnancies. Many of these women gave birth at the hospital or at home with a midwife in attendance and were then followed up postpartum at the health center. Their infants received care from birth onward. Walker explained that it was "quite a change . . . from the days when Sister Mary Stella and Aase [sic] Johansen saw many mothers for the first time when they were ready to deliver—or had delivered—and from the time when little children never saw a doctor or nurse until they were so ill with diarrhea or pneumonia that it was touch and go to save them." She added that the "two nurse midwives have helped in prenatal care or delivery of over 100 babies, all living, many at home, but now most mothers have their babies in the hospital."[112]

Ultimately, the Tufts-Delta Health Center brought poor blacks in the Delta the basic and preventive health services that were available to most other populations in the United States by 1966. But, unlike with most other hospitals serving the poor in America, in Mound Bayou the poor provided and managed much of their own health care. The health center workers, many of whom were drawn from the local population, including the physicians, nurses, nurse-midwives, nurse's aides, sanitarians, and health outreach educators, were black women and men who understood that African Americans had been neglected and even abused by mainstream (white Jim Crow) health provision in the past. Clinic staff also addressed fundamental factors contributing to ill health that few people had defined previously as legitimate to a medical practice. As Dorsey explained, they had created a farm collective because they believed that the only antidote to hunger was food.[113] Lack of food was a medical issue. Geiger pointed to the success of the cooperative farm: "In one spring and summer, they have grown one million pounds of food, enough to end hunger in Northern Bolivar County—sweet potatoes, Irish potatoes, snap beans, butter beans, black-eyed peas, collard greens and the like."[114]

Were the NHCs Successful? Mostly Praised . . . but Also Criticized

Certainly, a targeted focus on funding and delivery of health care to address health problems among the poor helped bring medicine to many patients never before seen by a doctor. But money is not the only reason many of these programs succeeded. According to Dr. Joseph English, administrator at HEW, some federal health care programs were unsuccessful despite targeted funds. He noted that $.5 billion a year went to fund grant-in-aid programs in Alaska but did little to alleviate the vast health problems in that state, particularly among Native Americans, who had some of the highest infant mortality rates and lowest life expectancy rates in the country.[115] A Neighborhood Health Center in Lowndes County, Alabama, however, did demonstrate success. Lowndes County, like the Mississippi Delta, was one of the poorest places in the country, without jobs, adequate roads, housing, or any health facilities before the NHC arrived in 1969. The county had only three doctors, one of whom was in his late seventies. Locals involved with the health center pointed out some fundamental barriers to fostering good health among the poor that needed to be addressed for the health center to succeed. These included locating health facilities within walking distance or providing transportation to clinics. Also, showers and coin-operated laundries needed to be in health stations so that individuals could wash before seeing a doctor. Many local individuals felt too embarrassed to see a doctor without having washed and in dirty clothes. Other innovative solutions included a sewing machine at a clinic so that those without adequate clothing could make or repair clothes; another station included a kitchen in which nutrition demonstrations took place. As in Mound Bayou, patients were seen by nurses and community health workers recruited from the area.[116]

The difference between Alaska and Lowndes County or Mound Bayou was not money flowing from the federal government into a poor and underdeveloped region. Rather, the difference was in the design of the programs delivering the services. A comprehensive set of linked services planned by those who needed the services achieved good health for the individual and the community because locals were involved in communicating which barriers stood in the way of their health. Some of these barriers were transportation, cleanliness, housing, jobs, education, sanitation, and nutrition, and they all needed attention. Sometimes that attention needed to be tailored to a particular community.

On the whole, NHCs were praised for successfully achieving their goal of providing comprehensive health care and linked services to the poor in the 1960s and early 1970s. They received broad congressional support and continued funding even after other War on Poverty programs were dismantled during the Nixon administration. A 1971 evaluation of the NHCs also indicated that they had a significant impact on ideas about health care delivery within the medical establishment. The NHCs were part of a shift in health care delivery towards preventive services, which gained support as government agencies looked for ways to cut public health spending while also promoting a healthier population. The American Public Health Association, for example, began to increase its emphasis on primary care as the successes of NHCs became known. Although at first skeptical, the American Medical Association and state and local medical societies also expressed support for the NHCs. One public health evaluator writing about the health centers noted that papers delivered at AMA meetings "have all but endorsed the concept [of

NHCs] and have at least moved to the point where they encourage local medical societies to participate in, if not endorse, these projects."[117] Evaluators also found that NHCs were cost effective. On the whole they were no more costly dollar for dollar than health care provided in the private sphere, but they also offered an array of services not available among private providers.[118] The employment of locals in the programs also helped support the argument that the NHCs offered economic advantages. With 50 percent of their staff from the neighborhoods they served, NHC supporters asserted that money spent on the health centers was a positive economic stimulus. The majority of projects provided curricular support as well as on-the-job training to foster local employment. These additional services incurred a cost, but arguably one that returned to the community as people became trained for employment.[119]

The NHCs, however, were not without their critics. Some black rural and urban physicians worried that the NHCs would compete for Medicaid patients.[120] A 1971 exchange between Dr. Jack Geiger and Dr. Howard Levy of the Medical Committee for Human Rights (MCHR) and Health-PAC, a New York–based New Left think tank devoted to medical issues, also revealed a negative view of NHCs from a progressive point of view. This exchange revealed that not all members of the movement to transform health care in the United States were happy with the NHCs. Levy critically assessed the NHCs as tools of a medical establishment bent on collecting Office of Economic Opportunity federal dollars without delivering any real transformation of health care or empowerment of the poor.

Much of the debate over the value of OEO-supported NHCs within the movement for health care reform played itself out within the ranks of the Medical Committee for Human Rights and the Student Health Organization (SHO), an off-shoot of MCHR. In the late 1960s MCHR's political critique of entrenched establishment medical services mainly targeted the American Medical Association (AMA). They argued that the AMA represented self-interested physicians who viewed medicine as a privilege for the poor rather than a right. Dr. Fitzhugh Mullan, a member of the Chicago MCHR and SHO, wrote, "[T]o many of us the American Medical Association symbolized medicine in America. Overfed and complacent, the 'voice' of organized medicine seemed completely self-serving and ignorant of the health problems that beset many

Americans."[121] Forcing the AMA to end racial segregation stood as one of MCHR's great successes. They pressed the AMA to expel medical societies that based their membership on racial or religious criteria.[122]

The AMA, however, was not their only target. Younger MCHR members, who often joined the SHO to distinguish themselves from the older MCHR, became active in health care politics in the late 1960s, after the organization had shifted away from its origins in the civil rights movement, the Mississippi Summer Project, and desegregation. The younger participants often identified as part of the counterculture and the New Left.[123] Levy allied with this cohort of young medical activists. Geiger, alternatively, represented the older incarnation of health reform activists who cut their teeth during the civil rights movement of the mid-1960s and were more amenable to building partnerships among the federal government, established medical institutions, and local grassroots organizers.

Despite their differences, Levy and Geiger both wrote from the perspective of wanting to transform what they viewed as a bloated and ineffective medical delivery system that did not serve poor patients very well. Levy believed, however, that Geiger's OEO-funded NHCs only made the problem worse by accepting federal "establishment" dollars and imposing an outsider's will on local health care providers by tying medical schools and medical elites to local projects. Indeed, over 50 percent of U.S. medical schools had been involved in NHC projects. Levy wrote, "It could have been predicted that the interests of the professionals, not those of the people, would be preserved when medical schools, chasing after the federal dollar, boldly stepped into poor communities, medicine bag in hand."[124] Levy argued that real experiments in community-driven health care delivery could be found in Black Power clinics provided by nationalist organizations like the Black Panthers. He also pointed to a critical letter that appeared in a local newspaper written by a Mound Bayou Black Power group opposed to the Tufts sponsorship of the health center in Mound Bayou as evidence that local blacks were not supportive of the project. Levy suggested that architects of the Tufts-Delta Health Center, Geiger in particular, never intended to alter medical delivery significantly. Rather, he believed that because the health center existed with federal financial support and medical professional guidance from mostly northern and white outsiders, it could not represent any real transformation of health care for the poor. It was, instead, an example of a kind of medical missionary project that maintained hierarchies between medical administrators/physicians and the recipients of care.[125]

Geiger countered that the Black Power group in question was never representative of the Mound Bayou community. They were an assertive group of activists who put themselves in the public eye, but that in no way gave them community authority. Instead, he noted, the Tufts-Delta Health Center had acquired "a staff and leadership that is 95 percent Black and 90 percent from Mississippi—and those percentages include the professionals: Black health center director, business administrator, clinical director, director of environmental health, social services director, director of training, and Black youth organization leaders, southern pharmacists, nurses, sanitarians, data processors, and three of the nine physicians."[126] He continued, asserting that locals "organized themselves first at the grassroots. . . . And in any given month 700 people come to a health association meeting."[127]

Yet, in his critique, Levy raised important questions about the OEO-sponsored health centers and the extent to which they could provide real transformed medical care that not only expanded resources for the poor but also fundamentally changed the way health care was provided. Levy and Geiger fundamentally disagreed as to whether OEO-supported NHCs were the proper vehicles with which to meet their common goal of creating a health care system that no longer neglected the poor. Levy argued that storefront clinics provided by groups such as the Black Panthers were better examples of reformed medical institutions for the poor because they were funded and operated entirely by black activists (although they also employed white medical professionals from entities such as the Student Health Organization to staff the clinics and raised funds from white supporters). Geiger countered that these were patchwork measures and largely ineffective because their services were so limited. He believed that federal dollars linked to an established medical delivery system in the form of hospitals, medical schools, and local departments of public health could be effectively utilized by local health care activists to achieve successful health reform.[128]

Most examples of SHO and Black Panther attempts to provide clinics for the poor confirmed Geiger's criticism. White volunteer medical students who provided medical support in SHO summer clinics (which did receive federal funding through OEO) in poor urban areas and in

Black Panther clinics often found that they garnered important educational experience from the work but did little to change overall medical provision for the poor over the long term. A handful of clinics set up to serve the poor, most of which, like SHO summer projects, were also temporary, could do little to transform a medical system that failed to provide for the vast majority of the poor in both large cities and rural areas. SHO disbanded its summer clinics for this reason.[129]

Levy's critique of and Geiger's support for the NHCs hinged on what each meant by community control and, specifically, on whether they thought that involvement by the "establishment" negated community control. Did community control necessarily mean that white professionals and federal government support needed to be absent? Geiger insisted that the resources held by professionals, medical institutions, and the federal government were too important to reject. He wrote,

> Those resources are now in the hands of the Establishment institutions—the medical schools, the hospitals, and all the rest—and the funds needed to operate significant health services must come from the Establishment, and overwhelmingly from government itself. These institutions are now, properly, damned for their racism, their elitism, their indifference and hostility to the community, their exploitation of the poor, and their refusal to surrender even a share of their control to community/worker groups. But what if they are dragged by the community, or the workers, or the students, or some of their own professional staff into primary care and community action and community service, or even into new institution-building under community control?[130]

If we accept Geiger's assertion that the presence of the "established" medical and government institutions did not by itself hinder health care reform, did NHC programs foster a real partnership between traditional medical providers—public health administrators and medical professionals—and local poor residents and consumers of health care? From evidence gathered for this chapter, it appears that the NHCs were mostly successful in their effort to involve the community in health care provision and in broadening the meaning of health care to better serve the real needs of poor communities. Much of that success, however, depended on the quality of community representation at a particular

NHC. Hatch explained that "OEO programs were often planned as if poor communities had no viable social organization or structure. They, therefore, sought to create or sanction new structures rather than to conduct a hard analysis of what existed."[131] Geiger agreed with Hatch that community boards at NHCs could be more or less effective depending on how representative board members were of the local community. He also asserted that community worker involvement in the clinics impacted medical delivery much more consistently than did community board involvement. Medical administrators reported that community outreach workers often improved contact with and design of programs within a particular neighborhood. Maximum utilization of community workers, however, also required adequate training programs, which were also unevenly operated at the NHCs. In some of the more successful cases community workers were hired for nonprofessional reasons such as their intimate knowledge of the community but then trained to develop new career tracks as professional employees.[132]

It is very unlikely that such an extensive program of health care reform could have been realized or even minimally successful without strong federal support and some help from established medical providers.[133] The program required both money and medical expertise ideally guided by those who most needed and used the resources but provided in dialogue with professionals who delivered technical expertise and services at least until community workers could be trained to deliver services themselves. A less successful (and much smaller) health care reform effort that took place in 1970 at Lincoln Hospital in the South Bronx, a city-run hospital affiliated with Albert Einstein College of Medicine, lacked both federal funding and broad support from the medical administration. This program's failure to establish lasting reform lends credence to Geiger's contention that some federal money and established medical involvement combined with community input were essential for any real sustained change.[134]

Community Control at Lincoln Hospital in the South Bronx

The Young Lords, a Puerto Rican nationalist organization modeled on the Black Panthers, and other activists involved in Lincoln Hospital reform efforts shared the goal of improving health care and its delivery within a very poor community with multiple socioeconomic problems that deeply affected health. Originally built in the nineteenth century for use by freedmen and women, Lincoln Hospital had long been considered a woefully inadequate provider of charity health care to the mostly black and Puerto Rican residents of the South Bronx. The vast majority of health care providers and staff at the hospital lived outside of the South Bronx community and did not use the services of the hospital. By the mid-1960s, senior medical staff, residents, and interns at Lincoln hospital became affiliated with Einstein Medical College, improving medical care somewhat. Yet, Einstein interns and residents who rotated through Lincoln to complete their medical educations had little commitment to the Bronx community. Most of the young physicians were foreigners from outside of the United States who were only in the South Bronx to complete their medical training. Furthermore, senior medical staff on the faculty at Einstein Medical College utilized the patient population for instructional purposes, often with little or no sense of obligation to the community.[135]

Health care reform activists contended that community involvement needed to be at the center of any reform effort so that Lincoln would serve the health needs of the neighborhood. Several protests occurring in 1969 and 1970 involving Young Lords and other community activists attempted to further this goal. In the first protest in July 1969, community workers who had been trained in the Lincoln Community Mental Health Program, operated out of an old nurses' residence at the hospital, focused on gaining more community-worker control over the mental health services. Cleo Silvers, one of the staff protesters, recalled that they demanded that psychologists consider that poor people had very specific problems that could not be solved by middle-class theories of mental health care. They called for the replacement of the two psychiatrists who ran the program and for a section of the mental health unit to be devoted to welfare and poverty issues. After the protest, the worker/activists became more involved with local branches of the Young Lords and Black Panther Party.[136]

Nearly a year later, in June 1970, at Lincoln Hospital, another health care reform effort was organized by workers, community members, and the Young Lords. This diverse group called themselves Think Lincoln. To illustrate their demands for more community-worker input into hospital policy and health care delivery, activists staffed community complaint tables in the lobby of Lincoln Hospital. As health care reform activist Fitzhugh Mullan recalled, "The complaint table was intended as a mechanism to stimulate patient awareness and participation in the hospital." Those who staffed the complaint table handed out leaflets and pamphlets about patient rights and community control. Signs placed near the table instructed patients to lodge grievances about the hospital at the table because it was "their hospital."[137]

In many instances, activists at the table also acted as patient advocates. If a patient had complaints or questions that could be directed to a particular staff member, a Think Lincoln activist would help the patient locate the appropriate hospital worker or workers to find the answers. Often this system worked and many patients viewed the complaint table as a positive benefit that demonstrated that someone in the community cared enough to improve patient care at Lincoln. Some staff, however, felt under attack by the Think Lincoln activists in their advocacy role because they believed their competence was being questioned. At the same time, many staff supported the action as a way to better serve patients in an extremely busy and understaffed hospital.[138]

A group of pediatric interns and residents, including Mullan, who had specifically chosen to work at Lincoln because of his interest in community medicine, also sided with the Think Lincoln activists. This group of doctors called themselves "the Lincoln Collective" and had connections with both the Medical Committee for Human Rights and the Student Health Organization. The newly minted doctors believed the Think Lincoln tables provided "a ready-made political role for the Collective" as supporters of Think Lincoln community activists.[139]

Despite support from this group of young doctors on the house staff at Lincoln, as protests escalated at the hospital, divisions increased between the activists demanding greater community control and the Lincoln Hospital administrators who had no real interest in significant reform of health care delivery or community control. Without significant collaboration among health care activists, hospital administrators, and federal or local funds to sustain innovative programs, reform efforts were short-lived at Lincoln. Yet, even short-lived reforms revealed a demand for community involvement in health care delivery in the South Bronx that, while not met, clearly carried weight among young activist physicians, members of the Young Lords, and other members of the South Bronx community. One Young Lord, Carl Pastor, wrote of community control in the Young Lords publication *Palante*, "Who can better determine what's best for ourselves than us? If this is the richest country in the world, why is it that this country is 13th in the world in health care?"[140] I focus in some detail on these particular protests at Lincoln Hospital to demonstrate that demands for community control thrived outside of programs sponsored by established physician-reformers and their federal government supporters at the NHCs.

The first escalation of demands for reform at Lincoln Hospital occurred on July 14, 1970, about a month after the complaint tables appeared in the lobby. This action involved a Young Lords' occupation of the Nurses' Residence (a former nursing school) at Lincoln Hospital for about twelve hours. The Lords presented a list of demands to hospital administrators that included a community preventive medicine program, a free day care center for children of patients and workers, a free breakfast program for children, health education classes, and a community-worker board to run the hospital. They asked why tuberculosis and lead poisoning, both preventable, were rampant in the South Bronx, suggesting that the hospital neglected the basic health needs of the community. The occupation garnered attention immediately. Police surrounded the building and the press flocked to publicize the Young Lords' challenge to a city-run institution.[141] Mullan recalled the experience from the perspective of a physician who lent his support to the community takeover: "The Nurses' Residence suddenly had the fantastic, intoxicating air of a liberated zone. . . . The Lords had risen up and were telling the stories of the women and children waiting endlessly in the clinic, the old folks dying for lack of a Cardiac care unit, the humiliations of the Emergency Room, the flies, the pain, the degradation."[142] After police ordered the building cleared, the Young Lords and the interns and residents supporting the action left the building peacefully, ending the occupation. Permanent staff physicians at Lincoln generally did not support the action.[143]

The next protest and escalation of tension between activists and hospital administrators and permanent staff physicians revolved around the abortion death of a young Puerto Rican woman, Carmen Rodriguez. Sometime in the middle of July, Rodriguez had been diagnosed with rheumatic heart disease and told that a pregnancy endangered her life. She was scheduled for an elective abortion at the end of the month. The gynecologist performed a saline abortion, which ended tragically. Rodriguez died four days after the procedure. When it became apparent that a mistake might have been made at the level of medical malpractice, Think Lincoln and the Young Lords began to publicize the death as a murder. In response to the uproar over the Rodriguez death, Lincoln Hospital administrators announced that they would hold an open meeting with the community. The interns and residents involved in the protest called the meeting the "first People's Clinical-Pathological Conference" (CPC) in reference to the medical school practice of analyzing difficult cases collectively. Mullan recalled the success of this People's CPC: "At the least, it was a real and significant instance of physicians being called to account by community people. . . . [It] stood as a victory for community participation in the hospital."[144] Activist residents and interns shared Rodriguez's autopsy records at the "People's CPC" in order to assert the community's right to access medical information that is usually kept by medical staff.[145]

At the CPC, the Young Lords, Think Lincoln, and other South Bronx residents asked questions of the senior staff physicians, including the director of the Department of Obstetrics and Gynecology. They wanted to know why a saline abortion had been performed on a woman with a disease that contraindicated the procedure. Think Lincoln and the Lords concluded that Rodriguez's death, while not malicious, did stand as strong evidence that Lincoln Hospital provided insufficient and even dangerous medical care. They argued that the pivotal failure in this case had been lack of continuity of care, a common problem in an urban hospital catering to poor people without access to private physicians. Although Rodriguez had been treated for a drug addiction at the hospital and referred to ob/gyn for an abortion because of her pregnancy and heart condition, her case was unknown to the ob/gyn department. Better communication would have saved Rodriguez's life. Think Lincoln and the Lords called for the ouster of the director of the Department of Obstetrics and Gynecology and for a worker-community board that would help design and oversee hospital policy. As a result of the protest, the director of ob/gyn resigned and an interim director took his place. Ultimately, however, the hospital retaliated against the activists, filing an

injunction against the Young Lords and Think Lincoln that forced them
to remove their complaint tables from the lobby.[146]

After the Rodriguez death, the hospital administrators took no actions to increase community control over hospital decisions although
the Young Lords and Think Lincoln continued to organize around
health care reform. The supportive residents and interns in the Department of Pediatrics experimented with increasing community involvement in their department. Mullan, another physician, Paul Bloom, and
some former members of Think Lincoln helped organize a Pediatric
Parents Association that would function like a Parent Teachers Association, allowing parents of young patients to have input in hospital
policy. The group recruited parents in the hospital emergency room
waiting area and in the pediatric clinic. A group of about ten parents
met biweekly for several months to attend lectures about community
health issues such as lead poisoning and to meet with physicians and
staff. The parent group opposed budget cuts at the hospital and helped
select the new house staff (interns and residents). After interviewing
applicants, with particular attention paid towards candidates' attitudes
towards blacks and Puerto Ricans, the parent group made hiring recommendations to Dr. Helen Rodriguez, the new director of the Pediatrics
Department and a strong advocate of community involvement in health
care design and delivery. Less successfully, activist residents and interns
also attempted to integrate worker input into the Pediatric Department.
Nurses, secretaries, aides, and clerks, however, were suspicious of the
physicians' motives since they had never before been asked for their
input. The nonphysician staff also brought their own hierarchy and
disagreements among themselves to meetings, which inhibited free discussion. Unsurprisingly, many staff felt uncomfortable speaking freely
among doctors in a workplace that had long operated along rigid lines of
hierarchy and power. All of these factors contributed to a failed attempt
to level hospital hierarchy.[147]

The physician residents and interns and the community activists,
which included the Young Lords, pitted themselves against an intransi-
gent group of hospital administrators who, in the end, stood in the way
of any real transformation of Lincoln Hospital's services, although they
did succeed on a few fronts. Dr. Harold Osborne, an MCHR activist and
intern at Lincoln, recalled that the interns were more successful at re-

forming the internship process than ending poverty-related health problems in the South Bronx.[148] It was impossible to implement these sorts of reforms without some support from entrenched powers, even when those in powerful positions were also targeted for change. NHCs, with their federal mandate, congressional support, and national scope, were much more successful at bringing those with some entrenched interests in sustaining medical hierarchy—but also with interest in delivering quality medical care—together with community members who could help shape health center offerings to best meet their community's needs.

Multiple studies support the contention that NHCs had many successes. One national study found that Boston, Chicago, and Portland hospital admissions were lowered for target populations. Researchers also noted a reduction in hospital stays as well as a reduction in the number of hospital days per capita. Several other studies showed a reduction of hospital admission up to 44 percent and a reduction of hospital days per capita from between 25 and 62 percent in communities with NHCs. Other studies of Medicaid users revealed that those using NHCs had 50 percent lower hospital rates than nonusers and reduced infant mortality rates, particularly among African Americans. These studies revealed too that when NHCs reduced hospital admissions, costs also fell in comparison to hospitals that employed high-tech solutions to low birth weight and premature births, such as neonatal intensive care units.[149]

There is less agreement about precisely which factors contributed to these improvements. Was it the geographical location of clinics in poor neighborhoods, the low cost to patients, the use of community outreach workers, or the use of community boards? It is outside the scope of this chapter to attach particular successes to specific reforms. It is also necessary to consider to what extent the NHC model really transformed health care delivery. Although health care and health improved markedly in neighborhoods with federally supported health centers, the solution was still hospital centered, technical, and entrepreneurial. Geiger, too, is critical of the form community health centers took over time as they lost their focus on community empowerment. He wrote, "After too few years the window that was open to expanded programs and community development began to close. This happened in part because of program costs and in larger measure because conservative national administrations were (to put it mildly) not overly interested in community empowerment and social change." He explains that health centers became more traditional in their delivery of medical services rather than focusing on ending poverty or transforming social inequalities.[150] Other critics of NHCs argued that although power was no longer held by individual physicians, it shifted to hospital corporations and insurance companies that made decisions about patient care rather than being distributed to community residents. Certainly, with the end of the War on Poverty, the gradual shift away from federal spending on social services in the 1970s, and the more onerous cuts in the 1980s during the Reagan presidency, community control of social programs no longer had many federal champions.[151] Yet neighborhood health centers have continued to be a fundamental part of health care provision for the poor and uninsured in the United States. Today there are twenty million people each year who use community health centers. Twice as many will probably use the centers, with eleven billion new dollars from the Obama health care plan (the Affordable Care Act) and $2 billion in stimulus monies going to health centers. With this sort of long-term and future investment in community health centers, it is imperative that we attend to how and why health centers were created nearly a half-century ago and how and why they succeeded, even though success may have been uneven.

In the next chapter I turn to the feminist women's health movement that grew, in part, from the health reform efforts of the civil rights and the New Left NHC movement. Feminists also built neighborhood-based health centers with local, federal, and private support, but they also challenged what they viewed as socially embedded gender hierarchies in health care delivery that were connected to a larger context of uneven social power between men and women. With less federal support than that garnered by NHCs, feminist women's health centers also struggled to survive through the decade of the 1970s. When they provided abortions, their survival was threatened by a burgeoning and passionate anti-abortion movement.

"Thank You for Your Help . . . Six Children Are Enough"

The Abortion Birth Control Referral Service

Community and neighborhood health clinics, grounded in the civil rights and New Left movements, provided intellectual, political, and practical experiential precedents for the women's health movement. By the early 1970s, with the explosion of Women's Liberation participation in cities around the country, feminists began to create new health institutions for themselves and other women. The feminists who built these institutions perpetuated the earlier health reform commitment to reaching people without access to health care. At the same time, they also wanted to expand women's sexual and reproductive autonomy and dismantle sexual and reproductive double standards that seemed natural and normal to many but actually stemmed from deeply entrenched, yet socially constructed, gender roles. As women met and discussed which social mechanisms perpetuated sexist gender roles, they came to the conclusion that gender inequalities could not be transformed unless sexual and reproductive autonomy were also secured.

With Women's Liberation, women's increasing expectation that they be able to freely explore sexual feelings and desires became linked to the need to dramatically improve abortion and birth control access. Women's Liberation groups across the country were demanding free, legal, and easily accessible termination procedures performed in safe and nonjudgmental environments. Yet, even as abortion became legal in a handful of states, including Hawaii, Alaska, California, New York, Washington State, and Washington D.C., many women still found it difficult to locate providers of safe abortions in supportive environments. As Carole Joffe has shown, abortion was still not commonly available in U.S. hospitals or other medical institutions even after *Roe v. Wade* made abortion legal in 1973. For this reason, feminists created abortion referral services to help women secure abortions both before and after *Roe*.[1]

This chapter traces the history of one feminist abortion referral service, the Abortion and Birth Control Referral Service (ABCRS), founded by feminists who were members of the University of Washington YWCA (U of W YWCA) in Seattle. It also examines some of the varied attitudes towards abortion in the 1970s expressed by women who used the service and reported their feelings after their abortions on feedback forms collected by the ABCRS.

Washington State, after a two-year campaign led by Washington Citizens for Abortion Reform, became one of the first states to legalize abortion before *Roe*, and the first to legalize abortion through popular referendum. On November 3, 1970, 56 percent of those who voted agreed that abortion should be legal up to sixteen weeks' gestation. Leading up to the vote, there had been broad political support for the referendum from the Republican governor of the state, Dan Evans, Republican state senator Joel Pritchard, who helped draft the referendum, and other lawmakers. The law required that abortion be performed by a doctor in a licensed medical facility, that the patient reside in the state for ninety days, and that minor patients notify their parents and married women notify their husbands of the abortion.[2]

Yet, the new law didn't provide any mechanism to help women access abortion, just as it did not require doctors or hospitals to provide abortions. Feminists associated with the U of W YWCA realized that women still needed help figuring out where to acquire a safe, legal, and compassionate abortion. Jan Krause, then program director of the U of W YWCA, recalled working with Planned Parenthood director Lee Minto to compile a list of medical doctors from the Planned Parenthood Medical Advisory Committee who would be available to an abortion referral service housed and funded by the YWCA.[3] Since hospitals were not quick to establish abortion services after legalization, it fell to individual doctors to provide them after the law changed. Many individual doctors were also reluctant to provide abortions after legalization, often because of religious reasons but also because those who performed abortions were still stigmatized as "quacks" or as greedy, a legacy of the pre-*Roe* era. Those who did provide abortions often did so only for their private patients, making abortion less accessible to poor and young women who did not have an established relationship with a physician. Freestanding clinics eventually became the most common abortion providers and helped make abortion both affordable and easily accessible.[4]

According to Patricia Valdez, a volunteer coordinator for the ABCRS referral service, the purpose of the service "was to try to give women a good, safe, and reassuring referral to a good, safe, and reassuring practitioner who would be sensitive to their needs and all the negative projections about abortion at the time."[5] Some of these women would also be traveling to Seattle from out of state because abortion was not yet legal in their places of residence or because it was expensive and difficult to access. The ABCRS volunteers acknowledged the residency requirement by informing out-of-state women of it, but still referred them to physicians in Seattle willing to perform their abortions.[6] Thus, due to the referral work of services like ABCRS, legal abortion gradually became more accessible even before the Supreme Court's decision in *Roe v. Wade* made abortion legal in every state in 1973.[7]

Seattle feminists decided to continue to organize for women's sexual and reproductive health and autonomy after Washington State legalized abortion because they contended that the new abortion law was only a first step towards full gender equality that would allow women to make unencumbered choices about their sexuality and sexual and reproductive health. They decided that an abortion and birth control referral service would best meet their immediate goal of helping women access pregnancy testing, legal abortion, and contraception, while larger educational and activist strategies also associated with the YWCA were designed to educate women about their bodies, transform their relationships with medical providers, and interrogate socialized gender roles that perpetuated sexual and reproductive double standards.[8]

Birth control counseling, referrals for pregnancy tests, adoption information, and prenatal care information were all part of the service from the beginning, but the emphasis was on assisting women who wanted safe, legal abortions within a social and historical context in which abortion had recently been illegal and socially stigmatized. Although abortion was newly legal in Washington, most women still didn't know where to terminate a pregnancy. They needed to know which doctors were willing to do the procedure and who among these would be safe and reliable. They also needed to know which doctors would treat women humanely and refrain from punishing women for sexual "transgressions." Some women also still lived in parts of the state with no doctor willing to provide an abortion. Since the law required doctors to perform abortions within a ten-minute radius of a hospital equipped to provide medical backup in case of emergency, large areas of rural parts of the state remained without any abortion services after the referendum passed. These women would also have to travel for abortions, although they were residents of a state that had legalized the procedure. If a woman traveled to Seattle for her abortion from another part of the state or from out of state, she also might need someone to stay with if she didn't have friends or family in a strange city; and she might require transportation if she didn't have a car.[9] Out-of-state travelers also needed information about which doctors would ask to confirm a Washington State address to prove residency.[10] At first, Seattle U of W YWCA feminists assumed the service would be a short-term necessity, helping women to access abortion until the procedure became more readily available. Clearly, the organizers underestimated the long-term need for an abortion referral service. The "service," as local feminists called it, closed its doors in 1994, well after abortion became legal in every state.[11]

Feminists operating the referral service also aimed to make abortion and contraceptive services part of a reformed medical system that would empower women to make informed and autonomous decisions about their reproductive and sexual lives. To these ends they made educating obstetricians and gynecologists about issues of women's health and sexuality a priority. They also focused on educating themselves and the women who used the service about reproductive health care so that women could not be duped into accepting inferior or even dangerous care. They argued that high-quality women's health care coupled with knowledge about women's health and sexuality would empower women to become stewards of their own reproductive and sexual lives.[12] Valdez recalled that she trained volunteers staffing the telephones at the service to provide information their clients needed in order to empower patient judgment rather than impose a political perspective:

> I trained volunteers to be able to answer the phones in a caring way and not [be] overly dogmatic about what [clients] should do, to talk to them about what they wanted and needed to do. A lot of the time women had

already made up their mind that they wanted an abortion and didn't want to carry it to term. We didn't push any philosophy but we would run through a description of the different clinics that were performing abortions at that time. We tried to give them an idea of what the clinic would be like. Some women felt more comfortable with a homey and feminist environment and other women were more comfortable with a high tech and more professional environment. We had a wide range of referrals depending on what women told about themselves.[13]

By responding to patients' needs, ABCRS volunteers affirmed a pregnant woman's decision-making capacity. The YWCA feminist volunteers who ran and staffed the service presumed that women needed information that would empower them to make their own informed choices about their reproductive and sexual lives.

Seattle feminists were not the first to set up an abortion referral service. Other services had existed since the middle of the 1960s in California, New York State, and Chicago, as well as in other cities. According to historian Leslie Reagan, the first abortion referral service started in 1966 in San Francisco when Patricia Maginnis began handing out flyers that detailed information about doctors willing to perform abortions outside of U.S. borders. Maginnis's organization was known as the Association to Repeal Abortion Laws (ARAL) and, as the name suggested, it had as its goal the eradication of all U.S. anti-abortion laws. Maginnis's abortion referral work centered on the "list," as it came to be known, which included names of abortion providers as well as the cost of the procedure and what women should do to prepare themselves for the abortion. Most of the women who used the "list" traveled to Mexico, but providers in Japan, Canada, and Sweden were also included. Maginnis's organization ensured that those on the "list" were providing safe abortions by checking on the physicians' credentials, by inspecting them on site, and by gathering feedback from women who used them. ARAL used the guarantee of referrals to pressure the abortion providers to ensure safe procedures. Providers not conforming to ARAL's standards were removed from the "list." ARAL's referral service was an important mechanism to help women find safe abortions, mostly across the border in Mexico, for the years immediately preceding legalization.[14] Like the Maginnis group, the Clergy Consultation Service also referred women to illegal abortion providers both abroad and within U.S. borders, with the ultimate goal of overturning the illegal abortion laws.[15]

Physicians, too, referred their patients to other local doctors who performed abortions. With an estimated 1.2 million illegal abortions occurring each year within the United States, it is certain that both lay abortionists and medical doctors were performing illegal abortions, often without complications. The problem for most women was locating a person willing and able to perform the abortion, either a physician or a lay provider. Secrecy, police payoffs, and low rates of prosecution and conviction of physicians made it possible for many physicians to perform illegal abortions without terrible risk to their practices. Yet, perception of risk, the vagaries of a shifting and uncertain legal climate that might cause local officials to stop tolerating illegal abortion, and seemingly arbitrary decisions about what constituted a legal "therapeutic" abortion in a hospital context all contributed to many physicians' belief that abortion laws needed reform.[16]

Probably the most well-known feminist abortion-referral service, first called the Abortion Counseling Service of Women's Liberation but later referred to as Jane, was created by Heather Booth in 1968 to provide referrals for illegal abortions in the Chicago area. The group was organized and staffed by women active in the Chicago Women's Liberation Union, although many women not associated with a women's liberation organization became involved with Jane either as volunteers or as patients, and in some cases as both.[17] For much of the time that the organization existed, participants in Jane counseled women and arranged for illegal abortions but did not provide the abortions themselves. By 1970, however, after learning that the man performing abortions for the organization was not a doctor, women in the group learned to perform abortions themselves, which helped them lower their prices to make abortion more affordable to poor women who could not fly to New York State from Chicago for a legal abortion. Learning to provide abortions also empowered women in Jane to take control of women's medical care and provide it in a context and in a manner that they believed was more respectful and caring than that supplied by established providers. Like other women's health movement participants across the country, Jane volunteers demystified medical care by training themselves to be health providers and educating their patients about their bodies. The organization disbanded in 1973 after the *Roe v. Wade* Supreme Court decision overturned the Illinois anti-abortion law.[18]

In 1971 members of the Los Angeles Feminist Women's Health Center, the first explicitly feminist clinic in the country, also started performing abortions using a procedure invented by Lorraine Rothman, one of the founders of the clinic, called menstrual extraction. Menstrual extraction allowed lay women organized in feminist self-help groups to perform very early abortions (usually from the time a period is expected up to two weeks after a missed period) by inserting a small plastic cannula into a woman's uterus and gently extracting the contents of the uterus into a small bottle attached to the cannula. The device was called a "Del-Em" by Rothman. Feminist self-help groups, including groups associated with the U of W YWCA and the Aradia clinic, founded in 1972 by Seattle feminists at the YWCA, also used menstrual extraction to treat particularly painful cramps or other symptoms of menstruation. Menstrual extraction was usually not used in the context of feminist health clinics, however, although there was a doctor at a women's health clinic at Harborview Hospital in Seattle who performed some menstrual extractions as very early abortion procedures. Feminists usually performed the ME, as it came to be called, at a private home in the context of independent feminist self-help groups devoted to learning about the reproductive body through self-examination and the examination of each other's cervixes.[19]

Both abortion referral services and legal abortion providers working in hospitals and in freestanding clinics proliferated between 1970 and 1973 as abortion gradually became legal in the United States. Women who did not live in states with legalized abortion before 1973 needed to travel for a legal procedure and often utilized an abortion referral service to find out where to go. Some for-profit abortion referral services that also thrived during this period took advantage of confused or desperate women to charge a fee for a referral and earned profitable kickbacks for making hotel and travel arrangements. Often these for-profit referral services were not looking out for their clients' best interests and so might refer women to doctors who were not providing high-quality care, who were expensive, or who were unsupportive of a woman's decision or emotions.[20]

Feminist abortion referral services, like the Seattle service, competed with these for-profit organizations by evaluating physicians, hospitals, and clinics for their safety and for the compassionate and respectful attitudes of the physicians and the other medical personnel. Their standards for care focused on medical safety, compassionate treatment, and affordability. Valdez explained that client "feedback was shared with the doctors when we met with them. We were sensitive not to come in and tell them how to do their job. The doctors were as receptive as they could be."[21]

Evaluation of physicians, hospitals, and clinics based on patient feedback was centrally important to ensuring quality abortion experiences. ABCRS feminists believed that caring treatment was as important as safety. Ann McGettigan, who coordinated volunteers and visited the clinics used by the referral service, recalled

> being the one who went out to observe abortions at every clinic. There were places that focused on providing abortions as a very lucrative clinical service. I saw some practices that were trying to fit in as many as possible in a day versus other places that did a much better job ensuring that there was enough time for someone to be well taken care of. Those practices where people were better taken care of got better feedback and got our referrals.

The feedback process, which included providing patient comments and complaints to physicians and staff so they could improve their services, was meant to ensure that patients received a higher-quality abortion procedure. ABCRS could press doctors and clinic staff to make improvements to their care if they received critical or negative feedback. McGettigan recalled that "[m]ost clinics were open to hearing feedback that we had and were willing to work with us and make changes."[22]

At the same time, some early reports about doctors who performed abortions were so negative that they were never included on the ABCRS referral list. One hand-written file created by ABCRS volunteers in 1970 titled "Bad Feedback on Doctors" revealed some of the reasons a physician on the list would be disqualified from the referral service list. One Renton, Washington, doctor tried to discourage a patient from having an abortion when she asked him for one. Another informed a patient of her pregnancy and, at the same time, told her she should marry soon. A doctor who apparently held religious convictions prayed over his patients during their abortions. And, finally, another doctor recommended contraceptive foam as birth control to a patient who subsequently became pregnant twice. After two abortions he prescribed the pill for her. These sorts of reports disqualified physicians from the ABCRS referral list.[23]

Other negative reports came from feedback forms solicited by ABCRS from patients after their abortions. Volunteers flagged patient feedback forms that were particularly negative. One report from a patient and her mother created reservations about a doctor. The young woman who had the abortion reported that the doctor, while giving her a shot, rudely told her to "be quiet, I don't want you to drive out all my patients, or I won't do it." Her mother, writing on the same feedback form, reported that she was concerned about the pain her daughter felt during the abortion. Jan Krause noted on this form that it should be returned to her for personal followup with the doctor.[24]

It was often important to women who used the service and reported about their experiences on their feedback forms to receive respectful and compassionate care from the doctors and their staff. The single most common complaint from women who used the service was that doctors were cold and too clinical. Many of the women described their abortions as emotional experiences. They wanted physicians, nurses, and support staff to understand the emotional context and respond in a manner that acknowledged that a woman might want sympathy when she had decided to end a pregnancy. One woman who had a positive experience in 1972 wrote the service that her doctor "made me feel very comfortable and was very obliging in every respect. I only wish there were more doctors like [him], it would make the abortion problem a less embarrassing procedure and also less frightening."[25] Of course women did not always agree as to which bedside manner they preferred. A few women reported that they preferred the doctor not engage them in conversation during the abortion.

Seattle feminists wanted women to be able to access safe, caring, and legal abortions. But like other feminists active in the women's health movement, they also emphasized the need for transformation of what many women experienced as alienating, hierarchical, and gender-biased medical practices.[26] Women from all over the country complained that doctors often did not put the needs of their patients first, were condescending and patronizing, withheld medical information, and at times used their power to manipulate or physically abuse female patients. Feminists also argued that the power dynamic between doctors and their female patients reflected pervasive gender inequalities that permeated the rest of society. Doctors and medical science, they declared, had long justified women's subordinate social role with biological arguments about the demands of a female reproductive body, which supposedly necessitated that women devote all their energies to it. They also noted that medical institutions in many ways reflected gendered roles in society; male medical doctors were the central players, the most respected, and the highest paid, whereas women played secondary roles as nurses or other support staff. Feminist women's health movement activists intended to transform these gendered hierarchies by providing alternative institutions and reforming existing ones.[27]

Feminist volunteers involved with the ABCRS were interested in both institutional reform and institution building: they acted as liaisons between women and abortion providers, ensuring that physicians provided high-quality health care, and later created Aradia, a feminist women's health center controlled by women to redress entrenched gender bias within health care institutions and in the wider society. In their first years, the ABCRS pressured doctors to comply with feminist demands for high-quality care; if they failed to deliver care that was up to standard, the Women's Liberation group would no longer provide referrals. In this sense, the ABCRS, like ARAL before it, acted as a consumer protection organization that ensured a safe abortion and minimized discomfort. Just after they set up the service, members of the group advertised in the local feminist newspaper:

"We're stressing the idea that it would be just another human being the woman talks to—not a doctor or a hospital administrator," explained a committee member. Homes for women to stay in when they come to Seattle for abortions will be needed. Anyone who could offer her home or who is interested in the referral service may contact the committee.[28]

In this advertisement, ABCRS feminists suggested that doctors and hospital administrators were a group apart from the women volunteers at the service, implying that women could understand and support other women better than medical professionals could do.

About two-thirds of the calls to the ABCRS hotline were from women with unwanted pregnancies asking for referrals for terminations. Other callers wanted information on birth control or had other health questions.[29] A year into their existence, the referral service had expanded, with telephone hotline volunteers available daily from 11:30 a.m. to 2:30 p.m. and 5:00 p.m. to 10:00 p.m. on weekdays.[30] In the second year calls were up to about eighty-five a week.[31] According to Valdez, the service hotline was staffed with a live person during most days and evenings, but if a volunteer staffer could not be scheduled, patients could leave a message.[32] Krause explained that there were usually two volunteers working at a time. A more experienced volunteer would train a new volunteer on the job.[33] Many women did not want to leave a message and be called back at their homes by a volunteer. Thus, women often called the service back if they didn't reach a volunteer on their first call. Some women complained on their feedback forms that the service was difficult to reach. A few of these offered to volunteer to staff the hotline so other women wouldn't have trouble accessing the service.[34] In addition to the hotline, the service could provide "a 'comrade in arms' to give moral support when a woman goes for her abortion. Overnight housing ('straight' and 'hip') for out-of-town women, transportation to and from bus stations and airports and daytime babysitting are some of the other services which will be offered."[35]

Valdez also pointed out that many women called the service in order to discuss with a volunteer deeply personal and emotional issues related to pregnancy and abortion. Volunteers often spent a lot of time with a client going over options as well as clients' emotional responses to their pregnancies and plans for abortion. Valdez explained that the service provided detailed information about doctors, their offices, and which services they performed. She recalled that "we did interviews with the doctors and we checked out their clinic so we could accurately describe it and met with the doctors and discussed how they are dealing with the women. [We would learn] which doctors would do later term abortions and the doctors who wouldn't."[36]

Krause explained the process of training the hotline volunteers: "[T]he women on the phones are more informed about abortion techniques. We have a special orientation for all women who want to work on the phones, and if a prospective volunteer hasn't had an abortion herself, we encourage her to go to a clinic or hospital and view the operation." She continued, explaining the importance of providing support and advocacy for women who had traveled to Seattle: "[T]he escort and driving service is the most difficult to arrange, but the women who use it critically need it, especially those who are alone in the city. . . . The driver becomes an advocate for the woman . . . [S]he looks out for her interests and gives her support during what can be a very traumatic experience."[37]

Some women also asked for information on how to acquire an abortion paid for with Medicaid. Volunteers were trained to walk poor women through the process for acquiring an abortion. Since women risked a more dangerous and expensive late-term procedure if they could not get an appointment in their first trimester, and many doctors did not accept Medicaid payment, particularly in the first few years after legalization, poor women, in particular, needed to be referred quickly. In 1970 only three Seattle-area doctors provided abortions to Medicaid patients in their offices; because of high demand for their services, poor women were referred to these doctors first over women with resources to pay for the procedure.[38]

Paying patients, alternatively, could be referred to a variety of doctors performing abortions in their offices, in Seattle-area hospitals and in free-standing clinics. A first-trimester outpatient abortion cost about $150 in 1970, but more than $300 for a second-trimester saline procedure if the patient needed to stay the night in a hospital. Most hospitals, clinics, and doctors in their offices provided dilation and evacuation abortions up to twelve weeks' gestation, but saline-method abortions were also available after twelve weeks. These abortions took place overnight—a patient went through labor—so if she stayed in a hospital the abortion was more expensive. A second-trimester abortion also required a lot more personal coordination if a woman had a family to care for, if she had traveled to Seattle for her abortion, or if she was trying to keep the abortion secret from parents, a boyfriend, or a husband.[39]

Abortion became more available and affordable in Seattle after it had been legal for several years. By 1974, the referral service had a list of fifteen doctors who performed first-trimester abortions in their offices, in clinics, or in local hospitals. One doctor's office was near the SeaTac airport and was advertised as "adjoining a motel for out of town patients." In 1974 a first-trimester abortion had become cheaper—the cost ranged between $90 and $140. All but three of the doctors on the 1974 list provided Medicaid abortions as well. Sixteen doctors provided the more expensive second-trimester saline procedures, which still cost around $300. Clearly at this point, in the immediate post–*Roe v. Wade* era, Seattle physicians were willing and able to perform abortions and made their services available to poor women who couldn't pay for their procedures. Opposition to the use of public money for abortion, however, quickly made it more difficult for poor women to access free or subsidized abortions.[40] In 1976 Henry Hyde introduced what is popularly referred to as the Hyde Amendment, attached to a Labor-HEW appropriations bill, which prevented federal money from being used for pregnancy termination.[41]

The referral-service feminists did as much as they could to make abortion affordable for all women. This meant finding funding to provide free or subsidized abortions for women who did not qualify for Medicaid. At the same time, it was important that each woman pay as much as she could for her abortion to preserve what reserves the service had amassed from donations for women who really could not pay. Volunteers needed to try to assess a woman's financial situation and even press her to think of all her possible financial resources.[42] The efforts the group made to fund abortions were duplicated among other abortion referral services around the country.[43]

Feminist recognition that some women could not pay for abortions while other women could demonstrates that despite a tendency to draw attention to women's similarities during the early 1970s, particularly with respect to the reproductive body, feminists also recognized socioeconomic differences that divided women. Abortion referral provided a very concrete service that forced feminist volunteers to confront in material terms the social, economic, and biological factors that made some women's experiences common and others quite unique. A more theoretically inclined group might have focused more intently on women's similarities—as sometimes happened within small consciousness-raising groups comprised of a group of friends or women already familiar with one another. But the abortion referral service volunteers could harbor few illusions about women's different circumstances. It was starkly apparent that for some women accessing an abortion was relatively simple if they had money and lived in a metropolitan area with numerous physicians willing to provide an abortion procedure. For other women, such as those living outside of Seattle, quite young women, and women with few material resources, abortions were difficult to acquire even after they were legal.

Feminists at the service were also conscious of racial differences among women. Valdez, who identifies as a Hispanic woman of color, explained that there were black women in Seattle who did not want abortions because they believed "it was part of racial control." They viewed abortion in the context of conversations among black nationalists about low-cost or free abortion and birth control services as genocidal for blacks. At the same time, there is an abundance of evidence that black women in Seattle and elsewhere wanted to control their fertility and voluntarily used birth control clinics.[44] White volunteers at ABCRS wanted to be receptive to women of color callers, and Valdez recalled that YWCA feminists also wanted women of color to volunteer at the service in order to better serve minority women who needed abortion referrals or contraceptive advice. Yet, the volunteers for the service remained predominantly white. Valdez explained to white feminists that sometimes feminism didn't appeal to women of color because they perceived it as splitting them from "their men" by "elevating women."[45]

The referral service also received numerous calls from women whose complicated lives made acquiring an early, inexpensive abortion more difficult. Krause explained, "A lot of our calls are problem cases, those who've tried everywhere else first." These women—often young and without resources—called the service in desperation. Krause detailed the process counselors used to determine a woman's circumstances:

First we ask them . . . has the pregnancy been confirmed? If not we have a list of pregnancy detection clinics. If the pregnancy has been confirmed how far along is it? . . . How much can the woman afford to pay? Then we refer her to one of the doctors on our cards and she makes the call herself. If he turns her down for some reason, she can call us back for another name. If she needs transportation, we can pick her up at the airport or bus terminal or at home and drive her to the doctor. And we have homes where out-of-town women can stay overnight. We even have women who'll visit a patient in the hospital or just babysit her other kids or hold her hand and give her someone to talk to.[46]

Whatever a woman's dilemma, the service tried to address it. Money and emotional support were in frequent demand. Service feminists also stressed contraceptive education to each woman they helped. Krause noted, "It's better than abortion any day. We ask if they have been using contraception and if they know where they can get contraceptive information to prevent this happening again."[47] Valdez also recalled that

> we did do a lot of consultation around birth control. It wasn't just about abortion. We kept our statistics very up to date about different methods and where you could get birth control. I trained the volunteers to ask if women needed birth control after the abortion. Having an abortion was a very difficult, hard thing to do. Women were really receptive to [birth control and often expressed,] "I don't want to go through this again."[48]

Women often called the service and traveled from rural areas outside of Seattle and from other states to acquire their abortions. Women came from Oregon (where before 1973 abortion was only legal under limited circumstances, including to save a woman's life), Idaho, North Dakota, Montana, Nevada, Alaska (where abortion was legal but more expensive), and even Canada for their abortions. Before 1973, out-of-state patients were breaking the Washington State residency requirement to acquire their abortions, but the service sent out-of-state clients to doctors who didn't check for residency or they provided fake addresses to the women and sent them to doctors who didn't ask to confirm an address with identification. Other restrictions such as parental and spousal consent, both part of the new Washington State law, could further hinder some women from getting the abortions they wanted. The ABCRS publicized its willingness to help women get around these legal restrictions, but they also explained that women should know it when they broke the law. One counselor writing to a women's health center in Oregon explained, "[T]echnically the women you are referring are getting illegal abortions. There are ways around most of the restrictions as you can imagine, but I think all the women you refer here should know this fact." Other similar letters were sent to Planned Parenthood affiliates, health departments, and health centers in the states that regularly referred women to Seattle.[49] This emphasis on full disclosure to the women using the service conformed to feminists' larger commitment

to treat women as competent adults who could make their own decisions about the risks they were willing to take when acquiring an abortion. This attitude was meant to counter what feminists often viewed
as patronizing behavior by established medical doctors who, feminists
argued, too often withheld information from women on the assumption
that doctors knew better than the women themselves about managing
their medical care.

ABCRS feminists also strongly supported a young woman's right to
choose abortion without notifying her parents or guardians. In 1972
Dr. Frans Koome, one of the doctors the service used frequently for referrals, was found guilty of performing a termination procedure on a
fifteen-year-old. At the time of her abortion the girl was a ward of the
King County Juvenile Court and in custody with Catholic Children's
Services. The superior court approved the girl's abortion at ten weeks'
gestation, but the Catholic agency and the girl's parents appealed the
decision. Approval for the abortion was suspended pending a hearing.
At the young woman's request, Dr. Koome went ahead and performed
the abortion the next day despite the lack of legal authorization. Seattle
feminists publicly protested Koome's conviction for performing the illegal abortion and demanded revocation of all state restrictions on abortion, including parental notification and spousal consent.[50] Dr. Koome
was sentenced to a year's probation and a $500 fine. He explained that
he knew the abortion was illegal but he believed all women, regardless of
age, should have access to voluntary pregnancy termination.[51]

Koome had also performed illegal abortions out of his Renton
general-practice office before the 1970 referendum, so he was not un-
familiar with lawbreaking around abortion. Koome was an outspoken
supporter of abortion law reform as well. In 1969 he publicly invited
arrest, hoping to mount a court challenge to the state anti-abortion law
by announcing his illegal practice in a letter to Governor Dan Evans and
in front of the media. Koome was not arrested, however, after his an-
nouncement. He continued to flout the law by performing over twenty
abortions a week in his private office. Apparently, the King County
prosecutor could not find sufficient evidence to bring charges against
Koome because no patients would come forward to testify.[52]

Koome was also a strong supporter of feminist women's health practice. According to Dr. Mary Ellen Walker, a Seattle family practitioner

who worked in Koome's office in the early 1970s before she went to medical school, Koome hired and trained people engaged in women's health provision in Seattle-area community clinics. Walker volunteered at both the Open Door clinic, a community health clinic in the University District in Seattle, and at Aradia, the feminist clinic established by the U of W YWCA, and trained to perform pelvic exams with Koome. She also recalled that before the referendum made abortion legal, Koome trained nonphysicians to perform abortions in his office. She explained that it was a relatively simple procedure and that by training assistants, Koome could perform more abortions each week. Walker recalled her observations of Koome's abortion services:

> Frans was an early feminist I would say. Everyone who worked there [at his practice] was a woman. He knew women were much more comfortable with women in that setting. Women were also more available and willing to work in that situation. We would bring patients back to explain the procedure and get them ready and he would come and do the procedure and then we would help the person down from the table and then let them rest and take them to a room and he would talk to them before they would have someone take them home.[53]

Elaine Schroeder, who volunteered at ABCRS and at Aradia, also worked in Koome's office. She recalled, "I took a job as an assistant to Dr. Koome. The job wasn't to do anything medical. He had an extra person standing there—me and a nurse and him. I did the pre-abortion counseling. I essentially distracted her and talked to her. I'd say things like oh, you're from Olympia. . . . Sometimes she didn't even notice it [the abortion]; sometimes they'd look at me and ask when is it going to start?" To have a support person in the operating room was not standard practice in the clinics or the offices of those who performed abortions in the early years of legal abortion. Feminist clinics pioneered the practice. As freestanding clinics began to dominate abortion provision, pre-abortion counseling and patient advocacy became commonplace.[54]

While providing access to safe abortions in a compassionate context was important to ABCRS and YWCA feminists, they also wanted to effect change in other areas of women's lives. In 1970, in addition to establishing ABCRS, U of W YWCA feminists created a women's divorce clinic; a support service for women entering the trades, called "Mechanica"; a service for women who experienced sexual assault, referred to as "Rape Relief"; and a Lesbian Resource Center. And, they began planning a feminist women's health center, Aradia, which would open in 1972 and be housed next door to ABCRS. All of these autonomous yet interconnected groups within the U of W YWCA reflected Seattle feminists' broad interests in the promotion of gender and sexual equality in health care, in the workplace, and in their personal relationships.

Most of the women who used ABCRS, however, were not involved with the U of W YWCA or with other feminist groups in Seattle, although some of them went to the feminist clinic at Aradia for their health care. The women who used the service came from all walks of life: some were married, some were divorced or separated, and some had always been single; some had their abortions with the support of boyfriends, husbands, or family, and others felt alone; many had children, and many did not; and they were of all ages, from teenagers to women in their forties. Regardless of their personal situations, the vast majority of reported feedback from women who used the service was positive and appreciative that someone had been available to help them access an abortion. This 1971 letter to ABCRS from a woman who traveled to Seattle from Nevada for her abortion represented many clients' gratitude to the service: "I can only say thank you for helping me, I truly feel it would have ruined my life if I would have had to bear the child, therefore I am extremely grateful to your service for helping me out, I would like very much to send you a contribution as soon as we are financially able." The referral service arranged for a volunteer to meet this woman's plane. She stayed overnight at a Renton hotel. Another volunteer escorted her from the hotel to the doctor's office in the morning. The volunteer also stayed with the woman through her abortion.[55]

To find out how well physicians on their list performed abortions—and whether ABCRS volunteers had provided sufficient information and support to clients—ABCRS collected feedback from patients. Patients received feedback forms at the doctors' offices, clinics, or hospitals at which they had their abortions and were asked to return the forms to the service afterwards. Negative as well as positive feedback helped the service improve abortions provided by ABCRS-recommended doctors. The feedback forms were comprehensive and included questions about a doctor's medical performance, a patient's wait time, the attitudes of the physician and the staff, what information a patient had been given about birth control, what information she had been given on the abortion procedure, the level of pain she had experienced, the medications that had been prescribed after the abortion, any complications she might have experienced and how these were treated, what the patient paid for her abortion, and her attitude toward abortion and how that might have changed since the termination. Many women who used the service filled out these forms diligently—there are hundreds of them in the YWCA archival collection at the University of Washington—reporting on the problems they encountered and their appreciation of the help they found at the service.

Comments on the forms were highly individual, although the majority expressed some form of relief that the procedure was over and gratitude to the volunteers at the service for their support. Studies completed during this period of early abortion legalization that investigated women's psychological experiences with abortion found that the overwhelmingly common response to abortion was relief. The highest period of stress usually came just before the abortion experience.[56]

Many of the comments on the forms were about attitudes of doctors or nurses at the abortion clinics or doctors' offices. A patient who went to the office of a doctor recommended by the service complained that before her abortion she was left in the office for an hour and a half without explanation. She also noted that this doctor did not provide information on contraception and his explanation of what she should expect to experience after her abortion was too vague.[57] Another woman complained that a doctor discouraged her husband from a vasectomy even though the two of them had asked him about it. Apparently, the doctor declared to the husband that he would never have a vasectomy himself. A volunteer from the referral service attached a note to the feedback form indicating that she would follow up with this doctor about his position on male sterilization. A third patient reported feeling particularly nervous about having an abortion, but her experience with the doctor who performed it turned out to be positive. In a section highlighted by the service, this patient wrote,

I called Dr. Harberts' office and he immediately came to the phone and reassured me of everything and said he would look after my problem immediately, and he did. He made me feel very comfortable and was very obliging in every respect. I only wish there were more doctors like [Dr. Harberts] it would make the abortion problem a less embarrassing procedure and also less frightening.

Feedback like this woman's report helped the service decide which doctors to use and in which circumstances. That Dr. Harberts could be particularly supportive and reassuring to a nervous patient might mean that volunteers would refer anxious patients to him.[58]

The last section of the feedback form was more open ended. Patients were asked, "What is your attitude toward abortion now?" This question evoked many long and often very emotional responses about how clients felt about abortion both before and after the procedure. I will quote some of these responses at length as they provide valuable insight into the personal opinions and emotional reactions of women who acquired an abortion relatively soon after abortion legalization. The comments on these forms were made before the anti-abortion movement launched its very public campaign making debates between anti-abortion activists and abortion supporters commonplace. The feedback provided by women who used the service between 1971 and 1979—forms from later years were not available in the YWCA collection—allow us a glimpse into how women felt about abortion before it became a divisive and controversial political topic in the 1980s.[59]

The responses reveal that many women's feelings about abortion did not fit neatly into a pro-abortion or anti-abortion category. Some women's responses on their forms expressed strong support for abortion legality and access, while others wrote about doubts they had about terminating a pregnancy. Most articulated some form of relief even when they hesitated to support abortion in unqualified terms. Some women wrote that they were not entirely "for" abortion, yet they appreciated that they had relatively easy access to the procedure. Others had heard that abortion was dangerous, like the woman who wrote in 1978, "I always maintained that I'd never get an abortion . . . because I'd heard about awful things like women dying of blood loss and infection." She added, "I thank you for your help and I hope that many girls who are in trouble seek help from you instead of doing something dumb like cheap abortions or self abortions." From this woman's remarks from 1978 it is apparent that some women recalled, from nearly a decade's distance, horror stories they had heard about the era of illegal abortion. Historical research on the pre-*Roe* era has taught us that illegal abortion was actually less dangerous before legalization than this woman believed. Yet stories clearly circulated about dangerous back-alley abortions that affected women's attitudes towards their abortion experiences in the post-*Roe* period.[60] Another woman writing in 1973 also acknowledged that the legal status of abortion affected her experience positively, although she still found it to be "traumatic." She wrote, "Certainly the legality of abortion made it a minor trauma."[61] A woman writing on her 1972 feedback form recalled trying to find an illegal abortionist in 1967. She failed, so she married and gave birth to her first child. She wrote, "At that particular time, no amount of money (and I had it) would have bought me a safe abortion."[62] The women who recalled the illegal period from the perspective of being able to secure a legal abortion were appreciative of the changed law.

Women writing in the early 1970s easily recollected the campaign for the referendum. Several women commented on their feedback forms that they were involved with the campaign. One woman, writing in 1972, referenced "stories" of illegal abortions that might have been circulated during the political debates that occurred during the campaign. She explained, "I certainly hope abortion remains legal—the frightening true stories around about illegal abortions; they're sad, very sad. . . . I might have killed myself if I were unable to get an abortion." Another woman also referred to rumors of dangerous illegal abortions: "I am thankful that the abortion law was passed so that I could be cared for by a physician and not by some 'alley butcher.'"[63] The tropes of both suicide (among women forced to carry pregnancies or threats of suicide used to convince hospital panels to approve therapeutic abortions) and "back alley butchers" were staples of the campaign to legalize abortion and continued to be in circulation after the procedure became legal.[64]

Many women expressed that their desperate personal circumstances made abortion their best decision. One woman reported having six children already, explaining that she just couldn't care for another. She detailed her situation:

> My feelings about abortion are . . . all women should have the right to determine what they're going to do with their own body. In my case,

six children was enough. My last child has a serious birth defect. He requires a lot of time and care. There's not enough time in the day now for
the things I have to do for my children. With another baby, I just felt I
wouldn't be able to cope with it.[65]

Many women discussed not being ready or able to cope with a pregnancy for various reasons, but, like this client, they also discussed
struggling emotionally with the decision. A woman reported, "The only
pain involved was the fact I was losing my baby but I knew I would not
be able to give the baby the things necessary as we are not in the financial position to bring another baby up."[66] Another woman explained
that she needed to finish school and couldn't find affordable day care
so she chose to abort even though in different financial circumstances
she would have continued the pregnancy. She wrote, "I wish that I
could have gotten a good babysitter 3 or 4 hours a day while I went to
school, then I could have time to spend taking good care of my baby."
She continued, expressing that women's ability to live autonomous lives
depended on both legal abortion and financial support for wanted children. She wrote, "Women can't be free when they are forced to have
abortions they don't really want. . . . Welfare isn't sufficient." Yet, she
wrote, "I am still absolutely prochoice as far as abortion is concerned."[67]

Another patient responded to her abortion in 1972 with ambivalence
toward the procedure, indicating that while she thought abortion access
helped women avoid even worse circumstances, an abortion was not an
appropriate solution in all cases: "Abortion is certainly not an answer to
birth control or even the lack of it, but it is at least a choice or possible
solution for something that could be far more devastating. Yet it can also
be a means toward avoiding responsibility—a very fine line that may
not be easily determined." She concluded her response, "As a procedure
I would not wish it on anyone."[68] Referral service volunteers circled and
starred her response, yet it remains unclear how they planned to follow
up on it. It is possible they were concerned that her procedure had been
painful or otherwise physically difficult. If that was the case they could
follow up with the woman's physician to ensure that other women did
not experience discomfort. Sentiments echoing this woman's fear that
abortion was treated too casually appeared multiple times on feedback
forms from other patients throughout the decade. Another patient wrote

of her abortion experience in 1977, "That some women regard it as a method of birth control is totally reprehensible."[69] A third patient writing in 1973 confessed that she had treated abortion like "birth control." She explained, "There seems to be one freedom of legal abortions that being the woman using abortion as birth control. This was my 3rd abortion in one year." She indicated that she had difficulty finding a contraceptive method that worked for her: "I pray someday to be at peace with the form of contraceptive I may choose."[70]

It is not clear that these ambivalent comments about abortion and its accessibility were related to an increasingly public anti-abortion sentiment since the anti-abortion movement didn't become highly visible until the 1980s, although mostly Catholic anti-abortion activists began to organize immediately after *Roe*. The first and third comments were made in the first part of the decade, well before a public anti-abortion movement had gathered steam in response to *Roe v. Wade*. Ambivalence about how abortion was used—if it was used as "birth control"— appeared to have existed among some women who had abortions both before and after *Roe*. There is evidence that "experiencing greater difficulty or conflict in deciding to terminate a pregnancy is associated with poorer adjustment after the abortion."[71] If this is the case, then it is possible that women who expressed ambivalence about the procedure had personal reasons for their critical perspective. These expressions of ambivalence may have reflected individual contexts that made choosing abortion difficult. At the same time, some women were critical that other women were using abortion in a cavalier way. They suggested that their reasons for abortion were legitimate, but other women were irresponsibly using abortion as "birth control." This opinion may have reflected a latent anti-abortion perspective that became more public later with the anti-abortion movement.

Of course, all of the women using the service chose abortion to control their fertility. For whatever reason—a failed contraceptive, failure to use a contraceptive, or changes in personal circumstances—many women who wanted to end their pregnancies expected to be able to access legal abortion even if they felt ambivalent about the choice. According to the Alan Guttmacher Institute, most unwanted pregnancies that end in abortion are the result of failed contraception. With increased access to birth control, including the pill, with its low failure rate, delayed marriage and childbearing, increasing rates of divorce, and greater access to higher education and the professions, many women in the 1970s expected to be able to use abortion as a back-up method of birth control (even if they didn't call it birth control) if their first contraceptive method failed to ensure personal autonomy over their sexual and reproductive lives.[72]

Abortion rights advocates have emphasized that abortion is experienced without negative emotional repercussions for the vast majority of women. For the most part, evidence bears out this assertion. Women reported in the early post-*Roe* period that legal abortion allowed them to continue to live lives they had chosen for themselves.[73] Yet, women's responses on feedback forms filled out after their abortions indicate that, while not depressed or experiencing "postabortion syndrome," some women's feelings about abortion were complex and at times ambivalent. To achieve a better understanding of how abortion was lived by women just after legalization, it is important to acknowledge and examine these complex feelings.

A woman writing in 1974 also expressed ambivalence about the abortion procedure but reported that the opportunity to speak with a phone counselor at the service helped her to adapt emotionally to her decision to terminate her pregnancy. She wrote,

> A young woman named Barbara answered my call at the referral service. It is very difficult to explain how she seemed to be the only person in the whole world who was going to help me and understood the mental part of my deciding to have an abortion. One minute after speaking with her gave me the first clue that I could cope with the situation.[74]

Another woman also described the mental strain of going through an abortion. She wrote, "The abortion was a bad experience mentally and would have been no matter what type of treatment I had." Fortunately, she received care that helped her through the ordeal. She reported, "The doctor and nurses were very sympathetic and tried to alleviate my fears of the procedure. This helped quite a bit."[75] Even more plainly, a woman wrote, "An incredibly sad, painful experience, but, damn, I'm glad I have the choice."[76] Other women reported feeling there was a stigma against abortion that made it difficult for them to speak about their experiences.

One woman wrote, "I only wish society did not consider [abortion] so evil. I do not feel I can tell the majority of my friends or family."[77] This response reinforces evidence suggesting that "a woman copes best with abortion when she experiences a low degree of ambivalence or conflict about her decision [and] receives support from significant others."[78]

ABCRS volunteers met monthly to go through the feedback forms and letters to address problems expressed by women who had used the service. Negative feedback often stressed dissatisfaction with doctors' sexist or uncaring attitudes towards abortion patients. To address these attitudes, the volunteers decided to provide doctors with "some educational materials . . . about sexist attitudes in medicine and positive examples illustrating more human behavior. Also, all doctors will receive copies of all negative feedback forms we receive." At one meeting, the group discussed negative feedback about two of the doctors they used regularly—Doctors Gold and Biback. Those attending the meeting decided to distinguish between feedback about medical incompetence and complaints about attitudes. A medically incompetent doctor would no longer receive referrals from the service. A sexist or chilly attitude, however, could be dealt with through physician feedback and warnings to clients.[79]

Women were also appreciative of the care they received from individual doctors. Sometimes there was contradictory feedback about a doctor. Dr. Gold, a problem for some patients, also received positive feedback from other patients. One young woman explained that she had never had a pelvic examination before her abortion and was very nervous about the experience. Dr. Gold allayed her fears, which she appreciated enough to report back to the service. She wrote,

> I highly recommend Dr. Gold to any girl that needs an abortion. He is a very kind, thoughtful gentleman. When I went into his office I was very nervous and afraid. The first thing he did was talk kindly to me, and tell me to relax. Then, he told me I would be alright and that it wasn't as bad as I thought.

Another woman compared an earlier illegal abortion to her procedure with Dr. Gold. She explained, "I had an abortion 7 years ago and find no comparison between the two. The first one I had was quite painful, I was not told what to expect, my blood type was not determined and I was treated like just another immoral victim. The treatment I was given by Dr. Gold was warm, helpful and very complete."[80] Another woman with very ambivalent feelings about abortion nonetheless appreciated her doctor's kindness. She wrote, "I'll never be in the position to have to go through with this again. I cried for 2 weeks—felt like a murderer—but it was something that had to be done I guess. . . . Dr. Callison is great and all his staff was very helpful and understanding towards my feelings and attitude."[81]

Women using the service expressed a wide variety of perspectives on abortion. One woman on her feedback form explained that acquiring an early abortion was important to her emotional acceptance of the procedure. She suggested that other women might feel the same way. She wrote,

> It is necessary for the girl to feel that she is just "pregnant"—rather than "expecting a baby." Having realized that she is pregnant and taking quick action before she can dwell on the fact is also important in readjusting herself. I personally considered myself as "pregnant" at a wrong time when I couldn't and didn't want a baby. If I would have considered myself as "expecting a baby" I'm certain I would have had problems adjusting to the fact of an abortion.[82]

For this patient, an important distinction could be made during a pregnancy when a woman began to think of the fetus as a baby. Another woman similarly commented, "I was only 8 weeks pregnant. I probably would have had qualms had the fetus reached a much greater degree of development."[83] A woman who wanted to be pregnant and have a child might conceive of her pregnancy as a baby immediately. Alternatively, women who knew they wanted to terminate a pregnancy might never think of being pregnant with a baby. Another woman who worked in the medical field couched her ethics of abortion in a trimester framework. She wrote, "I feel that as long as abortions are limited only up to 3–4 months of pregnancy . . . then it is permissible. Because I feel a fetus isn't . . . human yet."[84] A similar view of gestation divided into three trimesters was the foundation for the Supreme Court's decision in *Roe v. Wade*. According to that decision, abortion could not be regulated by the state in the first trimester, but it could be regulated according to state interest in protecting a woman's health subsequently. Only at fetal viability, or when the fetus could survive separate from the mother, could abortion be made illegal. Of course, the point of fetal viability has changed along with cultural and legal understandings of the fetus and its status as separate from the mother. By 1960, fetal status as a separate legal entity had been recognized in eighteen states, with damages awarded for "prenatal injury or death." Debates about fetal rights, fetal personhood, and viability escalated after *Roe* and have continued up to the present.[85]

Some members of the abortion rights movement have been adamant that a pregnancy at any stage should not be referred to as a baby. The anti-abortion movement has emphasized the opposite—that any pregnancy from conception onward is a baby. Women having abortions have usually defined for themselves when a pregnancy was too far developed to terminate or if the pregnancy should be thought of as a baby. Women often admitted that personal circumstances affected whether they felt they were carrying a baby or were "just pregnant." Sometimes, women wanted an abortion even when they believed it would kill a baby. This sentiment might result in expressions of guilt, too, but didn't necessarily stop a woman from terminating a pregnancy.

Another woman explained that her pro-choice position was strengthened through the abortion experience. She wrote that her negative association with abortion could be attributed to being raised Roman Catholic. After her doctor showed her the contents of her uterus following the termination procedure, the patient explained her changed perspective: "All it was was tissue, placenta, a fertilized egg. I laid back and felt incredibly good that it wasn't a human. It was only a human being in my imagination. I am proud that I made the decision to have an abortion and not let my imagination run away with me. I am glad not to be pregnant now."[86] In this case the abortion—and learning more about the procedure—helped strengthen support for the procedure.

Other women who used the service believed they had aborted a baby even when the abortion occurred in the first trimester. One woman wrote on her feedback form that the abortion cost her "$100 and a baby." Despite her belief that she had ended a life, she went through with the abortion. Her feedback about her attitude toward abortion doesn't tell us much. She just wrote "Thanxs," expressing gratitude for assistance from the service.[87] Another woman expressed more concern that she had ended the life of a baby. She wrote, "It makes me sick to think that

I could kill my child with such a small amount of pain to my body."
Yet, she too wanted to thank the service: "I want to thank you for your
help. I certainly could not have 2 children and raise them properly."[88]
This patient also seemed to reconcile herself to the necessity of "killing"
her baby, in this case, to raise her existing child "properly." Certainly,
"guilt" and "relief" were sometimes felt at the same time by women. One
woman wrote, "I'm certain I was nearing a possible suicide situation
because of guilt for becoming pregnant, guilt for wanting it terminated."
But then she added at the end of her form, "I couldn't believe my own relief when the doctor said that I was no longer pregnant. Another chance
to get back to my normal life."[89]

Having an abortion caused some women to change their opinion
about the morality of the procedure. One woman wrote in 1973, "I
wouldn't want to go through the experience again of course, but I'm
glad to know that there's help for people who need it as I did. I was
once against abortion. I now feel it's solving a lot of society's problems."[90]
Some women offered to donate money or even volunteer for the service
after their abortion. There is no evidence of how many of the women
who used ABCRS became involved with it, or became advocates for
abortion legality, but many women expressed their gratitude on their
feedback forms by expressing their intention to volunteer.

The majority of women expressed appreciation that they had attained
a safe abortion in a supportive environment even though some also acknowledged religious and ethical ambivalence about the experience.
Women revealed their own understandings of cultural forces that affected their attitudes toward abortion, such as a religious upbringing.
One woman wrote on her feedback form, "I believe what I did was the
correct thing to do. It was scary and painful, but there were many contributing factors—such as a Catholic background and low pain thresh-
old. To put it bluntly I was not psyched up for an abortion."[91] Another
woman confessed on her feedback form that she still "felt like a murderer," but she also wrote, "thank God it's over. I just hope he'll forgive
me."[92] These women's testimonies demonstrate the wide range of attitudes that existed towards abortion in the 1970s. Certainly it appears
that religion played a part in whether a woman felt she had "killed" or
aborted a "baby." Further investigation into attitudes about abortion by
women having the procedure, and how these have changed over time, is

necessary to determine which factors—the Women's Liberation movement, religion, or public anti-abortion sentiment—most affected women's attitudes toward abortion during this period.

Young women also used the abortion referral service. The referendum of 1970 required that minors notify their parents of the abortion, although the service often found ways to bypass the requirement. After 1973, Washington State had no parental notification or consent restrictions. Nor did the Washington State legislature pass any such restrictions at the close of the decade as other states began to pass restrictive anti-abortion legislation. Many young women voluntarily involved their parents in their abortions by confiding in them and relying on them for support. One sixteen-year-old client who had her abortion in 1972 did notify her parents and did not feel supported by them. She also seemed to regret her abortion. She wrote a long response on her feedback form that suggested she was looking for someone in whom she could confide her ambivalent feelings. From her response we also know that she felt her parents wrongly pressed her to stop seeing her boyfriend after the abortion. This client wrote,

> I wish now that I would have thought twice about it because my parents said nothing would "change" after I have the abortion but everything has changed. Like I'm not allowed to see my boyfriend. . . . I wish now that my boyfriend and I were married but I guess I'll just have to wait until I'm 18 years old. . . . I recommend all unmarried women who think about having an abortion be sure *to think twice!* [patient's emphasis][93]

Alternatively, another young woman affirmed her decision to abort on her feedback form and received strong support from her parents. She wrote, "I think abortion is necessary for a lot of young girls. I'm really glad that I had my parents to turn to because it was a really emotional time for me." This woman's mother also wrote on the same feedback form. She supported her daughter's decision despite her own ambivalence toward abortion stemming from religious beliefs. She explained, "I have taught Sunday School for years. But this was Jackie's body not mine, her decision not mine." The mother also detailed her frustration with her daughter's boyfriend, who denied he was responsible for the pregnancy.[94] Certainly some parents were more supportive of their daughters' decisions than others (as were some male partners). Another young woman didn't mention her parents' involvement at all. She reported that she learned of the ABCRS in her high school health class.[95]

Contemporary feminists have almost always opposed laws that would encumber a minor's right to choose an abortion autonomously on the basis that both pregnancy and its termination must be chosen freely by the individual with the pregnant body. The young woman who wrote on her feedback form about her regret over her abortion demonstrated the potential for young women to be influenced into a decision not entirely their own. How often did young women feel coerced to either bear a child or abort? We have very little documentation of the very personal process a family might go through when deciding to continue or terminate a teenager's pregnancy. These conversations almost always occurred behind closed doors. Yet, the feedback forms provided a little insight into the varying levels of support teenagers received from parents in making decisions about pregnancy and abortion.

ABCRS volunteers tried to expand women's ability to make autonomous decisions about their reproductive and sexual lives by providing information and material support like a ride to the clinic or babysitting during an appointment once a woman had chosen to abort. They could not, of course, provide much in the way of financial support, although they could help a woman navigate social services. One woman wrote on her feedback form that she and her husband went to the Aradia feminist clinic to have the abortion after speaking to an ABCRS volunteer. Once at the clinic they opted not to go through with the procedure. The patient explained, "I went into the Aradia Clinic and received very good support and information which I brought home for discussion. The Aradia people were completely neutral about whether or not to continue the pregnancy but the information they provided did help us with our decision."[96] We will never know what information Aradia staff gave this woman—probably it was information about the abortion procedure itself and possibly information on prenatal care and/or adoption—but we do know that the emphasis among feminist women's health movement activists was on empowering women to take control of their own reproductive lives and health care.

At times, however, women were not satisfied with the information they received. A woman who went through a second-trimester abortion reported being unhappy with information she received from the service. She did not expect to have a second-trimester saline abortion. She noted that at the clinic she received a description of the procedure and "the doctor and the nurse were kind to me." But she did not seem to understand that her pregnancy had proceeded too far for the simpler first-trimester method. She wrote the service, "I had heard good things about your referral service—but I don't feel I got much knowledge or information from you. Perhaps I didn't ask the right questions—but, then, I didn't know what to ask."[97]

Other women who traveled to Seattle from other states or cities often needed more support than a woman who lived in Seattle, including a place to stay and rides to and from the airport and clinic or doctor's office. This woman, who traveled from Montana for her abortion, explained, "Right now I'm very relieved that it is all over with. While I was in Seattle I felt very secure just knowing that if I needed anything I could call the referral service and they would help me out whether it be housing, a ride, information, or just someone to lean on."[98] Another woman who also traveled from Montana was particularly appreciative of her escort from the service, who stayed with her through the abortion. She wrote,

> I went to Seattle a little unsure—maybe even guilty—the woman who accompanied me from the plane, etc. was wonderful—very open, honest and understanding. . . . I panicked when the office said I needed a companion and home to stay in. We were having a hard enough time digging up the money for me much less enough for him [her husband] to come. You were so very efficient and good.[99]

A woman who flew to Seattle for her abortion wrote, "Charlotte picked me up at the airport and let me stay at her home overnight—I was really glad as I know no one in Seattle. And knew nothing about the abortion procedures. She explained it to me."[100] A second volunteer drove this patient to her abortion appointment the next morning. The patient wrote, "She drove me to the doctor's at 7:00 in the morning and . . . she had a family to take care of, yet, she had the time to take a girl she didn't know to the doctor's."[101] Doctors could also make a big difference in an abortion experience for out-of-state women. One woman who required a second-trimester saline abortion expressed that she felt particularly nervous. The night before the procedure her doctor came at 3:00 a.m. to the volunteer's house where she was staying to provide her with a tranquilizer injection.[102]

Previous to 1973, residency status was also a problem for women who traveled for abortions. Another out-of-state patient arrived at the doctor's office in Seattle unsure whether her doctor would quiz her about her address. She explained on her feedback form that she would have liked more information on what she should tell the doctor in order to receive what in 1972 was still an illegal abortion.[103] Similarly, another 1972 patient from out of town who used a fake address to acquire her illegal Washington State abortion recommended that the service "give out of state women the county in the cover address and remind them they will have to sign a consent to operate and that they may be asked questions as to length of residency."[104]

Women who traveled for their abortions faced other hurdles too. Their abortions were more expensive because they needed to travel to Seattle, some from as far away as Alaska, where abortion was legal but more expensive. Volunteers opened their homes to patients to help avoid the expense of a hotel room. An ABCRS volunteer who accompanied an out-of-town woman to her abortion at Dr. Gold's clinic in Lynnwood reported that the doctor provided a kitchen and a bed at the clinic at no cost for traveling patients.[105] Kathryn Draper, an ABCRS volunteer and later a nurse at the Aradia clinic, recalled hosting three second-trimester patients at her house in the early 1970s. She explained,

> We provided housing and support for women who were coming from out of state and having later abortions . . . [O]ne was really tough. She had not known that she was pregnant. She had kept having periods. It was better she had the abortion even though it was so late term. Not everyone would take the women in . . . [I]t was an individual thing.[106]

Another out-of-town patient who had a second-trimester saline injection abortion mentioned in her feedback form that Draper had been her overnight host. She too was thankful for the support she received as she labored to abort her pregnancy. She wrote of Draper, "She was a most wonderful person. Without her it would have been a lot harder."[107]

In 1983 Ann McGettigan began a postabortion counseling group with ABCRS. She explained that women would call the service wanting to talk about their feelings after their abortions. She also noted that the feedback forms often revealed complex emotions among women who had abortions. Indeed, many women felt both relief and ambivalence, like this woman, who wrote in 1972,

> My feeling about abortion now? I am happy to be free to live my life as I wish. The abortion made that possible. I am surprised, however, to find I have experienced a sense of loss, as though a friend were gone, the result of some inevitable separation . . . I cannot regret my decision—to have done otherwise would not have been in accord with goals of many years standing—but I am deeply aware that our child will *never* exist [patient's emphasis].[108]

McGettigan's postabortion counseling group was started amid growing anti-abortion activism in the 1980s when one might expect women to feel more ambivalent about their terminations. But from the feedback forms one can read that women revealed complicated feelings from the early 1970s onward, although usually not feelings of outright regret. McGettigan explained that she wanted a group to support women as they processed their emotions around abortion without seeming judgmental. Her position affirmed what many feminists in the women's health movement believed—that women were intelligent and moral individuals who should be given information to make sexual and reproductive decisions they felt sure about. Affirmation of a woman's sense of loss or ambivalence about abortion as a legitimate feeling that might need to be expressed in a group setting fit well within this ethical framework.[109]

Of course, safe, legal, and compassionate abortion was only one small part of the feminist women's health movement. Feminists of the early 1970s believed that abortion would ideally be provided in a medical setting controlled by women themselves, in which women provided the care and, most importantly, in which female patients would be empowered to become involved in their own health care delivery. To achieve these goals some of the women from the University of Washington YWCA, from ABCRS, and from the larger Seattle health reform movement founded the Aradia clinic in 1972.

3

Reproductive Control, Sexual Empowerment

The Aradia Women's Health Center and the Early Movement for Feminist Health Reform

Historical literature on the abortion and reproductive rights movement has often disconnected the movement for abortion legalization and, after legalization, abortion access from larger issues of reproductive health and sexuality.[1] This representational schism is inaccurate because the fight for legal abortion was only one part of a larger and more complex women's health movement. In the last chapter, I, too, focused on the Abortion Birth Control Referral Service to the exclusion of other reproductive health–and sexuality-related programs operating simultaneously among Seattle feminists. Women's Liberation participants of the 1970s did not disconnect abortion from their sexual experiences or from their desire for high-quality health care. Understandably, many women who wanted access to safe, legal, and compassionate abortion services were also very much attuned to issues of sexual autonomy and comprehensive reproductive health care access. Women wanted access to abortion in order to achieve greater control over their sexuality and sexual and reproductive health. They also sought health care, including contraceptive services, that was controlled by women themselves, in order to achieve more control over their reproductive lives. Recent historiography on the women's health movement demonstrates that feminist health movement activists made these connections among reproduction, health, and sexual autonomy explicit.[2]

Following in the path forged by these accounts of women's health movement activism, this second chapter on the Seattle women's health movement focuses on the attention feminists gave to improving and transforming women's health care and increasing women's reproductive and sexual autonomy by establishing a feminist women's health clinic controlled by women for women. In the last chapter I discussed the first of two health institutions founded by feminists active in the Seattle-based University of Washington YWCA (U of W YWCA): the Abortion Birth Control Referral Service (ABCRS). This chapter will attend to the Aradia Women's Health Center, called Aradia after the goddess of the healing arts. ABCRS helped women terminate unwanted pregnancies and provided information about birth control, a laudable but somewhat narrow feminist goal. Yet some of the same feminists active with the ABCRS also became involved with the Aradia Women's Health Center, which provided contraception and contraceptive counseling, preventive women's health care like pelvic exams and pap smears, information about childbirth options, breast-feeding, and childrearing, as well as public discussions and information sessions on women's experiences with sex, sexuality, and intimate relationships. For example, in 1971 the Seattle-area Feminist Health and Abortion Coalition, which later helped to organize Aradia, linked demands for greater access to abortion and contraception with aspirations for greater sexual freedom. They called for free abortions on demand, an end to forced sterilization, repeal of all laws restricting sexual expression among consenting adults, and an end to exploitation and abuse of women's bodies, which they tied to the advertising industry, prostitution, and police unwillingness to intervene in domestic violence situations.[3]

A group of Seattle women's health movement activists associated with the U of W YWCA also built alliances across lines of class, race, and ethnicity to underline the importance of women's health, including safe and legal abortion, access to contraception, and preventive care, to women of color. They argued that while all women needed quality health care and the means to make informed choices about their sexuality and fertility, not all women were in the same economic circumstances to achieve these goals. Some women's health movement activists suggested that women's health care reform should be linked to wider goals such as the eradication of racism and classism.[4] In one 1973 report on the Seattle women's clinics, Becky Ludwig, a contributor to the health reform publication *The People's Health: A Voice of the Seattle Health Movement*, commented, "The outrageous prices, the misinformation, the racist attitudes, the demeaning treatment of 'girls' of any age, and the [mis]treatment of welfare women by the majority of institutions must be stopped."[5]

Seattle-based U of W YWCA feminists founded the Abortion Birth Control Referral Service and the Aradia Women's Health Center to realize both reproductive control and sexual empowerment for all women regardless of socioeconomic status, race, ethnicity, or sexual orientation, although in the early 1970s they tended to serve white women dispro-portionately. The clinic was located in a neighborhood with a predomi-nantly white population near the University of Washington. In her response to a question about racial diversity at Aradia, Carol Isaac, one of the founders of Aradia, recalled, "We had two black women who were volunteers in Aradia for various amounts of time, one Asian woman (paramedic), a few Mexican women (one as a paramedic and one as our bookkeeper), unattached to La Raza, and a Filipino woman as a long-time volunteer (paramedic). That was still a small number."[6] In 1972, however, to ensure that more women of color and poor women had access to health services and information on reproductive control and sexual autonomy, a group of YWCA feminists (both white women and women of color) created the Third World Women's Resource Center (TWWRC). TWWRC would, among other things, address the problem of reproductive health access among women of color by establishing an affiliated clinic dedicated to the needs of women of color called the Third World Women's Preventive Medicine and Health Education Cen-ter connected to El Centro de la Raza on Beacon Hill, closer to African American and Hispanic populations in Seattle. TWWRC also increased educational training for voluntary staff at Aradia on racial, ethnic, and class differences among women, so they could better serve women of color. Thus, very early in their organizing efforts Seattle feminists were attentive to the ways in which race and class affected women's reproduc-tive health access.

The Aradia Women's Health Center: Feminist and Neighborhood Health Center Roots

While ABCRS opened in response to an immediate and urgent demand—the need among women in the Pacific Northwest for infor-mation on how to acquire legal and humane abortions after the 1970 Washington State referendum—U of W YWCA feminists began planning to open a clinic in 1971 with Title X family planning and Department of Health, Education, and Welfare (HEW) funding with the broad goal of transforming health services available to women in the city. HEW funded the clinic for their first year at a level that would allow treatment of approximately one thousand women per year. Clinic organizers reported, however, that there were 870 visits to the clinic in the first five months. The clinic also received funding to pay part-time employees through the King County Public Employment Program.[7]

Seattle feminists involved in the women's health movement and the creation of Aradia wanted to transform women's health care to incorporate a nonhierarchical and compassionate atmosphere that validated women's experiences with and knowledge of their bodies and affirmed their reproductive and sexual intentions, whatever those might be. Carol Isaac, who was one of the creators of Aradia and was present at the first meetings about feminist health care reform in Seattle, along with Moosh Graber, wrote about the philosophy behind health care reform that led to the creation of Aradia: "[Our] objective is legal ownership of, and medical control over, our own bodies." This meeting, attended by "[t]wenty five members of various organizations such as Radical Women, the King County Health Department, International Socialists, Group Health, the different women's clinics in the city, and the University YWCA," generated a broad list of demands, indicating that Seattle feminists initially focused on much more than access to abortion and contraception. For example, those who attended the meeting demanded an end to forced medical procedures on "Third World people and prisoners by drug companies" and "forced sterilization of welfare recipients." They also wanted to expand "research staffed by women and minorities to study the medical needs of the poor, women, and minorities." And they called for "affirmative action and preferential hiring of women and minorities in medical research and medical schools."[8]

Along with planning for a clinic, YWCA feminists also began to provide public workshops on sex and sexuality in order to connect abortion to issues of sexuality and reproductive health. Each workshop was open to the public and lasted eight weeks. Women volunteers from the YWCA gave the workshops. As they explained, the series was "an attempt to deal with the physiological, psychological and social determinants of sexuality and the consequence of such learning for human (sexual and nonsexual) relationships." Their lectures and discussions were open to both men and women, yet they always devoted a portion of the series to female sexuality because they believed that "women do face a special disadvantage in lacking accurate knowledge of their sexuality." Some of the topics covered included "anatomy and physiology of intercourse; conception, contraception and abortion; venereal disease; female sexuality: myth and reality; the politics of rape; prostitution; female homosexuality; male homosexuality."[9] There was also a particular focus on exploring topics related to sexual identity, lesbianism, and gender identity. Isaac explained,

> Lesbianism was an entirely new subject to most of us to talk about, and we had rap groups addressing that. We had one person who today we would say was transgender, assigned male but now out as female. It was much more a phenomenon of stretching our understanding by learning about those two gender differences that were not before even a subject to talk about.[10]

The addition of a women's health clinic to the already active ABCRS helped the Seattle women's health movement remain cohesive (Aradia remained open until 2006)—and even grow—once abortion became both legal and more readily available. Other women's health movement services that focused on abortion referral and provision exclusively, like Jane, the illegal abortion service in Chicago, closed after *Roe v. Wade* (although women from Jane remained active in the feminist and women's health movements). Jane provided a much-needed service and dissolved once that service was no longer required. The organization had satisfied its goal—to provide abortions when they were illegal. Aradia's mission was quite different from Jane's or from ABCRS's. Aradia and other women's health clinics addressed a broad array of interconnected health needs related to reproduction and sexuality.[11]

In April 1972, the Aradia clinic first opened for three days and two nights per week with a staff that included one female doctor, Barbara Puckett, and several codirectors, including Carol Isaac, Allysen Hathaway, Penny Teal, Dyan Edison, Nancy Stokley, and Moosh Graber, who was a licensed physical therapist and had experience with the local Country Doctor clinic.[12] The founders decided to call themselves "codirectors" to avoid reproducing hierarchies in traditional clinics. As Isaac recalled, "We were all codirectors . . . of the lab etc., codirector of this and that, codirector of liaison and no hierarchies."[13] At first the clinic was housed in a storeroom at the U of W YWCA offices in the University District. An all-woman construction crew under the direction of architect Donna Thompson built the new space for the clinic in the same building almost immediately.

To administer the daily activities of the clinic, a group of clinic workers, volunteers, and patients met monthly in what they called a "coven" to make collective decisions about the clinic operations. The coven consisted of eighteen women—thirteen from the Aradia Clinic and five from other U of W YWCA programs, including the Lesbian Women's Resource Center, the Abortion Birth Control Referral Service, Rape Relief, Mechanica (for women in the trades), and the Ad Hoc Committee on Menopause. Coven members headed several committees that took care of necessary details associated with running a clinic. The committees consisted of Educational, Medical Practices (which always included the staff gynecologist), Business, Paid Staff, Volunteer Staff, and Advisory—the last intended to be a group health professionals available for consultation.[14]

Like other feminist clinics around the country, the Aradia clinic was created to provide reproductive and gynecological care in a feminist setting.[15] Clinic organizers outlined their objectives: "Improving the quality of health care; educating women to self-help; provid[ing] gynecological services within the framework of feminism." The clinic would provide contraception, including pill prescriptions, diaphragm fittings, IUD insertions, or vasectomy and tubal ligation referrals; venereal disease screening and treatment; community health education on issues related to sexuality, reproductive health, birth control, abortion, and pregnancy; and a community clinic that encouraged patients to become involved in their own health care provision. Clinic staff could also provide referrals to patients whose health needs were outside the scope of what Aradia provided. The ABCRS hotline remained in the same building and the two organizations were affiliated, reflecting the Seattle activists' emphasis on preventive and well-woman gynecological care in addition to crisis care when a woman found herself with an unwanted pregnancy.[16] Women who came to Aradia with unwanted pregnancies were referred to the abortion referral service down the hall to help arrange their abortions. If an abortion service volunteer wasn't available, clinic staff had access to the referral information and could also give a woman a list of doctors to call. Aradia volunteer JoAnn Keenan recalled walking down the hall for abortion referral information for patients and even arranging her own abortion using the referral service lists.[17]

In addition to demands among women for a nonhierarchical clinic without gender bias that would offer more personally responsive gynecological care in a feminist context, founders of the clinic also responded to countercultural demands for alternative health care facilities specifically for women. U of W YWCA feminists felt an affinity with a countercultural community, mostly made up of young people, increasingly residing in the University District neighborhood adjacent to the University of Washington in the early 1970s and the home of both Aradia and the ABCRS. Although other free and low-cost health options existed in the city, YWCA feminists explained that young women who identified with the counterculture were often more willing to attend a clinic fully staffed by their female peers. When Aradia applied for HEW funding, a student clinic at the University of Washington as well as sixteen other alternative free clinics, including the Fremont clinic, Country Doctor on Capitol Hill, and the Open Door Clinic, Seattle's first neighborhood clinic also in the University District, already existed in Seattle and served about fifty thousand patients per year.[18] Among these clinics only Fremont and Aradia focused exclusively on women's health. Neither Country Doctor nor Open Door served women only, although both of them reserved one evening a week for services for women in response to feminist complaints that gynecology was often a low-priority medical issue when general health care was the main focus of a clinic.[19]

Social movement cross-fertilizations between New Left and antiwar activists and feminists were common in Seattle and helped solidify the links between the broader health reform movement and the feminist women's health movement. Women who had been active in the New Left and antiwar movements often shifted to Women's Liberation as that movement gained strength. For instance, Country Doctor's founders were mostly active in the New Left antiwar and Black Power communities in Seattle. But they also had connections to the feminist movement that gave birth to Aradia.

The Country Doctor clinic, founded in 1971 on Capitol Hill by a collective of New Left activists interested in health reform among other social justice issues, was one of the first community-based clinics in the city. Most of the founders had some medical training and one had been a medic in Vietnam. Organizers of Country Doctor clinic collaborated with a group of Black Panthers in Seattle who had already created the Sidney Miller clinic in the Central District. According to Linda McVeigh, one of the founders and currently the executive director of Country Doctor, the health collective that would become Country Doctor went to Sidney Miller and asked how to create a community clinic. After acquiring advice from the Black Panthers, particularly Carolyn Downs, a member of the Panthers with the strongest interest in health reform, members of the collective went door to door in the Capitol Hill neighborhood to find out if people had a need for a local health care collective in the area. They found that over 75 percent of Capitol Hill residents, many of whom were elderly and low-income, did not have access to regular health care services. The clinic first opened in an abandoned fire station donated to the clinic by the city. Country Doctor dedicated one night a week to women's health exclusively. McVeigh recalled that women who staffed the evening women's clinic went on to work at both the Fremont clinic and Aradia. Country Doctor also dedicated one night a week to an elderly clinic and one night a week to pediatrics. General medicine clinics were held two nights a week.

McVeigh recalled that abortion became a divisive issue early in the existence of the Country Doctor clinic. Some of the clinic's collective members with links to the Women's Liberation movement in Seattle wanted to provide abortions. They had also been active with the campaign for abortion legalization by referendum in 1970. But others in the group feared that abortion was too controversial and would alienate the clinic from the community. When the collective voted, opposition to abortion fell along gender lines. With a majority of men voting, the decision was made to forego the procedure. Although McVeigh and others disagreed with the decision, ultimately, by not providing abortion, Country Doctor remained eligible for federal Neighborhood Health Center funding. McVeigh also noted that feminists at Country Doctor conceded abortion provision, but fought to provide home births and train midwives as central services of the clinic.[20]

Feminist activists, who were first involved in the broad health reform movement in Seattle and helped to organize women's evening clinics, eventually founded Aradia. Nancy Stokley, for instance, founded the evening women's clinic at Open Door.[21] She recalled creating the Open Door woman-only Sunday evening clinic after being a patient at the general health clinic. Her experience at the general clinic was so alienating that she decided to attend a community meeting at the clinic to help improve it. But when she asked staff when and where community clinic meetings were held, they responded that they didn't exist. Stokley decided to take action by publishing her critical comments about the clinic in the *Open Door Clinic Newsletter*, which earned her an invitation to meet with Open Door staff. She and a group of about fifteen other women used that opportunity to push for a women's clinic after discussing that "as women, a lot of us found that the Free Clinic was really ignoring our female health problems."[22] When feminists at the YWCA decided to create Aradia, they turned to Stokley with her experience at Open Door to help them design a full-time women's health clinic.[23]

Experiences of feminist volunteers at the Open Door and Country Doctor women's evening clinics helped shape goals that would be pursued further at Aradia. For example, feminists at all three clinics emphasized connections among reproductive health, sexual health, and sexuality. In an educational flyer prepared for a rap session on women's health for Open Door volunteers, Open Door feminist organizers explained that they believed "gynecology is clearly related to sexuality" as well as to a series of other linked issues that female patients might want to discuss in relation to their health care, including "frigidity, advertising, prostitution, orgasm, heterosexual intercourse in detail, lesbianism [and] celibacy." In addition to a discussion of these topics, women would also learn to do a pelvic exam during the rap sessions and at "pelvic parties." Pelvic exams performed by feminists on each other expanded their general knowledge about women's health as well as personal knowledge about their own healthy bodies. The parties also encouraged volunteers to train as paramedics or community health care workers.

Feminist health movement activists around the country were interested in eradicating the hierarchies that structured the chain of command in traditional medical contexts. They also wanted to deconstruct traditional interactions of unequal power that existed between medical providers and patients. In order to collapse these relationships of power, community health care workers, paramedics, or "paras," as they came to be called for short, took over most of the daily medical provision at the community clinics. As historian of the feminist women's health movement Judith Houck writes, "Women themselves, sometimes trained through state-sanctioned programs, sometimes merely guided by more experienced women, could identify their anatomy, understand their menopausal experiences, treat their menstrual cramps, all without the help of physicians."[24] Stokley recalled that doctors originally trained paramedics as a volunteer support staff for the neighborhood clinics, but the paramedics quickly expanded their role to perform pelvic exams and pap smears, diagnose vaginitis, prescribe birth control and counsel about abortion, and train other women as paramedic volunteers. The physicians, who trained the first paras, eventually became the medical back-up for the volunteers at the Open Door women's clinic, Fremont, and Aradia as paras took over primary health care delivery. Patients at all of the women's clinics were also encouraged by the paras to learn about their bodies during exams by looking at their cervixes with a mirror and going to the lab to look at their own lab work through a microscope.[25]

The Fremont women's clinic also began as a neighborhood effort developed by residents of the Fremont-Ballard-Wallingford-Queen Anne neighborhoods in 1971. Although specializing in women's health care for low-income community members, the Fremont clinic offered basic gynecological services for women as well as preventive health care for both women and men. Fremont organizers explained their plans for the clinic: "Ideally, we'd offer week-long, full-scope service: pediatric care for children, gynecology for women, a senior citizens' clinic, general care for everyone. We'd provide everything from inoculations to birth control to pre-natal care, physical exams, and classes on nutrition, childbirth, sexuality, and first aid." The clinic also provided babysitting and transportation to the clinic to facilitate health care access. And they offered nutrition and budgeting courses, and self-realization courses for young women.[26] By the middle of the 1970s, state and federal funders pressured the clinic to become a full-service community clinic no longer specializing in women's health. Clinic staff and administration agreed to expand the clinic.[27]

The Fremont clinic founders first organized in response to a particular scarcity of health care providers serving the needs of the neighborhoods clustered in the Fremont-Ballard-Wallingford-Queen Anne geographical area. They noted that there was only one doctor for 3,804 people there, as compared with the King County average of one doctor for 486 people. Accordingly, they wanted to focus on community-based preventive medicine, targeting low-income women. Organizers explained in their application for federal Office of Economic Opportunity funding, "Low income women do not have sufficient opportunity to obtain treatment for illnesses or accidents that do not seem to be emergencies . . . [which] results in needless suffering . . . [and] increases the number of relatively minor health problems that develop serious complications." They also believed that low-income residents lacked the means to learn about their bodies and potential illnesses in order to maintain health. The Fremont clinic, like Aradia, focused on the provision of health care as well as on empowering women to understand their bodies and health care needs. Expanding knowledge, women's health feminists at Fremont, Open Door, and Aradia explained, led to increased involvement by women in their health, which motivated some of them to become voluntary health care providers themselves. Fremont organizers, like Neighborhood Health Center organizers nationwide, intended to "maximize community participation in decision making so that alienated people feel that they . . . decide what services the clinic will offer."[28]

Feminist organizers for the Fremont clinic, like the U of W YWCA feminists who planned Aradia, focused on women's health services, although the clinic never excluded men. They explained their reasoning behind their choice to concentrate on women's health needs: "Because a sizable majority of people who visit physicians and an even larger majority of the neighborhood residents are women, establishing a women's clinic is a practical matter." And furthermore,

> As feminists, we are especially sensitive to women's rights and needs. We feel that women must take responsibility for their lives, learning to make judgments about the institutions that influence them. One of these institutions is medicine. Women particularly have been taught to expect to have little knowledge or control of their own bodies. By emphasizing education and self-help, we hope to demystify gynecology.[29]

As at Aradia and across the country, Fremont feminists emphasized self-help and the creation of personal knowledge about the body, health, and illness from women's experiences of living with sexed and reproductive bodies in various contexts. Fremont feminists and other women's health care activists wanted to use this knowledge to wring power and influence from institutions that affected women's lives, particularly medical institutions that impacted how women understood and lived their sexual and reproductive lives. In 1973 Barbara Ehrenreich and Deirdre English wrote that self-help "arms us to demand what we need, not what someone thinks we should get. It gives us a vision of what medical care could mean—a system in which needs are not met at the price of dignity."[30] By knowing more about how their bodies worked, and by defining for themselves what they needed to promote health, feminist health movement activists believed they would gain greater control over their sexed and reproductive bodies, their sexuality and sexual expression, and their health, and thereby over what it meant to live within a female body. They also believed that greater knowledge of and control over the body translated into the ability to make more informed personal life choices about sex, reproduction, family, and intimate relationships.

"Demystifying Gynecology": Transforming Health Care

To prepare for the Aradia clinic opening, clinic organizers ran a series of educational programs on anatomy and contraceptives to encourage more lay women to become paramedical volunteers. Dr. Julius Butler of Harborview Medical Center also trained two women who would later volunteer at Aradia to do pelvic exams; these women could begin training the other women to be paras. Courses for volunteers continued to be offered at Aradia after its opening. The nine-week paramedical training courses included information on pelvic exams, contraceptive options, venereal diseases, and abortion counseling. Courses were taught by seasoned feminist health activists, some of whom, like Graber, a physical therapist, and Stokley, a nurse practitioner, already had medical credentials. Training courses taught women who had used the clinic or who were just getting involved in the women's movement and feminist health care medical skills so they could volunteer with Aradia.[31] Women could also volunteer and receive training to be lab workers or phone and desk workers. A volunteer could start in one area of the clinic and move around as she pleased. Clinic feminists encouraged experimentation by volunteers.[32]

The widespread use of paramedics in the Seattle women's clinics, and around the country in feminist-created clinics, was designed in part to dismantle what feminists believed were entrenched gender hierarchies in the medical delivery system, often appearing in the form of the knowledgeable and powerful male doctor and his female medical assistants. Contrary to this model, the female paramedics would perform pelvic exams and other diagnostic tasks at the clinic although they could not legally provide abortions. As mentioned in the preceding chapter, there is evidence that in some cases they did provide illegal abortions as well, usually through menstrual extraction.[33] By empowering women who were not physicians to provide medical care, women's health organizers hoped to convey to patients that specialized medical knowledge need not be the exclusive possession of men and/or trained medical doctors. Medical care could be demystified, they argued, and women patients and lay practitioners could be empowered to learn about their own bodies and become involved in their personal health promotion.[34] They could also help women feel more comfortable during pelvic exams, they argued, because "the 'paras' who perform pelvic exams are women who have a strong desire to eliminate the awkwardness and the confusion they themselves have often experienced during examinations."[35] Furthermore, as volunteers who were willing to donate their labor, paramedicals helped Aradia and other Seattle clinics to provide low-cost and free health care to all women who walked through their doors.

Some young feminists who trained as paramedical volunteers to work at Aradia went on to have long professional medical careers in nursing, as midwives, or as physicians. Aradia helped these women enter the medical professions, and in turn, these women transformed the medical professions over the course of their careers as they continued to apply feminist standards of care even after they left Aradia for more mainstream medical institutions. Dyan Edison, for example, eventually trained as a registered nurse but began her medical career when she first volunteered at the Open Door clinic and then joined Aradia shortly after its founding. She had come from a big family of medical doctors so the medical field was not foreign to her. Edison recalled that as an Aradia volunteer she was "an assistant in an exam room to provide material for paps and exams, providing a flashlight and mirror and the warmed speculum . . . that was revolutionary. [A] flashlight and a mirror [allowed] women to look from the outside to the inside of their vagina to their cervix." She continued, "For me, my life changed from that time on."[36]

Sharon Baker, another early Aradia volunteer, was already a licensed registered nurse when she started at the clinic but she participated in a federal training program to become a Women's Health Care Specialist. She and four other Aradia volunteers, including Graber, one of the founders of Aradia, trained in the three-week Ostergard Program, created in 1969 by Dr. Donald P. Ostergard, professor of ob/gyn at UCLA, and Duane Townsend, at Harbor General Hospital in Los Angeles. Women in the program learned "to conduct breast and pelvic exams, insert IUDs, fit diaphragms, and perform routine prenatal and other well-woman tasks."[37] This program was an HEW-funded initiative to train Women's Health Specialists, who, if they passed the exam, were licensed as physician assistants and could practice in Washington State, Oregon, Idaho, and California. According to Graber, HEW came to Aradia as their funding agent and insisted that some of their practitioners be trained in the program. The Ostergard program was open to both licensed nurses and unlicensed lay practitioners and included training to detect gynecological abnormalities that would need to be referred to a physician for follow-up diagnosis and treatment.[38] When women at Aradia returned from the Ostergard training they passed on the information to other women volunteers so they could provide medical support and assist with pelvic exams.

Baker, Edison, and Graber all remained in the health care field after their stint at Aradia and all suggest that their experiences at Aradia impacted their later work in health care. Graber, for example, became a licensed nurse midwife and started a rural women's health clinic in eastern Washington State in 1976. After her experience at Aradia, Baker went back to school for a master's in public health and became the director of Oakland Planned Parenthood and then returned to Seattle to work at Harborview Hospital in a women's clinic staffed by several Aradia veterans, including Graber before she left Seattle.[39] The Harborview women's clinic, which hired nurse practitioners and specialists in women's health to do pap smears, IUD insertions, and diaphragm fittings and provided other well-woman gynecological care to low-income women, many of whom had never had a pelvic exam before, is one example of how feminists at Aradia helped transform more mainstream medical institutions.

Graber recalled training medical student interns and residents at Harborview to do pelvic exams just as she had been trained in the Ostergard Women's Health Specialist program. She remembered that she would "stand there with the medical student and put my hand on their hand and make sure they weren't pinching and totally instruct them in how to do it. Then I would do it after them to make sure that they did it right."[40]

Many feminists viewed the women's clinic as much more than just a place to receive well-woman gynecological care. They believed medicine was a profoundly gendered institution that negatively affected the health care women received. The feminist clinic was meant to be a corrective to this gendered and hierarchical medical system that, Women's Liberation activists argued, sanctioned male doctors' power over women's bodies. They argued further that gendered medical authority not only often represented itself as an objective purveyor of women's health needs and information about women's bodies but also often justified women's subordinate status with medical science.[41] Feminists reasoned that training more women to practice medicine would empower them to be subjects directing their own medical care. Aradia founding feminists explained,

> Due to the lack of women in the medical profession many doctors cannot adequately relate to women patients and their lack of understanding of women's problems contributes to paternalistic and condescending attitudes. Women, by grouping together to demand conscientious and high quality medical care for themselves, will force a change in those attitudes and subsequently improve the relationships between doctors and patients in general.[42]

Edison recalled a particularly powerful incident with a patient that she believed typified the kind of transformative experience many women had at feminist clinics. Feminists attributed the transformative experience to an emphasis on communication between health provider and patient and also to feminist efforts to encourage patients to learn about their own bodies. In this example, Edison had just performed a pelvic exam on a young woman in the clinic accompanied by her mother. When the young woman had finished her exam, she asked her if her mother could have one too. Edison described her interaction with the young woman's mother:

The mother had had six children and was from the south . . . and the mom came in to have her exam and she was a little nervous. When she was on the exam table and we were going to do the exam, we said we're going to warm the speculum up so it's not cold in your vagina and we'll give you a mirror and speculum and you can see. And we said we are going to touch you before we touched her very gently on her thighs. [This] was huge for women and we always maintained that eye contact with a patient. The woman had tears streaming down her face, so I asked if I was hurting her. It was such a responsible position and a vulnerable position for a woman to be in. She said, "No, you aren't, but darlin' I've had six babies and I never knew where they came from. I knew that they came from somewhere down there. I want to tell you how much this means to me." We were giving gentle responsible health care for women. It was one of the highlights of what we were doing. Gentle responsible health care for women.[43]

Similarly, Graber recalled, "showing women their cervix and having women feel their cervix and they would sometimes break into tears and say that they were thirty-five and never dared [feel it]. They thought they'd hurt themselves."[44]

Seattle women's health movement feminists constructed their clinic around the assumption of a female reproductive body that women should manage among each other. All women, both patients and members of the feminist clinic, required health services, so at any given time patient and clinic member (health provider) might switch roles. The fluidity of these roles countered the notion that the feminist provider was the purveyor of knowledge whereas the patient was the object of that knowledge. Both the woman on the table being examined and the woman examining her were subjects and producers of knowledge about their socially situated bodies and about each other's bodies.

Paramedics-in-training and women just interested in learning more about their bodies also attended "pelvic parties," or self-help gatherings, often held at the U of W YWCA, at which women used plastic speculums and mirrors to investigate their own and other women's cervixes to learn about women's sexual and reproductive bodies first-hand. "Pelvic parties," which also occurred in other cities around the country with active feminist health movement organizations, had roots in the first women's health movement efforts to appropriate gynecological services from medical doctors by observing their own and each other's reproductive bodies.[45]

While feminists at Aradia were influenced by burgeoning challenges to the medical establishment, mostly in the context of the New Left and the abortion rights movement, as well as the rapid emergence of the Women's Liberation movement in Seattle and across the country, it is also likely that many of the ideas about feminist women's health generated by Seattle feminists can be traced to Los Angeles and Carol Downer's creation of feminist self-help. The story of Downer's invention of feminist "self-help" and her inspiration to teach women how to view their own and each other's cervixes has been recounted many times. However, I will briefly relate it here, because her impact was so influential on the feminist women's health movement.

Downer and several other women associated with the Los Angeles National Organization for Women wanted to increase abortion access for women beyond what the California State abortion law allowed, which was therapeutic abortion for reasons including rape, incest, and congenital fetal defects.[46] Rather than fight for greater access to abortion through legal channels, Downer, like the women in Chicago's Jane, decided that women should learn to perform abortions themselves. Performing abortion, however, would not be Downer's main contribution to the women's health movement. Downer's moment of inspiration came when she looked at a woman's cervix during an instructional IUD insertion with a physician who had agreed to demonstrate abortion as well as other gynecological health procedures to Downer and a group of five other women. After seven pregnancies, it struck her as remarkable that she had never seen her own cervix, so with a mirror and a plastic speculum, she looked at herself. Sheryl Burt Ruzek, early chronicler of the feminist women's health movement, explained, "Self- help gynecology was born on April 7, 1971, at the Everywoman's Bookstore in Los Angeles" when Downer demonstrated a self-exam on herself.[47] Very quickly Downer and others who had observed and learned the self-help procedure showed other women cervical self-examination. The simple self-exam spread like wildfire as Downer and Lorraine Rothman, the inventor of the menstrual extraction kit, demonstrated cervical self-exam at the 1971 national conference of the National Organization for Women.

Later in the year, they embarked on a national self-examination tour. When they returned to Los Angeles in 1972 they founded the Los Angeles Feminist Women's Health Center (LA FWHC).[48]

Downer and Rothman wanted to transform the medical system and decided that the best way to do so would be to establish a new medical infrastructure of feminist women's health centers. Certainly their efforts influenced the practices at the countless feminist health clinics that sprang up across the country at this time. Downer and Rothman also contributed to this explosion of new feminist health services with their plan for a National Federation of Feminist Women's Health Centers. Soon after creating the Los Angeles Feminist Women's Health Center clinic, which provided both abortion care and other contraceptive services, feminists with experience at the LA FWHC founded an FWHC clinic in Orange County and then in Oakland. In 1973 a group of women launched the Detroit FWHC. In 1974, another group of women founded a federated clinic in Tallahassee, Florida, then in Chico, California, in 1975. In 1976, FWHC clinics were founded in Concord, California, San Diego, Portland, Oregon, and Atlanta. All Federation of FWHC clinics placed self-help and well-woman care at the center of their health services. They called their well-woman clinic a "participatory clinic" that provided an opportunity for women to meet with trained lay health workers or female paramedics to discuss their health concerns and to learn and do vaginal and cervical self-exams. Health care at the FWHCs also included information about birth control so women could choose the method most suited to them, pregnancy testing if needed, detection and diagnosis of sexually transmitted infections, and abortions. All of these services were provided in a context of maximum information sharing and participation by the women who wanted the services.[49]

The idea that women could observe their own reproductive bodies and those of other women both to chart their healthy cycles and to diagnose illness or even perform an abortion became a fundamental part of the nationwide women's health movement and feminists' critique of established medicine. Nancy Tuana has argued astutely, "Women not only learned about and from their own bodies, they also learned to trust their cognitive authority and resist the authority of the medical professionals."[50] Susan Reverby, historian and women's health movement activist, also recalled, "Many women began to trust what we thought we knew and could learn—not what 'they' could or would tell us." Reverby, however, also questioned the quest for greater knowledge without an accompanying political strategy to demand real institutional and structural changes to the health care delivery system, particularly for women of color and poor women, for whom knowledge of their bodies might not translate into improved health care services.[51]

While demystifying medical care in self-help groups or at "pelvic parties," women examined each other's and their own cervixes and learned about self-help methods for treating minor health problems such as yeast infections. Women also learned to observe healthy changes in their and other women's cervixes or to recognize differences in a woman's cervix depending on whether she had given birth vaginally. But Seattle feminists also recognized that cervical observation was not for every woman; women could also attend lecture series on sexuality and reproductive health. Some women became volunteers at Aradia by attending a lecture series or a pelvic party and then training as a paramedic once they established a strong interest in women's health delivery.[52] Women outside of the city of Seattle also became involved in women's health provision. A group of Bothell self-described "housewives" created a free women's clinic in the basement of a Lutheran church. They explained that women often neglected their own health care to focus on the well-being of their families. They reasoned that a woman-centered clinic would encourage women to care for their own needs as well.[53]

Female paramedics were the primary means of transforming the delivery of health care at Aradia by demonstrating that knowledge about bodies and sexuality was accessible to lay women and that women could control their own medical delivery and decision making about health. Women without any medical experience could take courses on "the menstrual cycle and birth control, on pregnancy and its effects and prenatal care, on abortion . . . on urinary tract infection, vaginitis, sexuality (especially female sexuality), and on counseling on all these subjects." They also learned "on the job" in the clinic at Aradia, at the Fremont Women's Clinic, or at one of the women's evening clinics at Open Door or Country Doctor. While paras did not entirely replace physicians because of legal requirements that doctors perform abortions, paras could staff reception, provide educational forums, and both perform examinations and make diagnoses with a physician's backup. Legal stipulations requiring a doctor's presence at the clinic frustrated feminist intentions to free medical care entirely from established medical practitioners and hierarchy. To make clear that volunteer women had the real decision-making power over the clinic, feminist health activists emphasized that "paraprofessional workers, rather than the professional staff, control the clinic and determine its policies." They further emphasized that para-professionals were not nurses "who help doctors because women should help men so men should be doctors and women should be nurses." Rather, the feminist clinics hired doctors to back up the paraprofession-als and meet legal requirements.[54]

A more theoretical approach to a critique of established medicine was taken up by the Political Education group, a subgroup of the Aradia "coven," which reported to the rest of the group about their critique of what they believed was established and patriarchal health care. They argued that established medical institutions produced a "mystification of medicine to keep power and knowledge more securely in doctors' hands." In an analysis that brought together both socialist and feminist theoretical frameworks, they also argued that the "capitalistic base of traditional medicine keeps doctors' fees and drug prices high." In this line of reasoning, capitalism and patriarchy reinforced one another in a system that maintained a ruling class in which gender was one fac-tor that produced and reinforced individual social positions. Although women could be a part of the ruling class and could be beneficiaries of capitalism, they gained entry into the upper class through marriage or birth and were generally confined to private and domestic roles that did not give them access to the means of producing their own wealth or controlling capital. Professional segregation by gender reinforced this system by diverting mostly men into the high-paying and socially im-portant professions and diverting mostly women into the lower-paying service positions or into unremunerated domestic work as wives of pro-fessional men who could afford stay-at-home wives.[55]

The Political Education group explained that physicians further re-inforced gendered social segregation and women's subordinate status by treating women patients as ignorant and childlike. Other Seattle femi-nists concurred, explaining that "[t]hey [doctors] treat us as if we 'girls' wouldn't understand or be interested in all that medical stuff he knows about what goes on 'down there.'"[56] Feminists noted that shame coupled with ignorance played a large part in maintaining women's subordination as well. They explained that the more women believed their bodies were dirty, the less interest they had in feeling connected to and in control of their bodies. Furthermore, if girls and women were taught that their bodies were not for their own fulfillment and pleasure—and that if they did pursue their own pleasure they were even dirtier—they were less apt to want to use their bodies for their own ends. The female body remained an instrument of male knowledge, pleasure, and utility, the group reported.[57] Aradia volunteers sometimes joined the clinic because they had had negative experiences with their doctors treating them like ignorant children. Larraine Volkman, for instance, one of the few women in the group who had children before becoming an Aradia volunteer, remembered telling "my doctor that there was something down there that felt like the back of my thumb and the doctor patted me on the head and said don't worry about that stuff down there, I'll take care of it. Well, it was a prolapsed uterus."[58]

As Volkman's experience illustrated, Aradia feminists argued that established medical practice reinforced gendered hierarchies and social roles that disadvantaged women while giving men power over women's bodies, particularly over reproduction. They wrote,

> Most women who visit doctors are often faced with . . . numerous questions that are never answered. In the medical establishment men are the main providers of health care and reflect the attitudes of the larger society. These attitudes of women being "dumb," and "passive," and "baby making machines" are seen in the care they receive. They are not given any information about what is wrong with them . . . and told to "have babies" to remedy a variety of physical problems.[59]

Aradia feminists and other feminist health movement activists across the country repeatedly claimed that gender hierarchies were reinforced when doctors kept medical information from women. They argued that women needed to access this information to better understand the workings of their own bodies and to provide better medical care for each other. Better medical care, they theorized, would follow from the informed choices women could make with improved knowledge about the workings of their healthy bodies and their potential illnesses. Seattle feminists explained, "They [doctors] do not educate us about our bodies, or explain what procedures and tests they take; often they don't even tell us what infection we've got." They continued, emphasizing the unequal power dynamic this relationship reinforced: "Withholding information creates mystery and gives power to him who holds that information, so as long as he knows about our bodies and we don't, we must return to him for diagnosis and treatment of our problems."[60]

Women's health movement feminists also argued that purported medical objectivity and the separation of reproductive health from female sexual feelings also reinforced gendered power relationships founded upon women's ignorance about and alienation from their bodies. Medical claims to objectivity privileged physician control of medical information by associating it with science, dispassionate research, and professionalism, rather than the personal and lived experience of a sexual and reproductive body. A woman's knowledge of her body, alternatively, they argued, could be discounted as personal, unscientific, and tainted by sexual experience. They wrote, "He [the doctor] is not to 'enjoy' performing the exam, but is to remain objective. . . . There is no connection between the woman's face and mind, and her genitals, of what is going on 'down there,' of what is or isn't normal, or of what your infection may be and what caused it."[61] Over and over, former Aradia volunteers emphasized the importance of "the touch" as they called it— when they explained to a woman that they were going to start the pelvic exam and touched her leg. Instead of maintaining objectivity, the Aradia volunteers reinforced the connection among a woman's emotions, her body, and medical care. As Graber explained, this connection was often fundamental to doing a good exam, because a woman needed to relax before the nurse or para could feel her ovaries. A tensed abdominal wall made it difficult to feel internal reproductive organs.[62]

The corrective for established and patriarchal medical care, Aradia feminists asserted, lay within the walls of feminist-controlled women's health institutions like Aradia. Within the feminist clinic, women would learn from other women not to be ashamed of their bodies. Rather, they would teach each other to understand how their bodies functioned, particularly their sexual and reproductive bodies, since those aspects of the body had been most often employed to maintain women's subordinate status. Knowledge of the body would be acquired from a variety of sources, including establishment medical sources, but also from women's subjective experiences of their own bodies and what they observed in other women's bodies. They argued that "as women's attitudes toward themselves change, men and doctors will be forced to change."[63]

Seattle health movement feminists decided that men could also learn to provide nonsexist gynecological care. To this end they invited men to attend pelvic exam trainings. One class was set aside for male physicians and paramedics interested in volunteering in a women's clinic. But men were not to be passive observers; nor were they to take on the role of practitioner without experiencing what it felt like to be a patient too. The feminists required male participants to have rectal and urethral cultures taken during the session. The organizers of the training explained, "These men will leave with a better understanding of what women must endure for a pelvic, and we women will have a rare opportunity to perform these tests on a male subject." They continued, emphasizing that the exercise would help deconstruct gendered roles. They argued that the training was "a great opportunity for us to strengthen communication with our brothers who are struggling as we are to break out of conditioned roles."[64] This particular experiment in role reversal suggested that health movement feminists often believed that the way men and women experienced their bodies hinged on social context and that context could be manipulated by feminists to teach men antisexist behavior.

The Aradia clinic feminists also linked sexuality and reproductive health services from the beginning. Clinic services included "information and discussion of sexuality, including sexual minorities, information about menstruation, conception and menopause, contraception information, and pregnancy detection and counseling." Clinic volunteers placed a lot of emphasis on helping women find the best birth control method. They provided birth control pill prescriptions, fit women for diaphragms, or inserted IUDs; foam and condoms were also available. The clinic also provided referrals for tubal ligation and vasectomy upon request.[65] But they did not disconnect this vital information on contraception and reproductive health from information on sexuality. Edison recalled calling a pharmacist to find out how to acquire vibrators. He suggested she try a bookstore that sold pornography in the "red light district" in downtown Seattle. Edison called them and learned they could order vibrators in bulk, so she bought five and distributed them to other Aradia volunteers. When the vibrators proved popular, she began ordering them in batches of twenty-five from the same bookstore and Aradia began selling them at the clinic and recommending them to patients who had difficulty achieving orgasm.[66]

Seattle feminists, like other women's health movement organizers, often articulated a desire for women to provide health care to other women "because we feel that women can understand the problems women have better. It stands to reason just as a woman will never know how it feels to have an erection, a man can never know how it feels to give birth to a child."[67] In this explanation, an emphasis on women's shared embodied reproductive experiences took precedence over an exploration of women's potential for feminist alliance despite differences of class, race, ethnicity, sexuality, language, political orientation, or religion. Yet, Seattle feminists emphasized the power of knowledge to transform gender roles, which suggested that women's gendered and embodied experiences were situated socially and historically and subject to change. They explained, "[An all-female clinic staff] says that we have confidence in women's ability to learn skills and be knowledgeable about previously withheld information." Women who volunteered at the clinic might become introduced to feminist ideas critical of stereotypical gender roles. These women might start "challenging the structures that hold us back, experimenting, and introducing new and radical methods."[68]

The clinic organizers adhered to an intentionally nonhierarchical structure of medical practice in accordance with women's health and feminist movement activists' mistrust of consolidated power. Feminist organizations across the country experimented with "structureless" organizational frameworks with varying degrees of success. Their criticism of consolidated power and hierarchy, however, often did not erase unacknowledged hierarchies that developed among women on the basis of race or class difference.[69] In their attempt to erase hierarchy in women's health care provision, Aradia clinic feminists opened their "coven" meetings to the public. They explained, "Everyone is equal in these meetings, and encouraged to share her ideas. . . . We want everyone who works in and comes to Aradia to have a voice in what the clinic will do and hope she will involve herself in the decision making for the clinic."[70]

Yet, hierarchies did form, advantaging those with the most time to spend in the organization, those who were paid staff members, and those with race or class privileges.[71] Larraine Volkman, a volunteer at Aradia from 1973 to 1976 and also a member of the U of W YWCA board, recalled that "if you are an 18–25 year old professional woman and going to medical school is just one of your choices," that reveals a class bias. She explained that as a young woman who grew up on a farm in southern Idaho in Mormon country, she had never thought of attending medical school, but not just because of gender bias. Class also shaped what she saw as the career paths open to her. Volkman continued, "Many women [at Aradia] went on to medical school [and] many could go off and volunteer their time so supporting themselves was not necessary. They were getting checks from their parents" that made full-time feminist activism or volunteer work in a feminist clinic a possible choice. She added that "self-confidence and how you express yourself is all involved in your class background."[72] Both class and race shaped the way women experienced the women's health movement, as well as the kinds of institutions they demanded emerge from the movement. The next section will focus on the creation of the Third World Women's Resource Center and an associated clinic that would serve women of color.

Third World Women and Feminist Health

The national YWCA has a long history of participation by African American women and civil rights movement involvement, beginning in the 1920s with segregated club activities for African American women and girls. In the 1940s, at the behest of black club members, the organization began to press for reforms in southern states to allow blacks access to the franchise. In 1946 the YWCA desegregated all of its chapters nationwide.[73] In concert with that history, although also as a distinctly separate Women's Liberation entity, the Seattle YWCA feminists created a Third World Women's Resource Center (TWWRC) in 1972 with support from the National Student YWCA based in New York City to eliminate "racism wherever it exists and by any means necessary."[74]

The term "Third World" was preferred by feminists in the early 1970s to signify political and theoretical connections between the experiences of minority populations in the United States and colonial and postcolonial populations abroad. The establishment of a center dedicated to the needs of "Third World Women" and to addressing racism is an early example of Women's Liberation activist commitment to ending discrimination along the intersecting identifications of race, ethnicity, nationality, class, and gender. Women of color feminists would continue to criticize white women in the Women's Liberation movement for racism and classism, but this example demonstrates that in some Women's Liberation organizations, race and class issues were addressed in the early years of the movement. Women's health activists Ehrenreich and English in their popular feminist pamphlet *Complaints and Disorders* emphasized that race and class powerfully shaped women's medical access and needs. They wrote, "A movement that recognizes our biological similarity but denies the diversity of our priorities cannot be a women's health movement, it can only be *some women's* health movement."[75]

Theresa Saludo, Sarah Sakuma, Shelley Yapp, and Janet Krause, associate director and later director of the U of W YWCA, founded and secured funding for the TWWRC. Alma Arnold became the program director. The purpose of the TWWRC was to "increase its [U of W YWCA's] outreach to minority women by serving their special needs and interests." Founders also designed the TWWRC to "support Third World women who are using other services at the Y, such as the Abortion-Birth Control Referral Service and Aradia." The resource center also sponsored "rap groups" "to bring women together to share personal experiences as a means of gaining understanding and acceptance between women of different cultural backgrounds." Their goal was "not only . . . [for] white women to achieve a better understanding of women from other ethnic groups . . . but to increase understanding and knowledge between Black, Spanish American, Asian and Native American women." They planned to offer classes on subjects such as Native American women's literature and "Women in Black Literature" and support for English-as-a-second-language speakers.[76]

The TWWRC included a health care component from the beginning by pressing for improved contraceptive services for women of color at Aradia and elsewhere in the Seattle area. First, they sponsored educational workshops to train staff at family planning clinics around the city and the state of Washington to "raise . . . the consciousness of those workers that are involved in the delivery of educational and medical services to the thoughts and feelings of our people as shaped by our individual and unique cultures."[77] They also generated a "collection of info on family planning and writings by Third World people" to edu-cate those serving women of color in family planning facilities as well as women of color who used the clinics. They believed information pamphlets generated by and for women of color would be more sensi-tive to their specific health care needs and better promote health among women of color.[78]

In 1973 YWCA feminists focused more intently on expanding health care services to "Third World" women. First, Theresa Saludo, YWCA board member, member of the Aradia clinic "coven," and cofounder of the TWWRC, designed a workshop for Aradia clinic and other local family planning staff to increase their sensitivity and responsiveness to the reproductive health needs of women of color.[79] In the same year Saludo and Penny Teal also proposed expanding the Aradia clinic with HEW funding to provide a facility that would better serve women of color. They would train "Third World Women" to operate a family planning facility dedicated to the "Third World community" in Seattle, which would "provide medical services, counseling, educationals, and referrals to the people of the community." They called the new clinic the "Third World Women's Preventive Medicine and Health Education Center" and connected it to a new community facility, El Centro de la Raza, founded in the previous year on Beacon Hill, about ten minutes from downtown Seattle.[80]

Although family planning and contraception provision would be a central part of clinic services, Seattle feminists argued that the clinic should also include infertility testing and treatment because "[Third World] people are adamant about the right to have or not to have chil-dren."[81] Furthermore, the 1973 involuntary sterilization of the two Relf sisters, when they were only twelve and fourteen years old, in a feder-ally funded Alabama clinic heightened associations among birth con-trol, forced sterilization, and alleged genocidal intentions of the federal government against people of color.[82] Feminists planning the clinic explained that the "threatened sterilization of women on welfare, the fear of genocide, and the impact of the historical as well as present day treatment of people of color are seen by Third World Women as a real basis for mistrust and apprehension for Family Planning Programs."[83] They also explained that women of color often avoided family planning clinics because of cultural and language barriers and also, at times, because of a stigma associated with public conversations about sexuality. Family planning services needed to reflect these linguistic and cultural differences among clients, YWCA and Aradia feminists argued. Saludo and others encouraged women of color to participate in the Ostergard training of Women's Health Specialists so they could provide services at El Centro, at Aradia, and in the other clinics in the city. Finally, YWCA and Aradia feminists discussed the fact that services needed to be easily accessible (available in local clinics near women's homes) and affordable, if not completely free.[84]

Like Aradia, this clinic would link sexuality education, contraception education, and health provision. Its founders also planned to provide education about contraception to men of color, in part to counteract negative religious and cultural views about birth control, including ideas that linked contraception to genocide among people of color. YWCA feminists believed a clinic linked to La Raza that would primarily serve a women of color population could help solve several problems specific to women of color's experiences. First, they believed the new clinic would allow women of color "to operate within a facility that is [not] geared to the needs of white women"; second, it would provide a staff "that has . . . knowledge [and] understanding of [Third World women's] particular background and needs," including a medical and support staff that represented the variety of cultural groups using the new clinic. The clinic would be located in the southern part of the city on Beacon Hill, closer to neighborhoods where many minority residents lived. This location would be easier to access for women of color than the Aradia clinic in the University District, a historically and still majority-white neighborhood in the northern portion of the city.[85]

Saludo also wanted to gather information about Third World "peoples' feelings and opinions about Family Planning Health care and Sexuality to be used as the basis for a Workshop" to train clinic staff.[86] To meet this goal, Saludo designed and implemented a Third World Family Planning Needs Assessment Project that operated out of El Centro de la Raza community center to gather information that would help train medical staff and provide better services to this multiracial, multiethnic, and multilingual community. The project received Title X funding from HEW and began to gather information in 1973.[87] Saludo designed the Needs Assessment Project to evaluate the birth control practices of low-income women of color, including Asian, Latina, Native American, and black women. By gathering information on women of color's need for and current use of birth control, she hoped to improve contraceptive services at El Centro and at other clinics in Seattle.[88] She also wanted to find out if family planning clinics in Seattle optimally served women of color by charting how often women of color frequented clinics—neighborhood and feminist clinics like Aradia, Planned Parenthood, and county public health clinics—in different geographical locations of the city.

The project revealed that barriers to using contraceptives among women of color existed due to mistrust of family planning providers after the Relf forced sterilizations came to light in 1973. Women and men of color mistrusted the intentions of white birth control clinic staff. There were also communication barriers, particularly among non-English-speaking women, and/or because of technical jargon used among clinic staff. They also found that transportation and clinic costs sometimes prevented women from accessing wanted contraceptives. Finally, Saludo discovered that cultural sensitivity around sexual matters negatively affected many women of color's decision to use a family planning clinic.[89]

In other efforts to address intersectional race and gender issues, YWCA feminists, including Jan Krause and Jean Owens, coordinated a Feminism and Racism Rap Group in spring 1973 to explore the subject of racism within the feminist movement. The creation of this group, as well as the Third World Women's clinic at El Centro, and the Third World Women's Resource Center, suggests a certain level of feminist consciousness of racism within the movement in the early 1970s, contrary to some representations of early Women's Liberation movement activities as blind to racial difference and racism. The Feminism and Racism Rap Group provides evidence that conversations about race did indeed occur among white feminists even if many women of color still found feminist political strategies and priorities to be narrowly focused on an agenda that did not acknowledge or marginalized their demands. While many feminists certainly held racist beliefs, thus the need for a "rap group" on the subject, the existence of the rap group indicated intent to address that racism. Certainly, the intent to address racism and subtle patterns of racist exclusion could and did exist simultaneously. Furthermore, the existence of an antiracism rap group among YWCA feminists does not contradict assertions by white Aradia founders that sex, sexuality, and gender were their primary issues of concern in the 1970s. Isaac and Keenan clarified that at the time they did not often think about how sex, sexuality, and gender categories intersected with race, not because they were unaware that racism existed (some white Aradia and YWCA feminists had been involved in the civil rights movement) but because issues of sex and gender discrimination were new to them and at the forefront of their political consciousness.[90]

A conference and festival structured around the theme "Solidarity thru Sisterhood" sponsored by the YWCA TWWRC occurred on the University of Washington campus in early 1974. Seattle feminists hoped to "cultivate a harmonious intra & interracial unity . . . thru having more and frequent social interactions." They believed that women were better than men at creating ties with one another across racial and cultural divides because they were free of "the ego problems that many of our brothers are hung-up in . . . . so it is sisters who must make the initial steps to bring about our desired end."[91] One panel at the conference focused on the "politics of health care as they affect Third World Women." Other panels were on class and Third World Women, a celebration of International Women's Day, and a keynote address by Frances Beale, editor of *The Black Woman*, an influential early 1970s collection of black feminist writings. Workshop topics included Third World Women and the Law, Organizing Women, Third World Women and Prisons, Third World Women and Mass Media, Third World Women and Education, and Brother-Sister Unity.[92] Constance Hiller Engelsberg of the coordinating committee for the conference believed the meeting built on a burgeoning feminist movement among women of color in Seattle led by Seattle Third World Women, an organization affiliated with Third World Women's Alliance based in New York City.[93]

Conclusion

The Aradia clinic decoupled financially from the U of W YWCA in 1973, although it remained tied to the organization politically as women involved with the YWCA continued to be involved with Aradia. Aradia as an independent feminist health center continued to provide women's health services until 2006. During this time span, the clinic changed locations twice. It first moved to Capitol Hill and then to a larger, more accessible and modern medical facility on First Hill, near the Swedish Medical Center. Aradia staff helped train physicians at Swedish in the practice of feminist abortion.[94] Although methods of feminist and women's health delivery changed over the years—for example, less emphasis was placed on self-help and patient involvement in clinic services— many of the fundamental goals of the clinic founders remained. For example, Marcy Bloom, executive director of the clinic from 1987 until 2006, explained that "the model [of self-help] and the value of what it meant was not literal self-help of looking at each other's cervices—it was that women can be trusted to make decisions about their health care and women can be and should be partners in their own health care."[95]

Aradia's emphasis on partnering with women across lines of race, ethnicity, and sexual orientation to provide health services that affirmed women's different social contexts and life choices as well as their different economic and educational resources remained central to Aradia's mission until the clinic closed its doors in 2006. Throughout its existence the clinic prioritized the delivery of clinic health services to an increasingly diverse population in the city of Seattle. By the time the clinic closed, 70 percent of patients were Medicaid or Medicare recipients and a vast majority were women of color and/or immigrants. The clinic provided translators for non-English speakers in Spanish, but also in Chinese, Vietnamese, and Tagalog. Furthermore, Aradia staff sustained the clinic's original dedication to linking reproductive health with issues of sexuality through community health and sex education and outreach to local schools, other community venues, and colleges and universities in the area.[96]

During these years, Aradia committed to providing all women with a uniquely feminist and high-quality women's health experience, including abortions in a safe and compassionate environment, in line with ideals laid out by Abortion Birth Control Referral Service feminists in the early 1970s. Unfortunately, these services became unsustainable with increasing medical costs, a larger low-income population utilizing Aradia's services, and decreasing government support, including lower Medicaid reimbursements. The clinic closed in 2006 when the board of directors decided that it could no longer sustain the same high-quality services it had provided for over thirty years. These distinctive services included providing an advocate for each patient during her abortion and aftercare discussion of the emotional impact of the abortion if a patient required it. Executive director Bloom recalled that in the 1980s and 1990s the clinic staff spent a lot of time with patients and the public combating the stigmatization of abortion.[97]

After 2006, Seattle women could still access health care influenced by Aradia and other feminist health movement goals; for example, they might find that the physicians they went to for ob/gyn care listened to them and informed them of their choices; certainly abortion is still legal and usually very safe although not always accessible and often stigmatized. Yet feminist health care provided something more—an affirmation of a woman's sexual and reproductive choices without question and, perhaps even more significantly, a determination to increase women's knowledge of their bodies and their power over their destinies through high-quality health provision.

By existing into the twenty-first century, Aradia survived through much of the anti-abortion movement's most strident and violent attempts to close clinics providing abortion, feminist and nonfeminist alike. Fortunately for Aradia, Seattle was not a primary target for anti-abortion activity, although the clinic did increase security in the 1980s and 1990s as it responded to anti-abortion threats. Other feminist health clinics, however, were fundamentally affected by anti-abortion protests, blockades, and other vocal and even violent attacks. The Atlanta Feminist Women's Health Center stands as one example of a feminist women's health clinic that weathered these attacks as Atlanta became one of the primary locations for anti-abortion activity in the 1980s. The next chapter details the history of this feminist clinic to illustrate the different strategies feminists forged to meet vastly different contextual challenges as the revolutionary optimism of the 1970s transformed into a much more conservative and defensive era in the 1980s.

Conserving Feminist Health Care, Confronting Anti-Abortion

The Atlanta Feminist Women's Health Center

Feminists who founded and ran the Aradia Women's Health Center experienced the optimistic blossoming of Women's Liberation and the feminist women's health movements. Women's health reform was a fundamental component of Women's Liberation as that movement emerged in the late 1960s and early 1970s. As several women who were involved in the early days of Aradia explained to me, Women's Liberation health activists felt almost fearless, like they could do anything, including build a woman-controlled clinic with no formal medical training. Any of the fears they did have were quickly overcome by excitement about how rapidly things were changing around them.[1] The previous chapter on Aradia reflects those early days of the movement and that optimism. Yet, within just a few years after the first stirrings of a feminist women's health movement and then proliferation of women's health centers across the country, the movement experienced new challenges that feminists could not have anticipated in the early part of the decade.

The Atlanta Feminist Women's Health Center (FWHC), one of the most vibrant and influential women's health centers in the Southeast, was first created as a small and informal self-help "clinic" that met in Lynne Randall's apartment in 1975 to discuss feminist women's health issues and practice cervical self-exams. This small group included Randall, who became the first executive director of the Atlanta FWHC, Lynn Stoverson, and several women associated with the Tallahassee (Florida) Feminist Women's Health Center. The Atlanta group used its members' ties to the women in Tallahassee to learn about providing abortion in a feminist setting. Randall explained,

We had the ties. . . . [T]here was this small group of us that would actually
travel from Atlanta on Friday night and go down to Tallahassee, which is
more than a five hour drive, who would work their abortion clinic on Saturday. . . . And so we were starting to familiarize ourselves with how . . . this collective known as the Feminist Women's Health Center organize[s] and run[s]
clinics and meet the women who were involved as well as meet the women
who were involved with the broader Feminist Women's Health Centers.[2]

The Atlanta women also built ties with FWHC organizers in Los Angeles, Orange County, and Chico, California. The Atlanta FWHC finally
opened its doors in 1977 after the founders trained at the Tallahassee
Feminist Women's Health Center.[3] After struggling to find physicians
willing to perform abortions at the clinic, Randall employed two female
medical residents from Emory University, Beverly Douglas and Patricia
Ritchie Hanes. Both of them also trained at the Tallahassee clinic. At the
beginning the clinic was open one day a week and performed about four
abortions on each of those days.[4]

To understand the difference between the Atlanta FWHC and Aradia,
it is important to note that by 1977 the political context had changed
dramatically from the sanguine early 1970s as an antifeminist backlash
gained strength. This backlash included anti-abortion forces galvanized
by Roe v. Wade as well as a growing conservative antifeminist movement
represented by Phyllis Schlafly and Stop ERA (Equal Rights Amendment).[5] The 1976 Hyde Amendment, which cut off federal Medicaid
funding for abortion for poor women, was the first triumph of the anti-
abortion forces. The election of Ronald Reagan in 1980 marked a de-
finitive end to a heady era of social transformation that had fostered
the civil rights movement, anti–Vietnam War efforts, an expansion of
the social safety net, including the creation of Medicare and Medicaid,
challenges to establishment medicine by New Leftists and civil rights
activists, antipoverty work in the form of the welfare rights movement
led by the National Welfare Rights Organization, the Women's Liberation movement, and the gay and lesbian rights movement. The death of
the ERA in 1982 was for some a symbolic final blow to these feminist
and progressive activities in the United States.

While the opening of the FWHC in Atlanta in 1977 occurred near the
end of this period of powerful social and political upheaval and reform,

the Atlanta FWHC had advantages as an institutionalized product of earlier feminist struggles. Its structure, not as antihierarchical as earlier clinic experiments like Aradia, helped it weather new challenges, including the anti-abortion movement, the HIV/AIDS epidemic, and an increasingly diverse population of women who needed access to basic gynecological and obstetrical health services in an inaccessible medical marketplace. To grapple with these challenges, staff and administrators at the Atlanta FWHC strengthened their abortion services and fought the political and social influence of anti-abortion protesters; they also offered a diverse array of services to meet the demands of their clients, including information on HIV transmission and prevention, services tailored for lesbians, services for homeless and poor women, and health services designed for Atlanta's growing immigrant population.

This chapter, then, tells the story of the continued struggles of feminists to provide quality health services that were woman controlled and compassionate in a rapidly transforming political and social environment that most certainly changed feminism and feminist health provision, but did not end it. Anti-abortion movement activists did much to shape this new environment by employing a variety of methods designed to make abortion inaccessible to Atlanta women and women across the country. Thus, after describing the Atlanta FWHC's goals for providing high-quality women's reproductive health services with an emphasis on self-help, I turn to how anti-abortion forces in Atlanta attempted to circumscribe those services. They employed two strategies primarily, one legal and focused on passing state legislation restricting abortion providers and one illegal, including blockading clinics and harassing patients and clinic workers in a massive campaign in Atlanta. Both methods, refined against Atlanta clinics, were taken nationwide by anti-abortion activists. At the end of the chapter, I detail how the Atlanta FWHC continued to expand their services, particularly for women of color and poor women, despite these sustained attacks by the anti-abortion movement.

Self-Help and Feminist Health Reform at FWHCs

The Atlanta FWHC traces its roots to the first experiments with feminist self-help at the Los Angeles Feminist Women's Health Center, founded by Carol Downer and Loraine Rothman. As at Aradia, FWHC founders believed that women should be empowered to provide health services to each other, rather than relying on the "expert" knowledge of a medical professional. Female paramedics, or Health Workers as they were called at this clinic, collaborated in an information-sharing process with women who came to the clinic to participate in a group health care environment. They would "provide a comprehensive, community based program offering health services . . . based on the philosophy that women, given choice through knowledge, will seek women with whom to discuss their health problems. Women paramedics are trained to provide health services to our sisters and to do this with the empathy which comes from shared experiences."[6] The emphasis was on information sharing, rather than expertise. As at Aradia, clinic workers had information to share because of their experience and training. Training was "on-the-job" as workers "progressed through the various tasks involved in health care provision at the Center." Health Workers were eventually trained to "do every job from phones to assisting [abortions]."[7] The women who came to the clinic as patients were encouraged to learn and share information about their reproductive bodies and potentially become clinic workers themselves, if they chose.

Feminist clinics tended to have a few basic differences from each other, however, which, in part, reflected a shifting historical context. One of these differences revolved around the question of whether a clinic should radically challenge established medical structure and hierarchy. They also differed as to whether to charge fees and how much to charge for services. And, finally, feminist clinics varied according to the services they provided. A few clinics, like the Atlanta FWHC, offered comprehensive services that directly competed with the obstetrical and gynecological practices of physicians. These clinics might also offer abortion services. Clinics that offered comprehensive services including abortion, such as the Atlanta and Los Angeles FWHCs, threatened established medical practices and, in some cases, experienced counter-challenges from the medical establishment.[8]

Aradia feminists were particularly critical of traditional medical hierarchy; ideally, all volunteer positions were interchangeable, although this was not always their practice in reality as women learned certain skills that allowed them to specialize at the clinic and they hired women with medical credentials. Aradia also emphasized services offered on a sliding scale, asking women who visited the clinic to pay what they could. Finally, Aradia did not provide abortions until the 1980s. Women who came to the Aradia clinic with an unwanted pregnancy were referred to doctors or hospitals in the Seattle area for their surgery.

Alternatively, most of the health centers associated with the Federation of FWHCs, which included the Los Angeles clinic, the clinic in Tallahassee, the Atlanta FWHC, as well as other clinics across the country, eventually embraced both greater structure and variations on medical hierarchy, although they distinguished themselves from established nonfeminist medical institutions by incorporating a self-help model. As Randall explained, "[W]e agreed . . . that we wanted to do both. We wanted to provide direct services, and we wanted to be part of this network of women who were more serious about fundamentally changing the power relationship between women and the medical profession."[9]

Atlanta and the other FWHCs provided abortion from the beginning. Downer and others involved with the FWHC federation believed that professionalized abortion services, in the context of self-help clinics focused on well-woman care, was a fundamental part of feminist women's health care services. Furthermore, abortion could facilitate a clinic's independent survival by supplementing the cost of other non-revenue-generating services like well-woman self-help groups, although Downer argued that abortion should not be provided merely for profit. She explained in a 1971 publication written as a how-to manual for feminist health centers, "You must want to provide abortion care for its own sake, not because it's a money-maker or you can get funding." At the same time, she advised, "you must come to grips with nasty realities, such as charging money, insisting on standards of work of your staff, developing structures for your organization that enable you to function efficiently and productively."[10]

Downer understood that some collaboration with the medical establishment would be necessary, like consultation with and referral to medical doctors for certain procedures such as abortion. At the same time, clinics needed to be prepared to train doctors to perform abortions and other medical services in a feminist and self-help context. She continued, "It is important to find a doctor who is responsible and who will treat the women with the best health care AND respect and dignity (it is the responsibility of all of the Health Workers to confront the doctor if this is not the case and to fire the doctor if she will not cooperate)."[11]

Atlanta FWHC participants placed self-help at the center of their health care provision. They explained that

> Self-Help Clinic is not a place. It is any group of women getting together to share experiences and learn about their own bodies through direct observation. Women share with each other the techniques of breast and vaginal/cervical self-examination. Through observing the changes in their bodies during the menstrual cycle, women can learn what is normal for them and how healthy bodies function.[12]

Health Workers were instructed to guide women during self-help clinics that were mandatory for all well-woman care. Furthermore, Health Workers were "to maintain a Self-Help perspective in all aspects of clinic work and health work, not merely in the Self-Help Clinic."[13]

Emphasis was placed on information exchange and active participation among clients. Self-help groups facilitated by Health Workers guided clients through a process of information sharing that was designed to empower them to take more control over their health care. FWHC guidelines for Health Workers explained that a patient in a self-help group would learn "what is normal for her body and [have] the opportunity to share these experiences with other women" and asserted that in the process "a woman is educating herself and becoming a more active participant in her own health care."[14] Health Workers who ran self-help groups for FWHCs were instructed to present an "open and non-authoritarian manner. By listening to women, taking their experiences seriously, and learning from women, a Health Worker does not act as an authority on women's health. . . . When Health Workers present information in the clinics, they identify the source of their information— most often from other women sharing their experiences." A clinic worker, too, might learn from a client. In this sense, the Atlanta FWHC challenged traditional medical authority in a manner very similar to that embraced by feminists in the women's health movement across the country. Health Workers tailored a woman's health consultation to her particular health needs, although group self-help sessions were mandatory for each patient. Atlanta FWHC Health Workers learned to "find out what women want to know, what women are interested in, and facilitate a discussion that is relevant to the women's needs. The discussion is based on the experiences of the women in the group and the experiences and knowledge of the Health Workers, as opposed to a Health Worker presenting 'the facts.'" Health Workers were required to participate in self-help groups as well, further blurring the divide between patient and health provider.[15]

Yet, the Atlanta FWHC was more prescriptive than Aradia in its instructions for self-help groups. Basic self-help instruction required women to meet for four weeks in order to chart changes in their cervixes for a full cycle. But many groups were ongoing. Some self-help groups associated with the Atlanta FWHC adapted their focus to the interests of the women in a particular group. For instance there were "Self-Help Clinics for menopausal women, premenstrual women, women having interest in herbal health care, and women who just were interested in gathering as much health care information as possible." An Atlanta FWHC instructional guide for clinic participants and workers described self-help sessions: "A Well-Woman Participatory Clinic group usually consists of a group of five or six women and one to two Health Workers. Often, women who have similar health concerns are scheduled for the same group. Each woman discusses her reasons for visiting the clinic and begins a health record by discussing her health background." After discussing health history and health concerns, participants learned how to self-diagnose by discussing potential symptoms and variations among healthy women. The same Atlanta FWHC guide explained,

> A woman's subjective symptoms provide her with information, and she arrives at conclusions based on subjective data, objective measures and others' observations. Her experiences are validated in the Participatory group. The Feminist Women's Health Centers believe that when people have access to information about the options available to them, they can make responsible decisions about their own health care.[16]

Most patients at Atlanta FWHC attended well-woman self-help clinics for their routine yearly gynecological exam. They also attended to get information about birth control and learn which contraceptive methods might be best for their particular circumstances. Women in the self-help clinics were not required to learn how to do a self-exam, but they were given the option. Atlanta FWHC staff, however, encouraged women to try the self-exam because they believed that

> self-examination demystifies women's bodies and many of the screening tests and procedures that are done during examinations. A woman learns what is normal for herself, so she is able to detect changes to learn what these changes mean and to seek the advice of a more experienced or trained person when necessary. Knowing the normal, healthy condition of the cervix and vagina is no more a medical concern than is knowing the normal condition of the mouth and throat.

Women participants also learned how to do self–breast exams. Self-exams were followed by a pelvic exam with a physician, nurse practitioner, or midwife. A Health Worker was present throughout the exam to answer questions and provide support. Both home remedies and medical prescriptions were also available.[17]

In addition to self-help at the clinic site, the Atlanta FWHC offered self-help instruction off-site and visited community organizations. In their first year they held two self-help clinics at Spelman College, one in an Oglethorpe University dorm, three at Emory University as part of a campus "Women's Week," and one for the Emory Nursing School. They also held self-help demonstrations at both the Georgia and South Carolina State National Organization for Women (NOW) conferences and at the NOW national conference.[18] The Atlanta FWHC was integral to an active feminist movement in Atlanta.[19]

Like the paras at Aradia, Health Workers at the Atlanta FWHC were fundamental to the smooth functioning of the clinic. Unlike in the early years of Aradia, however, they held paid positions. Also unlike Aradia, the Atlanta FWHC detailed specific tasks to be performed by Health Workers in a formal job description. These tasks included running lab tests and sending samples to off-site labs as needed, running discussions and information sessions on birth control, assisting women with diaphragm or cervical cap fittings, maintaining paperwork and charts, making referrals, answering the telephone, helping to inventory supplies, cleaning up before and after clinic sessions, coordinating and participating in self-help sessions, and presenting women's health information at community sessions outside of regular clinic hours. Health Workers were divided into two carefully demarcated levels, which determined their pay. At the second level, Health Workers also did abortion counseling, supported patients during their procedures, and assisted during abortions.[20]

The Atlanta FWHC also hired medical professionals for more specialized health work. Nurse practitioners supervised Health Workers and assisted with abortions. Physicians performed vacuum aspiration abortions, inserted and removed IUDs, inserted laminaria for second-trimester abortions, followed up with complications or problems resulting from IUD insertion or abortion, and were prepared to accompany a patient to the emergency room in the event of a serious abortion complication. Physicians also prescribed medication and devices like the IUD. Atlanta FWHC administrators were more than willing to work with medical professionals like physicians and nurse practitioners, but they reserved the right to train them to perform medical tasks in a context that met with their feminist goal of empowering patients to be involved with and informed about their own medical care.[21] Most importantly, as at Aradia, physicians were not supposed to be treated like experts monopolizing all of the important information. FWHC guidelines

emphasize[d] the philosophy that in order for people to maintain their health and have control over their reproductive lives, it is essential that information be available. Not only is health education the mainstay of the Self-Help Clinic, but it is an integral part of community presentations by FWHC Staff Members, Telephone Counseling, Pregnancy and Childbirth Orientation, the Abortion Clinic and the Well-Woman Clinic.[22]

Despite their emphasis on defined job descriptions that maintained certain standard medical hierarchies, the Atlanta FWHC did not abandon the notion that patients needed to be empowered to have more control over their health with accurate information.

If a woman came to the clinic for an abortion, her interaction with clinic staff began when she called the clinic to make an appointment. She would initially speak to a Health Worker on the telephone who would explain "how the abortion is performed, the instruments used, how long the abortion takes, how long she will be in the clinic and what women usually experience during an abortion. The Health Worker also explains the cost and how she can pay for abortion. Women are scheduled into the clinic in groups." If a woman had questions, the Health Worker was prepared to spend significant time with her. Health Workers made "certain she [had] all the details relating to her appointment." Atlanta FWHC staff, like staff at other clinics in the Federation of FWHCs, did not counsel women per se. Rather, "at the Feminist Women's Health Centers, the word 'counseling' means sharing all the information that a woman needs and wants." If a woman chose to have her abortion at the FWHC, a Health Worker, often the same woman who originally spoke with her on the phone, would accompany the woman through the abortion, "providing coaching, hand-holding, explaining what will happen next, etc."[23]

Self-help and well-woman gynecological care continued to be fundamental to the services provided by the Atlanta FWHC through the 1980s. The Atlanta FWHC also participated in a national cervical cap study with Portland and Yakima FWHCs in the early 1980s. Thus, clinic administrators never limited the clinic's medical activities to abortion. At the same time, by the 1980s, abortions had become a large part of the clinic's service.[24] In its first year the Atlanta FWHC provided 198 abortions and 239 well-woman/self-help visits. They also saw 139 women for abortion aftercare. By 1980 they had performed 1,505 abortions in a year, and by 1984 that number had climbed to 2,609. The majority of women paid for their procedures, although the clinic used a sliding scale, accepted Georgia State Medicaid funds for abortion, and by 1992 offered abortions subsidized by the National Network of Abortion Women in Need (WIN) funds. If a woman accepted WIN funds, she was required to pay a portion of the cost; how much depended on her income and resources.[25]

By the mid-1980s the Atlanta FWHC and many other feminist clinics around the country were providing low-cost, safe, and compassionate abortion services for thousands of women a year; they also faced mounting challenges from the anti-abortion movement, including pickets, clinic blockades, and escalating violence and harassment. In 1985, Lynne Randall reported, "The most significant changes at the FWHC in 1985 were direct results of antiabortion activity: (1) the LAFWHC was completely destroyed by arson in April and (2) in July we were faced with an attempted clinic invasion by Joe Scheidler [Chicago-based anti-abortion movement leader] and subsequent weekly picketing and harassment."

Although the LA FWHC was rebuilt in the same year, the violent attack sent shock waves through the feminist abortion provider community. It seemed that the most extreme members of the anti-abortion movement would stop at nothing to prevent women from accessing abortion.[26] According to the National Abortion Federation, a federation of abortion providers in the United States, between 1977, the same year the FWHC in Atlanta was founded, and 1987, there were 104 incidents of bombings and bombing attempts at clinics nationwide. There were also 213 bomb threats and 216 clinic invasions nationwide.[27]

Anti-abortion confrontation was a daily reality at the clinic almost as soon as it opened and would affect Atlanta FWHC health care delivery for the duration of its existence. As Randall lamented in an interview with historian Johanna Schoen,

> I feel sad sometimes thinking about the women who had that as part of their abortion experience who so did not need that extra stress. I think as staff, we had stronger coping mechanisms for dealing with it, and it was still hard. But for each individual woman and her family who doesn't have the same environment to talk about it and to emote and sort of take it all in and take it more personally, I think that it's been horrible for them, more scarring for a lot of women who had that experience.[28]

The Anti-Abortion Movement Challenge: Legislative Restrictions on Abortion Providers

Regardless of where they fell along an ideological divide around organizational structure and hierarchy or whether they provided abortion care or not, feminist women's health center staff and administrators wanted to provide compassionate women's health care that would challenge inequalities grounded in social prejudices associated with gender, race, class, and sexual identity that they believed were embedded in established health care institutions. As opposition to abortion became more potent after *Roe v. Wade*, surviving attacks mounted by anti-abortion protesters that threatened clinics as well as female patients increasingly shaped feminist clinics' priorities.

The first significant challenge to abortion access was the Hyde Amendment, passed by Congress in 1976 as a rider attached to an HEW appropriation bill; it prevented any federal funding of abortion except in cases that threatened the life of the pregnant woman. A temporary injunction prevented Hyde from going into effect, but this was lifted when the Supreme Court found Hyde to be constitutional in *Harris v. McRae* in 1980.[29] This legislative success marked the first nationwide limit to abortion access. Not surprisingly, it affected the most vulnerable women, those too poor to pay for their health care. Anti-abortion movement activists did not, however, convince Congress to pass any other federal limits to abortion, although they pushed the Human Life Amendment (HLA), which would have made all abortion illegal.

State-based legislative attempts to limit abortion have also been used by the anti-abortion movement. Rather than overturning *Roe v. Wade*, these regulations were (and continue to be) designed to make abortion less accessible incrementally. According to the Alan Guttmacher Institute, "In the years immediately following the Supreme Court decision in *Roe v. Wade*, several states moved to impose strict regulations on abortion clinics, beyond what is necessary to ensure patients' safety."[30] At the same time, there were also abortion providers who quickly opened clinics after *Roe v. Wade* in order to make a profit. Some of these offered deceptive and even dangerous services. Some of these "clinics quickly acquired a poor reputation."[31] Thus, some form of regulation of clinics was not entirely unreasonable.

In Georgia one of the early attempts to limit abortion access came on the heels of several deaths due to abortion complications in local Atlanta abortion clinics (not at the FWHC), which aided the anti-abortion movement's representation of abortion as dangerous to women. The depiction of abortion as dangerous made state regulations restricting abortion more acceptable. The anti-abortion movement would continue to try to pass legislation putting limits on abortion and abortion providers throughout the 1980s and up to the present. In 1992 this strategy gained traction when the standard for restricting abortion in the first trimester was weakened by the Supreme Court in *Planned Parenthood v. Casey*. This decision opened the door for greater restrictions on abortion and abortion providers. Anti-abortion movement participants did not succeed at reducing the overall numbers of abortions in the country; women continued to have abortions at a similar rate—an average of just under thirty abortions for every one thousand women between the ages of fifteen and forty-four years. Currently, by the time women reach the age of forty-five, three in ten women have had an abortion. Abortion rates began to decline in the late 1980s and 1990s, but it is not at all clear that this decline was linked to anti-abortion activism.[32] Yet, the strategy to place hurdles in the way of abortion providers and women who wanted to end a pregnancy did make abortion more difficult to access and possibly more traumatic for those who had made up their minds that abortion was their best and freely chosen option. The anti-abortion movement also began to transform popular attitudes about abortion safety and women's right to control their reproduction balanced against the "rights" of a fetus carried within a female reproductive body.

In early June 1979, anti-abortion forces were quick to exploit a series of "abortion tragedies," including the deaths of three women in Atlanta, to push for limits on abortion providers. On June 2, 1979, two women were carried by ambulance from the Women's Pavilion clinic to Grady Memorial Hospital. Both were critically ill from anesthesia given during their abortion procedures and remained unconscious until, terribly, both died. The medical crisis began when nineteen-year-old Angela Scott had a reaction to her general anesthetic while in recovery after her abortion. Staff at the Women's Pavilion called the emergency department at Grady for an ambulance, which arrived immediately. The physician who had performed the abortion, Dr. Jacob Adams, also co-owner of the clinic, accompanied Scott to the Grady emergency department. Compounding the problem, when Scott reacted negatively to the anesthetic another abortion patient, fifteen-year-old Delores Smith from Athens, Georgia, also under a general anesthetic, was left alone by her nurse. The nurse exited the procedure room to assist with the Scott emergency. It was generally agreed that this nurse's failure to monitor her patient caused Smith to receive an overdose of anesthetic. It was also discovered that the nurse was not a licensed nurse anesthetist.[33]

When clinic staff called for a second ambulance they did not make clear that they had a second medical emergency. The emergency department at Grady treated the call as "routine"; they would not send an ambulance immediately unless the call was flagged as an emergency requiring instant response. Instead, the Grady dispatcher assumed a doctor was on hand to care for the patient so sent an ambulance twenty-five minutes after being called. Smith arrived at the hospital nearly an hour after her negative reaction to the anesthetic was identified. Since Dr. Adams had already left for Grady, another doctor needed to be called to accompany Smith to the hospital. Both of these young women would remain in comas until they died, Angela Scott on June 9 and Dolores Smith later in the fall. The Women's Pavilion, owned and operated by Dr. Adams, who performed the abortion on Scott, and Dr. Otis Hammonds, closed after the two women died.[34] In an unrelated incident, on July 18, Geneva Calton, a 21-year-old mother of two, also died from abortion complications at Northside Family Planning Clinic in Atlanta.[35]

The deaths of these three women may have resulted from medical treatment that was far less than ideal, including the administration of anesthesia to patients under unsafe circumstances and for a procedure that does not require the patient to be unconscious. Thus, the closure of the Women's Pavilion may have been warranted. At the same time, antichoice organizers used the deaths as an opportunity to try to restrict all Atlanta clinics, including the Atlanta FWHC, which did not use anesthesia under any circumstances because it was associated with greater risk for abortion patients.

Randall quickly called a press conference after the first of the two women died to discuss the nature of the complications. Since two of the three deaths resulted from complications related to general anesthesia, Randall was particularly careful to emphasize that the Atlanta FWHC performed abortions only with a local anesthetic in the first trimester. She commented, "It is important to realize that it appears that the woman suffered a complication from general anesthesia and not the abortion itself, that the risks of general anesthesia with any procedure are well known, and that a woman may choose to have an abortion without using general anesthesia."[36] She used the opportunity to emphasize that women needed complete information about their reproductive health options. With complete information a woman could choose the safest abortion procedure. Or, if she wanted to continue her pregnancy, she could acquire information on the most appropriate contexts for birthing. If she wanted to avoid pregnancy, she could obtain information on birth control methods. Randall continued,

Women must be given this information. . . . In no area of our lives do women now have complete control over our bodies and reproduction, nor do most women have adequate information to make the safest choices. Some examples of the choices we make are the choice between fetal monitoring and anesthesia in childbirth and having a natural or even home birth, the choice between the Pill and IUD and the diaphragm, and the choice between local and general anesthesia for an early abortion. Feminists will continue to provide health education and tools for self-help and to demand changes in health care institutions. In this way we work against all the tragedies which occur around women's reproduction.[37]

Randall asserted that making information available that led to informed choices about sex and reproduction would best maintain women's health, not the narrowing of reproductive options that the antichoice movement demanded. She also implied that women often were only told of high-risk technologies when they planned their reproductive experiences—whether they had an abortion, were carrying a pregnancy to term, or were choosing a method of birth control. Women's health movement feminists pointed out that the "choices" encouraged by the medical establishment often benefited medical professionals more than women themselves. Feminists argued that this hurt women by putting them at risk for complications related to abortion, birth control, and birthing, and did not respect women as fully capable of making their own informed decisions based on information about the risks and benefits of any medical procedure or method of birth control. To better inform the Atlanta public about anesthesia and abortion, the Atlanta FWHC planned a symposium for the media on the various risks of anesthesia to abortion patients.[38]

Joining the press release issued by the FWHC after the first abortion-related death, Lynn Heidelberg, an Atlanta abortion rights activist, warned that the anti-abortion movement planned to exploit the deaths to restrict abortion. She explained, "We do not want these recent events to give strength to those who would callously exploit the death of this woman to deny other women their constitutional right to have a safe abortion. Anti-abortion forces are calling for severe restrictions upon or elimination of safe, legal abortion. This will not result in fewer tragedies." She pointed out that legal abortion was much safer than illegal abortion. Thus, keeping abortion both legal and accessible would ensure women's ability to control their fertility safely. She continued, "We must never return to the day when abortion was illegal or so severely restricted that deaths from abortion were a regular occurrence. Despite our sadness, we must remember that abortion is safer than childbirth, and that abortion is safer today than it has ever been."[39]

The joint press release, issued two days before the symposium, emphasized that abortion in the first trimester was twenty-five times safer than childbirth, so forcing a woman who did not want to be pregnant to carry a pregnancy to term could not be justified in terms of her health or safety. Yet, the anti-abortion movement did just that—they argued that out-patient abortion clinics needed to be regulated more stringently to protect women. The proposed regulations sparked a battle in Atlanta between pro- and anti-abortion advocates that foreshadowed subsequent national debates around restrictions on abortion and abortion clinics and whether or not these were constitutional after *Roe v. Wade*.[40] Although in this instance pro-choice forces prevailed by arguing that increased "safety" measures in clinics were unnecessary, in the long run, the anti-abortion strategy of demonizing abortion as unsafe for women would become more successful in making abortion less accessible.

When the abortion deaths occurred, regulations called for by anti-abortion forces were already part of the 1978 Georgia state legislature's new health code amendment that included increased regulation of abortion in freestanding clinics. The Board of Human Resources drafted licensing requirements that incorporated these regulations before the abortion-related deaths but only released them the week after the abortion deaths.[41] The state regulations provided guidelines for all surgical centers, which would include abortion clinics under that heading. Some of the rules were clearly ideological, however, and targeted abortion clinics specifically. Other rules were not relevant to clinics like the FWHC that only performed abortions with local anesthesia. For example, a rule that was allegedly meant to facilitate the movement of patients from the operating room to the recovery room required widening the doors and hallways in all freestanding surgical centers, including all abortion clinics. Randall explained that this particular regulation was irrelevant to her FWHC because "[o]ur patients walk from the operating room to the recovery room."[42] It would be extremely costly for the FWHC clinic to widen all of its hallways and doors and would not increase patient safety.

Pro-choice advocates, like Randall and Lynn Thogersen, codirector with Randall at the Atlanta FWHC at the time of the deaths, argued that regulations would only add to clinic expenses, making abortion more expensive and less readily available to patients as some women's health facilities might find abortion too expensive to offer. Like the rules about the doorways and halls, they noted that rules that would require an increase in the height of ceilings and dictate the location of storage facilities also seemed unrelated to patient safety. Regulations also required abortion clinics to stock blood supplies. Clinic administrators pointed out that this requirement was also unnecessary since any patient needing blood would be transferred to a hospital. The regulation that all "clinics be no more than 15 minutes from a hospital" would put abortion clinics at risk for closure if they were not near a hospital. Another rule required that all facilities that provided obstetrical and gynecological services, including abortion clinics, make available bassinets and other equipment for emergency care of newborns. This starkly indicated that anti-abortion legislators meant to strap abortion clinics with costly and inappropriate regulations that emphasized the anti-abortion position that abortion was about killing babies. Proposed legislative regulations also required that the attending physician explain to the patient dangers involved in "the surgical procedure and cite the alternatives to surgery." Since abortion clinics already hired counselors (or Health Workers in the case of the FWHC) to provide this information, the rule appeared to be meant to increase the cost of the procedure by making higher-paid physicians spend their time counseling patients.[43]

Finally, the most telling anti-abortion regulation required that "a fetus 'capable of meaningful or sustained life,' must be given sustained aid." Given that abortion clinics like the FWHC only provided abortions up to twelve weeks, this requirement only underlined the anti-abortion mythology that physicians at abortion clinics actually killed babies born alive. A first-trimester or early-second-trimester fetus could not be born alive; most medical experts considered viability to be achievable at approximately twenty-four weeks. According to *Roe v. Wade*, states were required to allow abortions even after fetal viability to "preserve the life or health of the mother." Only trained medical personnel could determine both when an abortion was necessary to preserve life or health and when fetal viability had been achieved. These sorts of late-term abortion procedures were performed in hospitals, to which the regula- . tions didn't apply.[44]

Randall and Thogersen quickly moved to oppose the regulations as soon as they became public on the basis that according to the Supreme Court in *Roe* it was unconstitutional to regulate first-trimester abortions beyond requiring that they be performed by a doctor. The State Attorney General's Office also warned that the legislature's regulations were unconstitutional. Those who opposed the regulations pointed out that the Court in *Roe* had held that because abortion in the first trimester was safe, the state did not have a compelling interest to regulate abortion until the second trimester and, then, to preserve the health of the woman. This passage, written by Supreme Court Justice Harry Blackmun for the majority in the Court decision, was often referred to in debates over the legislative regulations:

> With respect to the State's important and legitimate interest in the health of the mother, the "compelling" point, in the light of present medical knowledge, is at approximately the end of the first trimester. This is so because of the now-established medical fact . . . that, until the end of the first trimester mortality in abortion may be less than mortality in normal childbirth. It follows that, from and after this point, a State may regulate the abortion procedure to the extent that the regulation reasonably relates to the preservation and protection of maternal health.[45]

Anti-abortion legislators and activists hoped to use the 1979 Atlanta abortion complications to challenge Blackmun's trimester framework and to popularize the idea that legal abortion was dangerous to women. They advocated for implementation of the state legislature's guidelines that specifically targeted abortion clinics. On July 26, anti-abortion groups in Georgia squared off against pro-choice advocates at a public hearing on the regulations. At the hearing anti-abortion groups called for even more stringent regulations that would require a "pre-abortion 'pro-life' presentation [to abortion patients], banning clinic advertisements and even mandating that aborted fetuses be given a 'proper burial.'" FWHC also sent representatives to testify on abortion safety at the hearings.[46]

Yet, in a concession to anti-abortion-movement rhetoric about abortion safety, some members of the pro-choice community did not oppose the regulations wholesale. After the June complications, Thogersen told reporters that "the clinic would challenge the state if it adopted regulations restricting first-trimester abortions" as such regulations went against constitutional protections. Yet, clinic administrators at other Atlanta abortion clinics publicly supported some of the regulations. Helen Ford, executive director of the Atlanta Center for Reproductive Health, announced that guidelines for outpatient surgical centers were appropriate but that excessive regulation would make abortion more expensive and less accessible.[47]

Terry Beresford, chair of the Board of Directors of the National Abortion Federation (NAF), a national professional association of abortion providers that included the FWHC, commented on the Georgia state regulations as well. She explained that abortion clinics already operated under regulations required for state medical licensing. She emphasized that more than regulations, what was needed was compassionate and caring abortion provision. She explained, "It's very hard to write legislation that will ensure that patients will be treated with dignity and respect; that no woman can be coerced into an abortion; that the doctors who perform the procedure are both experienced and competent. You can have minimum standards, but they certainly don't constitute a guarantee." She suggested that Georgia legislators who designed the regulations were not advocating for patients' best interests: "[W]e like to look at the motivation for state regulations (like Georgia's prospective rules). Does it serve the interests of the consumer, or is it designed to make it more difficult and expensive for women to obtain abortions?" She further explained that NAF had "developed a system for policing its own members. Each clinic must complete a detailed membership application and affirm that it subscribes to NAF's rigorous standards. Should NAF receive a consumer complaint about a clinic, it will dispatch a team to conduct an on-site investigation."[48]

Marjorie Pitts Hames, the Atlanta lawyer who argued *Doe v. Bolton*, the companion case to *Roe v. Wade*, in front of the Supreme Court, and remained an active abortion rights activist, also worried that the regulations were meant to make abortion more expensive and less accessible. She argued that medical incompetence would already result in the revocation of medical licenses, thus protecting patients. Inaccessible and expensive abortion, however, could potentially cause some women to put off their abortions, resulting in more frequent second-trimester procedures, which were more dangerous for women. Thus, the regulations could potentially make abortion more dangerous, the opposite effect of what legislators publicly claimed they wanted.[49]

Abortion rights supporters emphasized that first-trimester safety records in Georgia were already excellent despite the recent abortion deaths. In another Atlanta FWHC press release meant to counter anti-abortion contentions that legal abortion threatened women's lives, Thogersen explained,

> Less than one percent of abortions result in a complication. Complications from abortion occur far less often than with childbirth, tonsillectomy, appendectomy, or even a shot of penicillin. The two Atlanta women suffered complications from general anesthesia, not from the abortion itself. Abortions are safer when performed under local anesthesia with minimal or no sedation. Most abortions can be performed under local anesthesia and every woman should have that choice.[50]

As an institution dedicated to empowering women to understand their medical options, including the relative risks of abortion versus carrying a pregnancy to term, the Atlanta FWHC disseminated information because it believed women needed to understand the real risks of legal abortion. Randall explained in another statement on abortion safety made to the Georgia state Board of Human Resources that had drafted the regulations, "The removal of a mole under general anesthesia is a life-threatening procedure. First trimester, vacuum aspiration abortion performed under local anesthesia is a safe, simple procedure lasting two to five minutes."[51]

Dr. David Grimes of the Center for Disease Control's Abortion Surveillance Unit based in Atlanta also responded to the abortion deaths by pointing out that the state's first-trimester fatality rate was better than the national record. He argued that legal abortion was safe in Georgia and across the country. He also noted that no one had died from a legal abortion in the previous year. He continued, noting that the majority of abortion fatalities occurred in the second trimester:

There have been just six fatalities among the 116,000 women who opted for legal abortions in Georgia since 1973, when the landmark Supreme Court decision made first- and second- trimester abortions widely available. Four of those stemmed from hospital procedures, three from the induction of labor via saline injection—a mid and late-term procedure which carries a greater risk than early-term techniques.

The two June deaths at the Women's Pavilion were the only first-trimester abortion fatalities that had occurred in a clinic in Georgia since 1973. By contrast, "about 373 women died from childbirth complications nationwide in 1977, 18 of them in Georgia."[52]

By July, after a month of pro-choice publicity on the safety of abortion, legislators revised their original legislation. Abortion rights supporters had emphasized that any regulations that singled out abortion clinics exclusively unconstitutionally limited abortion in the first trimester. Legislators removed all mention of abortion clinics from the language of their document. Thogersen and Randall still worried that any regulations beyond the requirement that a licensed physician perform the abortion could "limit access to abortion and that means they are unconstitutional."[53] Billy McKinney, D–Atlanta, and chairman of a subcommittee of the Georgia House Health and Ecology Committee, tasked with evaluating the regulations for abortion clinics after the June abortion-related complications, became convinced by pro-choice advocates, including Thogersen and Randall, that "regulation will increase the cost of the procedure making it less available to the poor." McKinney's colleague, Representative Roy Rowland, D–Dublin, who was also a practicing physician, sided with McKinney, explaining that some of the Board of Human Resources regulations were "overboard."[54]

Both the Atlanta FWHC and Midtown Hospital invited the subcommittee on Health and Ecology to tour their clinics and witness medical precautions taken to ensure that patients received safe abortions.[55] After his tour of the two clinics McKinney decided not to recommend special regulations for abortion clinics. He was convinced by the argument that new regulations would increase the cost of abortion without increasing safety. He said, "More stringent guidelines would not be appropriate. . . . The overall cost to the patient would have to go up. Therefore, I would be against the regulation."[56]

In this instance, then, pro-choice forces staved off anti-abortion regulations that were nominally about protecting women, but according to pro-choice advocates were more about restricting abortion. Anti-abortion demands that the subcommittee chaired by McKinney investigate abortion clinics seemed to backfire when McKinney and the subcommittee sided with the pro-choice forces arguing that current regulations for abortion clinics were sufficient. Yet, the passage of state regulations would be a tactic used again and again by members of the anti-abortion movement to marginalize abortion as a medical procedure both culturally, by increasing its stigma as dangerous for women, and financially, by making abortion more expensive and difficult to access.

This strategy has continued well into the twenty-first century. For example, in 2011, Kansas instituted new health department regulations supported by the outspoken anti-abortion governor of Kansas, Sam Brownback, that required abortion providers to acquire a special license, prescribed drugs and equipment required to be available at the clinic, mandated that patient records be open to inspection, and established "qualifications for staff, set minimum sizes for some rooms and limit[ed] the temperatures in procedure and recovery rooms."[57] A 2012 Mississippi state law requiring physicians performing abortions to have local hospital privileges has threatened to close the only abortion clinic in the state because all of the physicians performing abortions in Mississippi commute from other states to provide the procedure.[58] Most recently, a 2013 Texas law bans "abortions after 20 weeks of pregnancy and hold[s] abortion clinics to the same standards as hospital-style surgical centers."[59] According to abortion rights supporters, these new regulations, like those narrowly defeated in Georgia in 1979, are thinly veiled attempts to increase abortion clinic expenses and make it more difficult for abortion clinics to remain open.[60]

In 1979, however, abortion rights forces in Georgia prevailed in the debate about whether abortion should be singled out from other medical procedures. As Thogersen stated, "[A]s far as these regulations should be concerned, abortion is a medical, not a political issue and should be treated the same as other medical procedures."[61] Given the heated political, religious, and emotional debates surrounding abortion, abortion rights advocates correctly feared it would be difficult to maintain this understanding of abortion—that it was a medical procedure necessary for personal and private reproductive control. A series of anti-abortion defeats in the 1980s, including the 1983 Supreme Court decision in *City of Akron v. Akron Center for Reproductive Health*, which found unconstitutional several state restrictions on abortion such as the requirement that abortion needed to be performed in a hospital, parental consent for unmarried minors, and a 24-hour waiting period, suggested that abortion rights supporters were succeeding. Congress also failed to pass the Human Life Amendment, which would have amended the United States Constitution to invalidate *Roe v. Wade*.[62] Unsurprisingly, the anti-abortion movement was not prepared to concede the debate in the early 1980s. As abortion entered its second decade of constitutional protection, anti-abortion activists escalated their protests against abortion clinics. And Atlanta and the FWHC became one of their primary targets.

Escalation of Anti-Abortion Tactics: Clinic Blockades and Violence

The Catholic Church led early anti-abortion opposition, both before 1973 and immediately after *Roe v. Wade*. For example, the National Right to Life Committee emerged from the Committee on Family Life of the National Catholic Bishops' Conference. Protestant fundamentalists mostly joined the movement after abortion became legal nationwide. Other anti-abortion activists linked their activism to nonviolent and antiwar ideologies rather than to religion, but these groups failed to garner the national attention that Protestant evangelical groups gained in the 1980s.[63]

Except for restrictions on federal funding for abortion, the anti-abortion movement achieved few successes through the late 1970s and most of the 1980s. That changed with two Supreme Court decisions, *Webster v. Reproductive Health Services* in 1989 and, in 1992, *Planned Parenthood v. Casey*. Together these decisions upheld state restrictions on abortion in the form of prohibition of abortion in public facilities and parental consent for minors. As noted earlier, the *Planned Parenthood* decision also paved the way for further restrictions on abortion and abortion providers.[64]

In the early 1980s, however, anti-abortion activists were frustrated that many of their legislative and legal efforts to block abortion had failed. For that reason they turned to direct-action protest and made Atlanta clinics one of their biggest targets. An increasingly radical anti-abortion movement also led anti-abortion campaigners to illegal and often violent protest activities. Clinic blockades and harassment of patients and clinic workers, bomb threats, bombings of clinics, and arson became commonplace across the country. In 1984, the peak year for abortion-clinic violence, there were thirty arsons and bombings.[65] From 1977 to 1993, "more than 1,000 acts of violence—including bombings, kidnappings and arsons—were reported against abortion providers in the United States."[66]

Operation Rescue (OR), founded by Randall Terry with help from Joseph Scheidler in 1986, is probably the most well-known nationwide Protestant evangelical direct-action anti-abortion organization in the United States. OR activists pioneered and popularized the escalation of anti-abortion protest. Terry, under the umbrella of OR, brought together thousands of increasingly outraged anti-abortion individuals into one organization that would amass evangelical Christian anti-abortion activists in front of women's reproductive health clinics in cities around the country. OR anti-abortion protesters were often willing to be arrested and spend time in jail as martyrs for their political beliefs.[67]

In 1988 Terry decided to make Atlanta during the Democratic National Convention the target for OR's biggest anti-abortion protests to date. Indeed, thousands of anti-abortion activists traveled to Atlanta during, and for three months after, the convention to protest the city's seven abortion clinics, including the Atlanta FWHC. Many protesters spent months in jail for refusing to give their names upon arrest.[68] At first, Terry dubbed his Atlanta campaign the "second siege of Atlanta," aligning his protest movement with General Sherman and the Union Army's sustained shelling of the city during the Civil War.[69]

As the clinic blockades and jail stints went on, however, OR decided to try to expand its ideological support in the city. Allying itself with the Union army was not a winning strategy in the South. Operation Rescue's spokespeople began to represent themselves as descendants of the civil rights movement for desegregation and racial equality in the 1960s. This description was, in essence, an attempt to cloak what was really a religiously motivated campaign against abortion in civil rights rhetoric. It was also designed to broaden the appeal of the anti-abortion movement as many Atlanta citizens had become outraged at OR tactics regardless of whether they approved of abortion or not.[70]

The anti-abortion protests in Atlanta revealed the extent to which anti-abortion activism now included, alongside legislative and other legal challenges, direct-action protest, clinic violence, and media spin. Yet, despite the fervent attacks of OR, the Atlanta FWHC continued to provide abortions according to a moderated but regular clinic schedule. Randall recalled that Atlanta clinics worked together to stay open and continue serving patients, allowing staff and patients to shift operations to another clinic if one clinic was blockaded by anti-abortion activists.[71] At the same time, things could not remain unchanged at the feminist clinic after the anti-abortion movement added direct-action protest and violence to the repertoire of anti-abortion movement activity. Atlanta FWHC administrators and staff confronted new fiscal restraints caused in part by the need for increased security to fend off anti-abortion protests and escalating violence. While they sustained their ideological, political, and practical commitment to providing high-quality women's reproductive health care, a new political atmosphere required new strategies for survival and growth. Yet, in the final analysis, OR's attack on Atlanta clinics, although costly, did not limit abortion availability significantly. Rather, the legal strategy of regulating abortion through the passage of state laws that were then tested by the courts did the most to make abortion less accessible over time.

Soon after its founding in 1986, Operation Rescue became well known for its clinic protests and blockades. It staged its first protest and blockade in Cherry Hill, Pennsylvania, in 1987. Clinic blockades were meant to close targeted clinics for the day and, thus, prevent abortions, although clinics usually stayed open and, when forced to close, rescheduled patients or scheduled them at another clinic not besieged as cripplingly. Operation Rescue took its name from these blockades, which it termed "rescues" because it believed that by closing clinics, even temporarily, and by informing abortion clients that they were about to "kill their babies," it rescued children.[72] Operation Rescue also used the blockades to harass clinic workers and to try to "counsel" patients not to end their pregnancies, which often amounted to harassment for patients as well. Atlanta was the organization's most sustained effort at clinic blockade at that point in the organization's existence, although after the Atlanta attacks OR protests also occurred at FWHCs around the country, including Los Angeles, Sacramento, Chico, Portland, and Yakima.[73] Operation Rescue protests in Atlanta became a model for anti-abortion movement clinic blockades and media campaigns nationwide. In the months immediately after the protests in Atlanta, OR staged 130 clinic blockades in 35 states and raised three hundred thousand dollars as publicity from its "rescues" spread.[74]

The OR protests had a profound impact on clinic finances, workers, and patients. Lynne Randall in her report to the FWHC Board of Directors at the 1988 annual meeting described the Operation Rescue campaign. She detailed nearly three months of protests and clinic blockades:

> Operation Rescue came and stayed thru October 6. Over 1300 people were arrested during that time. There were 20 days of arrests, 8 of those at the Health center. However, 20 days does not begin to describe the months of siege, of constant preparedness, and anxiety. I think we did an excellent job in keeping the clinic open, in organizing the providers and working with the police. Everyone should be very proud of the cooperativeness and commitment to our clients that was displayed during those months. . . . Energy, time, and money could be so much better used in positive ways. Operation Rescue tries to wear us down and has succeeded to some extent.[75]

Although Elizabeth Petzelt, director of the Atlanta Surgi-Center, told the media that the protests did not significantly reduce the numbers of abortions scheduled at her clinic, OR's blockades did reduce the average numbers of abortions performed at the Atlanta FWHC clinic from 104 per week to 70–75 per week.[76] Randall also reported that "Operation Rescue drastically affected the Health Center, both financially and emotionally, causing a lot of stress, tension, anger, and frustration. It consumed all of our attention, energy and money." Randall conservatively estimated that the OR attack cost the clinic about one hundred thousand dollars.[77] Sociologist Wendy Simonds, in her book on the Atlanta FWHC (thinly veiled by a pseudonym in the text), found that in August and October of 1988, the two heaviest months of protesting, "the Center suffered deficits of $23,000 and $61,000, respectively."[78] In her interview with Johanna Schoen, Randall elaborated further on the toll OR protests took on staff: "[W]e would rely on staff to be our own escort, so any time there were protestors, anybody who could put what else they were doing down and go outside and put on the little escort vest had to do that. . . . [I]t was pretty intense."[79] Randall recalled that they often lost staff who tired of the frequent protests and that staff often needed to work longer hours because of the protesters' disruptions of normal daily clinic work. All of this took a toll on the clinic staff emotionally and also affected the clinic's operations in terms of monetary expense.[80] At the same time, the siege on the clinic also produced camaraderie and mutual support among clinic workers.[81]

According to an injunction filed by the Atlanta clinics targeted by Operation Rescue, there were twenty-two clinic blockades during the three months of protest. Clinic administrators summarized the protest experience from their perspective, justifying the injunction:

> Upon arrival at their destination, the group trespassed on private property to blockade the means of ingress to and egress from the targeted building by locking arms and sitting or lying down. Emergency entrances, as well as entrances to the clinics and the administrative areas, were blockaded, trapping persons within the building as well as denying access to those physicians, staff, and clients who wished to enter. The protestors refused to leave when ordered to do so by authorized agents of the property owner and by police. When denied access to the private property, the group blocked the public right of way. When police barricades were in place, protestors crawled under the barricades separating them from the targeted facility. When placed under arrest, the group members refused to accompany police voluntarily and went limp, thereby forcing police officers to carry or drag them to police vehicles. Until the protestors were removed by arresting officers, the targeted facility was, in effect, shut down.

Protesters also crowded around patients' cars when they arrived in the parking lot of the clinic. When patients left their cars to walk to the clinic they were mobbed and yelled at by anti-abortion activists. These actions were typical of OR blockades around the country, which were modeled on what OR viewed as its success in Atlanta. Clinic staff reported that some patients expressed considerable anxiety when they finally reached the clinic and saw a staff member. According to papers filed in support of the injunction, some patients had elevated heart rates and blood pressures, putting them at greater risk for complications during their abortions.[82]

When Terry came to Atlanta, he planned to stage only a three-day protest at the Democratic National Convention from July 19 to July 21 while also simultaneously staging a series of blockades at the Atlanta abortion clinics. This three-day plan targeting the convention, and intended to attract media attention while Atlanta was in the political spotlight, turned into a three-month series of clinic blockades.[83] On July 19, OR began its first clinic blockade at the Atlanta Surgi-Center, without the blessing of Atlanta authorities. At this protest, 134 activists were arrested and refused to give their names to police after their arrests. This move won them even fewer supporters in Atlanta. They told authorities that they were "Baby Jane Doe" or "Baby John Doe" in a "show of solidarity with the pre-born children."[84] Their refusal to provide personal information to the authorities caused Atlanta jails to quickly fill with anti-abortion protesters since they could not be released on bail if authorities did not know who they were. According to reporters James Risen and Judy Thomas, OR members used their jail time to consolidate a "subculture of anti-abortion militancy and extremism." Housed together in Atlanta's Key Road jail facility, many prominent anti-abortion activists like Shelley Shannon, who would later shoot Dr. George Tiller in front of his clinic in Wichita, Kansas, and Father Norman Weslin, who became the leader of the radical anti-abortion group the Lambs of Christ, shared information and collaborated with other protesters during their time in jail.[85]

By early October there were varying reports as to how many OR protesters had been arrested at Atlanta clinics since the blockades had begun; the *Christian Science Monitor* reported that there were nearly eight hundred arrests with nearly three hundred protesters remaining in jail for failure to give names or addresses.[86] Risen and Thomas reported that there were 753 arrests by the end of August.[87] As the jails filled—it was estimated that over a thousand were arrested by the end of the campaign—OR leaders represented the jailed protesters as "political prisoners" willing to make large sacrifices for a just cause. As champions of what they viewed as society's weakest members—the unborn—they also depicted themselves as heirs to the southern civil rights movement and began referring to the Atlanta protests as the anti-abortion movement's Selma—drawing on imagery of the 1965 Selma-to-Montgomery march.[88]

For the most part, similarities between the Operation Rescue protests and civil rights movement activism were slight. Certainly, blockaders sang anthems like "Battle Hymn of the Republic" and "Amazing Grace" in front of Atlanta abortion clinics. "Battle Hymn of the Republic" resonated with civil rights history as the anti-abortion protesters attempted to ally themselves with the legacy of Martin Luther King Jr., who had invoked the lyrics of this song in his speech on the steps of the Alabama State Capitol after his Selma march and in his final sermon in Memphis, Tennessee. Yet, for anti-abortion protesters, the religious and Christian content of the songs' lyrics was probably more resonant than its civil rights legacy. The "Battle Hymn of the Republic" invokes imagery of a Christian God who will mete out ultimate justice. Operation Rescue anti-abortion activists had reason to sing about justice in the form of God's wrath because they, unlike civil rights activists, believed in the ultimate justice of a Christian rule of law, in opposition to a civil tradition that guaranteed all citizens, regardless of religious belief, equal protection in rules of law grounded in the United States Constitution. Operation Rescue activist Brynne Marshall revealed this position when she told the press, "'When any government does not fall in line with God's instructions, we are released from robot-like adherence to the law.'" Clinic escort Cathy Woolard told the same reporter that she didn't believe the anti-abortion movement had any similarities to the civil rights movement. She explained, "This isn't a civil rights demonstration. . . . What they're doing is trespassing on private property and infringing on other people's rights." She added, "They have a right to protests. . . . But they should be at the Supreme Court."[89]

Operation Rescue combined social justice and religious rhetoric in its protests. An OR flyer disseminated to potential protesters traveling to Atlanta informed, "By taking the alias Baby Doe, we (in a very small way) exemplify the injustice the children face, because we (for a short time) lose our names, our rights and our voice in court." Although the argument that life begins at conception was grounded in religious beliefs, the idea that the fetus might also enjoy rights in court as a citizen was grounded in civil claims. This flyer drew a parallel between the civil disobedience of the anti-abortion movement and the movement for de-segregation and voting rights in the South: "The sight of hundreds of blacks in jail for civil rights during the sixties helped their cause greatly." In the same paragraph, however, they revealed the fundamental religious significance of their movement with the claim that "[a]s the nation sees hundreds of decent, God-fearing Americans behind bars for fighting child-killing, it will give more credence to our rhetoric."[90]

Another informational flyer intended for protesters traveling to Atlanta for the abortion blockades after the Democratic Convention further revealed Operation Rescue participants' essential religious convictions. The flyer, written by OR head Randall Terry, intoned to potential activists that God would punish Americans if they did not mount a rescue of all potentially aborted fetuses and ultimately stop abortion. OR members believed that God's wrath would be turned on America as a nation if legal abortion did not stop. OR rhetoric, understood in a context of threats made by a Christian God, encouraged greater "sacrifice" among its members.

OR rhetoric also revealed that frustration with legal channels to decrease abortion motivated new direct-action tactics like the blockades. Any discussion of legal tactics, however, was also always strongly tied to OR's religious convictions. Terry urged protesters to understand that

> over 15 years of education and political lobbying have gotten us virtually nowhere. There has never been a debate in the House of Representatives concerning a Human Life Amendment. Over 25 million children are dead, and the situation is deteriorating. Euthanasia and infanticide are commonplace; school sex clinics are opening, and we have even entered the hellish practice of harvesting babies' organs for experimentation.

In the next passage, he drew parallels between the anti-abortion movement and other social movements in U.S. history:

> Even a brief overview of American history will prove that political change follows social upheaval. The birth of America, the end of slavery, women's voting rights, the repeal of the 18th Amendment (outlawing alcohol), the labor movement, the civil rights movement, the anti–Vietnam War movement, homosexual "rights," the "sexual revolution," and the femi-

nist movement all testify to one truth: that groups of Americans bring enough tension in the nation and pressure on the politicians that the laws are changed.

At the same time, Terry quickly discounted the notion that legal rights were paramount. Rather, he urged protesters to follow the law of God. He declared, "'civil disobedience' is NOT the issue, Biblical OBEDI-ENCE and our Christian duty to rescue innocent children from murder are the issues. The Scriptures consistently teach that when man's law and God's law conflict, especially when human life is at stake, 'We must obey God rather than men.'"[91]

Reproductive rights activists and other political commentators in Atlanta rejected OR's characterization of itself as the inheritor of a civil rights legacy. Dázon Dixon Diallo, at the time community relations coordinator at the Atlanta FWHC, explained that most black women resented the parallel drawn between the anti-abortion movement and the civil rights movement:

> "Operation Oppress you," as I have renamed Operation Rescue, ironically has indirectly called African-American women to respond to this issue. Operation Rescue constantly compares their efforts to deny women the right to abortion to the civil rights movement of the sixties; in fact, calling Atlanta the Selma of the anti-choice movement. Most women in the Black community resent this analogy. While some tactics of civil disobedience may be similar, the goals of both movements could not be further apart; the denial of rights vs. expansion of rights.[92]

Tom Peepen of the *Atlanta Journal-Constitution* also dismissed OR's civil rights claims: "Operation Rescue tries to pass itself off as an heir of the civil rights movement. Don't its members march, practice civil disobedience and get themselves arrested just like real civil rights demonstrators did? They do, but those are superficial similarities. You could do the same in any cause, however ugly." He continued, "The civil rights movement marched to give citizens access to rights they were being denied. Operation Rescue is acting up to deny women rights they have won, hardly a subtle difference."[93] Julian Bond, one of the founders of the Student Non-Violent Coordinating Committee and the first president of the Southern Poverty Law Center, also spoke out against the comparison between the OR protests and the civil rights movement. He told the media, "We wanted the Constitution enforced. They want to rewrite it."[94] Elizabeth Appley, a lawyer for FWHC, also disagreed that the actions of OR were similar to the nonviolent civil disobedience of the 1960s. Rather, she said that "blocking doorways and shouting was 'harassing patients' and violent."[95] Anti-abortion movement supporters appealed to Atlanta mayor and civil rights movement veteran Andrew Young to release the jailed protesters who would not give their names. He responded that he stood by *Roe v. Wade* and the protesters needed to give their names in order to be released.[96]

OR gained support from the Reverend Jerry Falwell, founder of the Moral Majority, who also called on President George H. W. Bush to support the protesters. Falwell donated ten thousand dollars to help pay fines accrued during the arrests. Pat Robertson also supported OR's actions and gave the organization national exposure on the *700 Club*. Yet, many Southern Baptist ministers distanced themselves from Operation Rescue and its direct-action protests. They argued that legal channels were more fitting for the anti-abortion movement. For example, the Reverend Charles Stanley, pastor of First Baptist Church of Atlanta and former president of the Southern Baptist Convention, told his congregation that there was "no strong biblical support for civil disobedience against abortion laws." Rather, because the United States government did not compel women to choose abortion, *Roe v. Wade* gave women moral agency.[97] He further explained that he opposed abortion but worried that OR's tactics could be "counterproductive to the cause of Christ."[98] Finally, he added presciently, "If blocking an entrance is permitted, then why not physical restraint . . . or even destruction of those who are performing the procedure? Anarchy and chaos will ultimately result."[99]

In order to prevent further OR blockades, clinics across the country filed injunctions that would require protesters to allow patients to freely enter and leave the clinics. The Atlanta clinics did the same in October 1988.[100] The preliminary injunction granted on October 4, 1988, went into immediate effect and was upheld against OR by the Supreme Court in 1990. It required abortion protesters to be at least fifty feet from the property line. It also limited a group of protesters to twenty at any one time. They were not allowed to crowd together, preventing patients from walking past them to the clinic. The injunction also defined a "free zone" around the parking lot and on the streets and sidewalks around the clinic. In this zone protesters could not distribute leaflets or display their signs. Nor were they allowed to "counsel" or disseminate flyers within five feet of patients unless they first received their consent. OR opposed the injunction on the basis of free speech claims. The Court argued that the injunction permitted protesters "to exercise their right of free speech by engaging in social protest, limited only by reasonable time, place and manner restrictions."[101] The injunction proved success-ful. Randall reported that it ended all Operation Rescue protests except for a small picket on Saturday mornings.[102]

Even though for the most part the clinic blockades ended after the fall of 1988, sustained clinic protests continued to have an effect on the Atlanta FWHC. In her 1989 report Randall explained that in that year there was only one clinic blockade and there were no arrests but staff members still received death threats, were stalked, and were threat-ened and harassed in public by protesters at the clinic. She noted that "[a]ntiabortion activity increased to almost a daily occurrence by fall of 1989." The Atlanta FWHC also needed to follow up on charges filed against the protesters for violating the injunction and for trespassing.[103] Randall further reported that it was more difficult to find physicians because of public harassment. After one of their long-term physicians, Dr. Orris Moore, left the Atlanta FWHC, Randall explained that it was difficult to find another doctor to take his place. They were also forced to downsize staff in 1989 as a result of the cost of anti-abortion protests; staff left and positions were not refilled.[104]

The Atlanta FWHC had experienced smaller anti-abortion protests before the summer and fall 1988 invasions of Operation Rescue. They had also already incurred expenses because of anti-abortion activities at the clinic. Starting in 1984, Joseph Scheidler had led a series of protests at Atlanta clinics. His protests galvanized local anti-abortion protesters to begin weekly pickets at the FWHC on Saturdays, which continued for several years. Picketers ranged from two to sixty at a time. Most stood in the entryway to block patients from entering the clinic. As a result of this protest activity, the FWHC hired an off-duty police officer and brought in volunteer escorts to be at the clinic on Saturdays. They also hired lawyer Elizabeth Appley to initiate injunction proceedings to force protesters to clear the entryway. Most costly, as a direct result of the pre-convention picketing, they lost access to their parking lot, shared by a neighboring methadone clinic.[105] As a direct result of this loss, the clinic had to find a new location with accessible parking in 1986.[106]

By 1992, however, anti-abortion protest activity had lessened signifi-cantly at the Atlanta FWHC, which allowed clinic staff to focus on ex-panding their health care projects.[107] The tapering off of anti-abortion protesting nationwide in the early 1990s was due in part to the applica-tion of the Racketeer Influenced Corrupt Organizations (RICO) law to anti-abortion groups bent on limiting patient access to abortion clin-ics.[108] The Northeast Women's Center in Philadelphia first used RICO laws against anti-abortion protesters in 1985, charging that the activists conspired to put the clinic out of business. This case, upheld on appeal, became the model for an effective lawsuit brought by NOW against Scheidler and other anti-abortion protesters. In 1988, after the Atlanta protests, NOW added Randall Terry and Operation Rescue to the suit. Pro-choice lawyers argued that RICO laws applied because anti-abortion protest organizations conspired to close abortion clinics.[109] National Abortion Rights Action League (NARAL) and NOW also sued OR for failing to comply with court injunctions barring the group from clinic entryways. Grassroots feminist pro-choice forces continued to challenge OR at the doors of clinics with volunteer patient escorts trained by the Feminist Majority Foundation, NOW, and other feminist reproductive rights organizations nationwide.[110] These renewed pro-choice activities did much to diminish OR protest activities.

Chroniclers of the anti-abortion movement suggest that Opera-tion Rescue's campaigns were part of a trajectory of increased violence among anti-abortion activists that culminated in the killing of doctors. Although OR did not advocate violence, it helped escalate much of the rhetoric against legal abortion providers. After the murder of Dr. David Gunn in 1993 OR set up "rescue seminars" that trained anti-abortion activists in harassment of providers and patients.[111]

Of course the anti-abortion movement was not uniformly in support of direct-action tactics. More moderate anti-abortion leaders warned that OR protest activity hurt the anti-abortion movement more than it helped it. For instance, Mike Schwartz, director of the Center for Catholic Policy, argued that the direct-action strategy was a reaction to the movement's failure to elect anti-abortion politicians and lobby for changes to abortion law. John Willke, president of the National Right to Life Committee, contended that "lobbying successes have been substantial, especially in cutting off federal payments for abortions. The US Supreme Court, too, has become a more promising forum for antiabortion rulings."[112] Indeed, the Supreme Court's decisions in *Webster v. Reproductive Health Services* and *Planned Parenthood v. Casey* impacted abortion clinics much more in the long term than did OR's direct-action tactics by allowing state regulation of abortion provision.

The Atlanta FWHC staff agreed that anti-abortion protest was more disruptive and costly than effective at stopping abortion and other women's health services at their clinic. Although in 1989, just after the OR attacks had ended, FWHC was forced to reduce the number of days they performed abortions each week from five to four to save money. By 1990, the clinic was seeing 189 patients per week and hired a new abortion doctor, Dr. Susan Allen, in 1991. In her Executive Director's Report, Randall wrote optimistically, "Georgia was ranked high on NARAL's list of pro-choice states, and no new anti-abortion legislation passed the Georgia legislature in 1991. Anti-abortion protest activity has decreased dramatically, and we have developed new ways for dealing with protestors who continue to harass us."[113] As staff and administrators at the Atlanta FWHC fought to continue to provide high-quality abortion and other women's health services during the anti-abortion movement campaign, they also struggled to expand their services to women of color and other women with the least access to high-quality health care.

"Do It Safe": Expanding Reproductive Freedom in the Age of AIDS

Abortion was certainly a fundamental component of the total reproductive health services offered at the Atlanta FWHC, and abortion subsidized the other health programs. Despite the attention abortion garnered from anti-abortion forces, however, it was never the only important health service offered by the clinic. As Randall explained, 90 percent of the clinic's income came from abortion services provided on a sliding fee scale. Yet, feminist staff and administrators at the FWHC understood that women required much more than abortion services to have healthy reproductive lives. Randall wrote in 1993 in her Executive Summary, "A respite from constant anti-abortion activity allows for attention to strengthen existing programs and develop new programs and services." Services offered in 1993 in addition to abortion in the first and second trimesters included routine gynecological services, birth control counseling, and provision of a full array of birth control methods, including the pill, the IUD, Norplant, Depo Provera, the diaphragm, and the cervical cap. The clinic also offered sexually transmitted infection counseling, a donor insemination program, and colposcopy for women with a negative pap test.[114]

Beginning in the early 1980s, as the AIDS epidemic grew, the clinic began to offer testing for HIV/AIDS. With the intent of expanding services for women of color in Atlanta, in 1987 it augmented its HIV testing services to become the Women with AIDS Partnership Project (WAPP) to educate women about HIV transmission and prevention. I focus on WAPP here to demonstrate that Atlanta FWHC staff was committed to offering a wide variety of specialized services to the most vulnerable women in the community even as the anti-abortion movement waged its protests on their doorstep.

In 1987, the year before Operation Rescue targeted Atlanta, FWHC community relations coordinator Dázon Dixon Diallo created WAPP to supplement existing reproductive health services. In a 2009 interview, she discussed the wide array of women's health services provided by the FWHC:

My work with the Feminist Women's Health Center took place from . . . early 1984 to the mid-part of 1989. . . . And it was a wonderful experience where I came in as a lay health worker working at an abortion clinic that also happened to be the only nonprofit clinic, so we were also an activist and advocacy organization. We provided contraceptive care, family-planning assistance, well-woman gynecological services. Eventually we even added services of artificial insemination for women, particularly lesbians who wanted to become pregnant. . . . I was the only woman of color among the health workers on staff, I was able to connect with other women of color—especially young women seeking abortion services—I think, in ways that other folks who were working at the clinic were not able to.[115]

As a woman of color, Dixon Diallo noted that she was also more aware that poor and black women in Atlanta were disproportionately being infected with HIV. Their poverty and lack of access to high-quality health care exacerbated HIV transmission. She pointed out, however, that many mainstream feminist organizations had not identified HIV/ AIDS transmission as a key issue: "I think that for a lot of reasons, because HIV and AIDS at that time was more indicative of poor women and women who were active drug users, that those issues did not necessarily connect for folks who were leading the movement for equality for women or for equal pay or for access to abortion."[116]

Dixon Diallo's concern for the reproductive health needs of poor women and women of color motivated her to advocate strongly that HIV/AIDS prevention and testing be fundamentally connected to other feminist health issues at FWHC:

> [I]t was already very clear to me the immediate connection between access to choice around reproductive health options and access to information and options for preventing HIV and STDs. And those things weren't readily available in the same place. And I found that to be problematic when it was time—at least in the mid-'80s—when it was time for women to be more engaged on behalf of women who were being affected by the AIDS epidemic. It made more sense to me, because I was at the Feminist Women's Health Center, that we should be the ones addressing this issue, and not letting the so-called AIDS community at that time address women's issues within that.[117]

She also explained that in 1988 the attacks by Operation Rescue drained the resources of the FWHC, which made it difficult to expand services needed by poor women with HIV/AIDS: "Operation Rescue . . . was very taxing on all of our clinics but particularly a provider like the Feminist Health Center, which was a nonprofit provider and really depended on donations, depended on funding, as well as the income from our services."[118]

The Atlanta FWHC had already been answering questions about HIV and AIDS and providing testing services as the epidemic reached increasingly larger populations of women. The health center often received phone calls from women asking questions about transmission of the virus. After several years of ad hoc information dissemination, Atlanta FWHC staff decided that a more systematic approach to educating vulnerable women in Atlanta was necessary if they hoped to contain the spread of the disease. In their first year, Women with AIDS Partnership Project reached over thirteen hundred people, including over seven hundred who attended "Do It Safe Parties," which were at the center of the project's activities. Dixon Diallo organized the "Do It Safe Parties" in settings that would reach women most vulnerable to transmission; these included public housing projects, drug treatment programs, transitional halfway settings after prison release, battered women's shelters, and homeless shelters. She also counseled HIV-positive mothers in Grady Hospital's Pediatric Clinic, which served poor women who had contracted the virus.[119] As a member of the Advisory Boards at the Center for Constitutional Rights' AIDS Education and Legal Advocacy Project for People and Women of Color in New York and of the Center for Women's Policy Studies' National Resource Center on Women and AIDS in Washington, D.C., Dixon Diallo had already placed herself at the center of the national campaign to raise awareness about the growing, yet mostly ignored, problem of HIV-positive women. She explained that "[t]he WAPP has defined its target population as women at high risk—which primarily consists of women of color, poor women, homeless women and women in public housing."[120] These women were at risk for the disease, but misinformation that HIV/AIDS was a "gay disease" often kept women from protecting themselves from infection.

"Do It Safe Parties," also referred to as "Safer Sex Parties" (SSP), were workshops "in which factual information concerning AIDS, including prevention, modes of transmission and assessing personal risk is shared in a group setting of women only. In addition to these issues, other issues that show the impact of AIDS on women, such as socio-political issues, economic issues and legal issues are also addressed." Dixon Diallo further explained that SSPs were offered in FWHC's self-help context. For this reason, they were "unique in many respects, but most notably because the tone is relaxing, convivial and non-judgmental. In a relaxed atmosphere women have the opportunity to discuss facts, fears, sexuality and safety, and to address barriers to practicing safer sex . . . and make it clear that sex can still be erotic and pleasurable, as well as safe from disease." Dixon Diallo continued,

If you've ever been to a Tupperware Party, then you are familiar with the SSP's set up. The party is hosted by a woman in the community. She is responsible for inviting the guests and for providing a comfortable space to hold the party. The party is facilitated by trained community educators who have invested interest in making sure women are aware of their risk for AIDS, understand the use and meaning of safer sex, and realize they don't have to compromise their sexuality for safety.[121]

SSPs, then, were modeled after women's health movement self-help and collaborative health care services. Women educated other women in a nonhierarchical context. In 2009 Dixon Diallo described the process as "a workshop that was intended to create safe spaces for women, particularly women of color, but for women to come and have a learning conversation around AIDS, HIV, sex, sexuality, prevention, empowerment, safer-sex negotiation—all of these new things that [women] had been socialized not to talk about."[122]

WAPP also reached into the community to educate target populations about HIV transmission and safer sex practices. Unlike with other services, Atlanta FWHC staff could not assume that the women most vulnerable to HIV transmission would come to them. Most of these women didn't know that they were at risk for HIV, which is why they needed to be reached before they acquired the virus. For this reason, WAPP included a speakers' bureau training for SSP facilitators who could then go out into communities, and HIV testing and counseling for poor women and their partners.[123] Dixon Diallo also networked with other community organizations focused on women of color and reproductive health like the National Black Women's Health Project (NBWHP), also based in Atlanta. WAPP and NBWHP collaborated on community education projects about HIV transmission. Dixon Diallo helped NBWHP design the HIV/AIDS education portion of its self-help groups. In 1988 NBWHP held a conference on women and AIDS at which Dixon Diallo spoke. When Spelman College sponsored a forum called "AIDS and Black Women: The Impact on Our Issues," Dixon Diallo, as WAPP director, spoke about the sociopolitical aspects of AIDS and issues of prevention and education in the black community. WAPP also held Safer Sex Parties at the University of Georgia's Student Health Services and at a University of Georgia Peer Sexuality Counseling class working on creating workshops for fellow students.[124]

WAPP organizers tried to hold SSPs where women lived. Workshops also needed to be held on a repetitive basis so that women could become comfortable with staff and volunteers and with sensitive ideas about sexuality. For example, WAPP held SSP workshops at housing projects twice a week for six months to reinforce information. They also went to the Atlanta Council for Battered Women shelter on a weekly basis. Weekly workshops at Metro Transitional Center for Aid to Imprisoned Mothers focused on risks associated with intravenous drug use and discussed methods for sharing and disinfecting needles in addition to safer sexual practices.[125]

Since the clients who attended SSPs were about 40 percent women of color and often poor, Dixon Diallo was attentive to the social context and needs of these groups, particularly African American women as the largest single group of women of color in Atlanta. Dixon Diallo explained that Atlanta FWHC staff and volunteers who led SSPs learned of attitudes often held by African American women that contributed to ignorance about HIV transmission. She wrote that these attitudes needed to be addressed so that women could empower themselves to take control of their sexual practices and sexual health. Dixon Diallo wrote in a grant application for WAPP,

> During the first two years of providing AIDS information and prevention education to black women, staff have noticed differences due to culture, lack of education, and poverty that have contributed to a high level of misinformation. Because of a lack of access to quality, affordable health care and a community that links a woman's self-worth with fecundity, many young black women still believe they have no right to control their bodies. Strong religious training in this community often mitigates against frank and open discussion of sexual practices, and the assertiveness that is required of women to take control of their sexual relationships. An AIDS education effort, therefore, requires direction from black women who can be sensitive to the needs and requirements of their peers in discussing and understanding the danger of AIDS.[126]

In this proposal Dixon Diallo linked HIV transmission to a variety of contextual factors, but she was also careful to connect it to a lack of comprehensive health care for poor women of color. In this way, she emphasized the link between the work WAPP did educating vulnerable women about HIV transmission and prevention and the larger mission of the Atlanta FWHC, which was the provision of comprehensive reproductive health services to all women.

In 1989 Dixon Diallo left the FWHC to form SisterLove Women's AIDS Project in Atlanta. She explained that in 1989 the FWHC "sunsetted our HIV program" but there was a group of women on the women of color advisory group that she had formed who argued, "We still need this to happen in our communities. And Dázon, if you want to do that, we got your back. And so that's when I left the Center, and a few months later we started SisterLove."[127] SisterLove focused on HIV/AIDS education and transmission prevention by facilitating "Party 'Til You Drop . . . Unsafe Sex Practices" workshops and "Healthy Love Parties." Healthy Love Parties, like SSPs, were designed to provide "factual information concerning HIV/AIDS prevention, modes of transmission and assessing personal risk." The group was funded in part by the Georgia Department of Human Resources. Like WAPP, SisterLove also maintained a speaker's bureau for educational forums on women and HIV/AIDS. They also sustained support groups for infected women and held an annual self-healing retreat in FWHC self-help tradition.[128] LoveHouse, operated by SisterLove, was a living program for HIV-positive women with support services including self-help support groups, retreats, transportation, childcare, networking, and advocacy services.[129]

Dixon Diallo added that SisterLove also worked with the Centers for Disease Control (CDC) to redefine AIDS diagnoses: "[I]n the early '90s, there was a situation where a lot of women . . . were dying from opportunistic infections that were not necessarily associated with AIDS through the Centers for Disease Control's definition of what an AIDS diagnosis was. And it was clear that these issues were gendered. There were issues, for example, with cervical cancer, that were obviously more prevalent in women diagnosed with AIDS." Dixon Diallo continued, explaining that SisterLove allied with ACT UP Atlanta to change the definition: "So we fought— . . . at a very local level, as a part of ACT UP Atlanta— . . . alongside other national activists to get the CDC to change its definition, to make sure that women's issues, women's critical conditions as a result of having HIV, were also included in that definition."[130] As historian Jennifer Brier explains, "For men, full-blown AIDS often caused KS [Kaposi's sar-

coma], while women experienced bacterial pneumonia, pelvic inflammatory disease, and cervical cancer. This meant that even as the number of
women with HIV increased during the 1980s, very few were actually diagnosed with HIV."[131] This changed in the early 1990s as feminists involved
with AIDS activism in organizations such as ACT UP began to focus on
women as vulnerable to HIV transmission and raise awareness about
their particular health problems and symptoms. For much of the 1980s
the primary focus had been on HIV transmission between gay men.[132]

After Dixon Diallo left the Atlanta FWHC, an AIDS Hotline for
Women at the FWHC remained allied with SisterLove to continue to
provide information on HIV/AIDS education and testing among Atlanta's most vulnerable populations of women. The FWHC offered the
hotline to provide "basic phone counseling to answer questions about:
HIV antibody testing, risk behaviors, sexually transmitted diseases,
housing, legal issues, pregnancy and pediatric issues, early intervention
therapies and treatment issues." The FWHC also established referral
and peer counseling partnerships with other HIV/AIDS organizations,
including SisterLove. SisterLove provided community outreach, so the
Atlanta FWHC could focus its efforts on staffing the information hotline. The hotline first received funding in 1991 from the Georgia State
Department of Human Resources. The funding application explained
why this service was important to maintain: "AIDS is now one of the
five leading causes of death in the United States in women between the
ages of 15 and 44, and in major cities (larger than one million) it is the
leading cause of death in this age group." They explained further that
"[f]ifty two percent of women with AIDS are Black, 20% are Hispanic
and 27% are white," which meant targeting women of color communities
for outreach and education. Despite evidence that women were increasingly vulnerable to HIV transmission, the Atlanta FWHC reported that
"virtually no research has been done on women with the HIV virus or
AIDS. We know that the life of infected white males can be prolonged
from 8–10 years, yet the average life expectancy of women in the high
risk categories is three years. This occurs because poor women and teenagers do not have access to AZT." Furthermore, due to gender bias in the
definition of diagnoses, "Symptoms are also not identified in women
because they are typical GYN problems." Women in vulnerable categories needed access to quality health and reproductive care to be able to

identify symptoms early and access treatment. The Atlanta FWHC, with its focus on reproductive health, also took on AIDS prevention because "[m]ost women who are infected by the HIV virus are of reproductive age and the impact has serious implications on future epidemic trends." HIV prevention, diagnosis, and treatment had become a fundamental part of total reproductive health services.[133]

In 1993 FWHC staffed the AIDS Hotline twelve hours per day with fourteen volunteer phone counselors. The primary goal of the service was to offer phone counseling to women by women. In addition to offering counseling for women on HIV/AIDS transmission and prevention, hotline volunteers distributed stickers and flyers with slogans like "Women CAN get AIDS," "Do you know how women get AIDS?" and "Lesbians can get AIDS." The hotline received 591 calls between January 1 and August 21, 1993. Eighty-five percent of callers were women. Nearly 60 percent of callers were white; 30 percent were African American and only about 2 percent were Hispanic. Native American and Asian American women made up about 1 percent each of callers. The remaining women who called did not identify their race or ethnicity or identified as "other." The women usually wanted information on symptoms and transmission. They also asked about risk reduction related to sexual behaviors and drug use. The service referred women for testing at the Atlanta FWHC and other testing sites around the city.[134]

HIV/AIDS education programs helped the Atlanta FWHC to address a perception in the Atlanta community that their services were largely for white women and largely confined to abortion services. In 1993 Randall addressed this perception:

> The FWHC is viewed by many outsiders as a white, elitist, liberal organization of radical women, mostly lesbian, whose agenda has been their own particular health needs. That is the perception. The reality is that the women who comprise the executive body are white, the political agenda can be considered "liberal" and it is an organization that is sensitive to the lesbian community.

The FWHC needed to dispel the perception that it was a "white" organization in order to better serve large women of color and immigrant communities in Atlanta who did not have access to high-quality reproductive health services. This process of reaching out to women of color may have been complicated by internal struggles around racism within the organization.[135] Randall also pointed out that the "abortion issue and the clinic have become larger than the organization and the mission." The FWHC mission since 1977 had been to "advocate, promote and protect reproductive rights for all women. Our goal is to enable women to make informed choices about their health care and reproduction through the provision of self-help health education and gynecological services. We work with others locally, nationally and internationally to ensure that women have the information and power to control their bodies and their lives."[136] Years of defending access to abortion at times obscured the broader intentions of the FWHC.

The AIDS Partnership Programs at the Atlanta FWHC and then the continued relationship with SisterLove demonstrated that women of color had impacted the women's health movement so that it better served their interests. Yet, the perception that the Atlanta FWHC served white women persisted despite efforts to reach more women of color. Women of color working at the Atlanta FWHC also reported that "covert racism and subtle exclusionism pervaded their work lives. In their view, the Center was a clinic run by white women who were part of a white feminist movement that was itself suspect because of its history of racism."[137] Women of color involved in the women's health movement often noted that feminist efforts to reach and include women of color fell far short of their recommendations and demands. Some feminist women of color chose to work within majority-white organizations in order to try to push them to be more sensitive to problems faced by minority women. Some of these women, like Dázon Dixon Diallo, also eventually left majority-white feminist organizations to build institutions focused on the needs of women of color. In the next chapter, I attend to Loretta Ross's work as a reproductive rights activist within the National Organization for Women (NOW) and her efforts to transform NOW to address demands made by women of color in recognition of their particular reproductive health contexts.

5

"All This That Has Happened to Me Shouldn't Happen to Nobody Else"

Loretta Ross and the Women of Color Reproductive Freedom Movement of the 1980s

At the same time that feminist women's health providers were fending off attacks by anti-abortion organizations, women of color were increasingly vocal about the failure of majority-white feminist, women's health, and reproductive rights organizations to prioritize the political and feminist demands made by women of color. Majority-white feminist and women's health organizations tried to address some of these concerns with varying degrees of success. One method of addressing the demands of women of color was to try to integrate more women of color into majority-white organizations. Black feminist and reproductive rights activist Loretta Ross was hired in 1985 for this reason as the National Organization for Women's (NOW) director of Women of Color Programs to build coalitions between NOW and women of color organizations and to bolster the participation of women of color in NOW. By hiring Ross in this position, NOW organizers signaled their receptivity to race and class issues, a response that grew out of criticism of mainstream feminist organizing by women of color in the 1970s and early 1980s. NOW members hoped to strengthen the feminist movement of the 1980s by involving women of color and addressing accusations of racism in mainstream feminism made by women of color. NOW leadership also needed to rethink the political focus of the organization in the 1980s. NOW had dedicated the vast majority of its resources to passage of the Equal Rights Amendment (ERA) between 1978 and 1982. When that measure failed, NOW found itself without a political focus and faced with criticism that the organization was irrelevant to the majority of American women because of its failure to adopt political issues put forth by women of color and poor women.[1]

Although Ross spent a total of four years working with NOW on its Women of Color Programs, she later admitted that she did not view her coalition work between NOW and women of color organizations as a total success. She gave one example of the kind of top-down organizing that she found to be a problem at NOW and that she believed was typical of national mainstream feminist organizations. Ross explained that she had asked the National Abortion Rights Action League (NARAL) and NOW to put up much of the money for the 1987 "Women of Color and Reproductive Rights" national forum at Howard University. This forum was a national reproductive rights conference for women of color held in Washington, D.C., and organized by Ross and Judy Logan White, the director and founder in 1984 of the Women of Color Partnership Program (WOCPP) within the Religious Coalition for Abortion Rights (RCAR). The D.C. conference was linked to a series of regional reproductive-rights "Between Ourselves" meetings dedicated to bringing women of color together to discuss how best to impact a feminist reproductive rights movement that often neglected their needs and demands. The regional forums led to the national conference. Ross believed the series of conferences gave women of color an opportunity to be the majority in forums in which they could articulate their particular experiences and politics of reproduction. To this end, she urged Kate Michelman, then president of NARAL, and Eleanor Smeal, then president of NOW and founder of the Feminist Majority Foundation, to avoid sending members of their organizations to the D.C. conference unless they sent women of color. Too often, she believed, women of color's particular perspective on what should constitute a reproductive rights agenda became subordinated to that of white feminists. She wanted to avoid that outcome at a conference organized by and for women of color. She explained,

> My message to all the pro-choice organizations was that, send women of color, if they're not the president . . . if they're in your shipping department, you need to have women of color speaking on behalf of your organization. . . . And that caused quite a bit of controversy, because I'm asking them to put up their money but they don't get the spotlight. They don't get to showcase themselves.[2]

Despite this assertion that white women should remain behind the scenes, Smeal was scheduled to give an address at a dinner at the conference. According to Ross, some at NOW believed that as primary funders of the conference, NOW should have "top billing." But Ross felt very frustrated by Smeal's address. She believed that Smeal did not listen to her advice, and, as a result, gave a speech that was not well received by the primarily women of color audience. She explained,

> The night before Elli [Smeal]'s talk, Elli calls me and I'm in the middle of organizing the conference. . . . "I don't know what I'm going to talk about tomorrow. What do you want me to say?" I said, "OK Elli. This is what you need to say. This is the frame you need to use. This is how to, you know, win this crowd. This is what they're talking about and if you echo back stories of sterilization abuse and how it's a feminist agenda to let women control their bodies and, you know, we need to fight racism both outside the movement but also inside the movement. These are the kind of things you need to say."[3]

Ross recalled that Smeal also called her press agent for guidance and gave a speech the next evening that diverged entirely from what Ross had suggested she address. Ross noted that the speech targeted women of color from the perspective of "what you people need to do." She found it insulting and reflective of larger problems of racism within NOW.[4]

This chapter is illustrative of the frustrations encountered by women of color feminists like Ross who collaborated with white feminists in multiracial forums to expand the reproductive rights politics of the mainstream abortion rights and feminist movements in the 1980s. I begin with this vignette, however, not to condemn all multiracial feminist organizing by mainstream groups as a failure. Some participants in the majority-white feminist movement were receptive to these attempts and helped build a broad coalition for reproductive freedom. These efforts to build multiracial coalitions in the 1980s marked a departure from feminist organizing of the 1970s that occurred within mostly racially homogenous groups.[5] In this sense, these collaborations represented important efforts among white feminists to expand their political agenda to be inclusive of the criticisms of feminism made by women of color in the 1970s and early 1980s. Often, however, these attempts fell short and women of color left mainstream feminist organizations in the late 1980s and early 1990s to create their own organizations dedicated to solving problems more specifically confronted by them.

Thus, the collaborations between women of color and feminists organized in the majority-white reproductive rights movement of the 1980s were often uneasy and short-lived. Yet, by looking more closely at Ross's writings and reproductive rights activism while she directed the Women of Color Programs at NOW, I argue that NOW addressed race and class issues both internally by examining their own racism and externally by broadening their agenda. These actions led to multiracial feminist collaboration. In this sense, Ross successfully broadened NOW's feminist activism to incorporate a raced and classed analysis of gender oppression and feminist demands for social change. At the close of the decade, however, Ross left the organization disappointed with NOW's failure to build a lasting coalition between mainstream and women of color feminist organizations.

"Simultaneity" and Women of Color Feminism in the 1970s

Ross is representative of a burgeoning reproductive justice and antiracist movement among women of color feminists in the 1980s, yet an earlier group of women of color feminists forged a theoretical framework about "simultaneous oppressions" and reproductive politics in the 1970s that informed Ross's own criticism of mainstream feminism in the next decade. The Combahee River Collective (CRC), for instance, a group of black lesbian socialist feminists, several of whom had been involved with the National Black Feminist Organization (NBFO) earlier in the decade, asserted in their 1977 essay "A Black Feminist Statement," "We believe that sexual politics under patriarchy is as pervasive in black women's lives as are the politics of class and race. We also often find it difficult to separate race from class from sex oppression because in our lives they are most often experienced simultaneously."[6] Several popular anthologies edited by black and women of color feminists and published in the early 1980s also influenced white feminists to attend much more closely to intersections among gender, race, and class in their organizing.[7] These arguments about the simultaneous oppressions experienced by women of color were highly influential and led to the attempts at coalition building discussed in this chapter.

"Bread and butter" economic issues were often the first to be addressed by women of color feminists in the 1970s due to their emphasis on simultaneous oppressions. They accused white feminists of failing to recognize the important links between sexism and poverty, particularly among women of color. Former NOW president Aileen Hernandez accused NOW of this blind spot when she participated in the creation of the National Black Feminist Organization (NBFO) in 1973 with Margaret Sloan, Pauli Murray, Cellestine Ware, and Florynce Kennedy.[8] One of the primary characteristics distinguishing NBFO from white feminist organizations like NOW was its attention to "economic survival issues."[9]

NBFO, CRC, and the National Welfare Rights Organization (NWRO), founded in 1967 by black women to address poverty as the primary source of their oppression, also made reproductive rights central to their political demands by linking a woman's right to prevent reproduction using abortion and birth control to the socioeconomic context that made the choice to have a child a reality.[10] Historian Deborah Gray White has explained that NBFO and NWRO "supported the African-American woman's right to work at a decent wage, her rights to education and job training, her right to medical care for herself and her children, her right to be safeguarded against sterilization."[11] According to these 1970s black feminists, real reproductive justice could only be attained when all women had both the means to prevent the birth of an unwanted child and the economic means and protection from reproductive abuses necessary to bear a wanted child.[12] Thus, black feminists in organizations such as the NBFO, NWRO, and Combahee insisted that freedom from simultaneous sexual, racial, and class oppressions could only be achieved with voluntary reproductive control.

Along with their support for birth control and abortion, women of color feminists singled out sterilization abuse as a fundamental political issue that needed to be addressed among feminists if feminism was really about addressing linked oppressions.[13] They asserted that forced and coerced sterilizations among women of color stood as painful reminders that sexual oppression was always "simultaneously" informed by race and class oppression as well. Poor women of color, they insisted, were disproportionately the victims of sterilization abuse.[14] Their impression was backed up by statistics: in the mid-1970s welfare recipients with three or more children were sterilized at more than double the rate of nonwelfare recipients.[15] Other studies found that half of the 100,000 to 150,000 women sterilized annually in federally funded programs were black.[16] The disproportionate sterilization of African Americans became a particular problem in the 1960s as poverty increasingly became associated with black single mothers. In North Carolina between 1964 and 1966, African Americans comprised 64 percent of state-sterilized women.[17] Women of color feminists of the 1970s were also attentive to the issue of sterilization abuse as a reproductive justice issue because white feminists tended to remain focused on maintaining legal abortion after the 1973 Roe v. Wade decision.

Several high-profile forced sterilizations in the 1970s, including the 1973 involuntary sterilization of the Relf sisters, ages twelve and fourteen at the time of their sterilizations, heightened attention to sterilization abuse as a concrete threat to the voluntary reproductive control of women of color. NWRO joined the Southern Poverty Law Center in a suit on the Relfs' behalf against the Department of Health, Education, and Welfare for the girls' sterilization. A class action suit brought by patients of Southern California/Los Angeles County General Hospital focused on the problem of involuntary sterilization of Mexican-origin migrant women. Native American and Puerto Rican women also experienced sterilization and sterilization abuse in high numbers.[18]

In my first book, Women of Color and the Reproductive Rights Movement, I argued that 1970s women of color feminists responded to the problem of forced and coerced sterilization by pressing the abortion rights movement to address the specific reproductive injustices experienced by poor women and women of color. Women of color principally insisted that the movement needed to couple anti–sterilization abuse with abortion rights access issues to emphasize that reproductive freedom also meant securing the right to bear wanted children.[19] Prominent African American feminist Angela Davis articulated the reproductive rights position of many women of color during this period: "What is urgently required is a broad campaign to defend the reproductive rights of all women—and especially those women whose economic circumstances often compel them to relinquish the right to reproduction itself."[20]

In response to the charge of racism demonstrated by the narrow list of issues majority-white feminist organizations chose to prioritize in the 1970s, NOW hired Ross to tackle its internal racism and to help make the mainstream feminist movement more politically accessible to women of color by pushing economic and racial issues higher up on NOW's agenda. NOW, like most other majority-white feminist groups of the 1970s, had focused pointedly on keeping abortion safe and legal and neglected campaigns against sterilization abuse and for economic access to legal abortion.[21]

The Shaping of an Activist Life: Recollections of Simultaneous Oppressions

Ross illustrated her long-term commitment to building a feminist movement that addressed both race and gender oppression in her narration of her life, recorded in 2004 for the Voices of Feminism Oral History Project at the Sophia Smith Library at Smith College. She also used her biography to demonstrate how personal experience can lead to political activism. Ross explained that key events in her early life contributed to her perspective on reproductive rights politics, particularly her belief that race and gender worked to "simultaneously" affect women's reproductive lives.[22]

Ross began her reproductive history with an account of her first pregnancy at the age of fourteen in 1968, which resulted from incest. The father of her child was her great-aunt's 27-year-old nephew. She also described the incest experience in a biographical article written for the *Black Scholar* in 2006: "Through incest committed by a much older cousin, I became pregnant when I was 14 and had my only child, a son. I did not know how widespread incest was in the African American community at the time. I just knew that it had happened to me."[23] Ross described this relationship as coercive although she didn't say she was violently assaulted. Given that she was only fourteen years old at the time of the conception, there is no doubt that her cousin had committed a felony by having sex with her. Ross had the baby at fifteen at a home for unwed mothers. She chose to keep her son with her, which required her to sacrifice a scholarship at Radcliffe College. She explained that her family contemplated taking her to Mexico for an illegal abortion but decided it was too dangerous. Ross's experience with the father of her child was not her first involuntary sexual experience. She had been raped previously at age eleven by a stranger.[24]

Ross represented both of these involuntary sexual encounters, the stranger rape and the statutory rape by the relative who fathered her child, as well as the contemplation of illegal abortion and the birth of her child, as pivotal events in the development of her awareness of gender oppression. Indeed, opposition to sexual violence and the reproductive rights of women of color became the two most important commitments in Ross's feminist activist history. Yet, she did not describe these events as overtly linked to racism. Although in the 2006 article she noted the prevalence of incest in black communities, she did not contend that it was any more or less common among African Americans than among whites. She explained that at the time of the incest she had no knowledge of its widespread occurrence. Her emphasis in the Voices of Feminism interview and in the *Black Scholar* article was on the gender injustice she felt as a young woman coming of age in a culture that denied women both sexual and reproductive agency.

In a 2009 interview, Ross contended that she may not have rendered her personal experiences of sexual assault and incest as a teenager as linked to racism because her primary goal as an antirape activist was to convince black communities that rape and incest happen among African Americans. She remembered, "The conversation in the black community was that it was a denial that it was a problem at all. That it was a problem at all was finally being acknowledged; this was significant in itself." Thus, in much of her work on sexual violence issues, Ross understood that she was talking about violence between black women and men. She explained, "When you talk about violence against women it is much more likely to be intraracial and incest is also within the community. We take it for granted that it is intraracial."[25] Of course, racism did have an effect on black women who experienced rape by black men. Most significantly, black women were often afraid to speak out about rape for fear that it would increase racist ideas about predatory black male sexuality. But this was not Ross's point of emphasis.

Events Ross chose to reveal about her college years echoed her teenage years. Again she encountered both a lack of reproductive control and sexual violence. In her first year of college at Howard University,

Ross was gang raped. She also became pregnant because she was having unprotected sex with her boyfriend. She explained that she was too young to obtain birth control, so they had sex without it. She ended the pregnancy legally in Washington, D.C., in 1970. The abortion was a late-term saline abortion that terminated twin fetuses.[26]

Ross also experienced her introduction to both feminist and Black Nationalist politics at Howard in the early 1970s. She explained that "[f]ellow students gave me my first political books: *The Autobiography of Malcolm X* by Alex Haley and *The Black Woman* by Toni Cade Bambara. It was this heady mixture of Black Nationalism and black feminism that initially defined my politics." Yet, "There was limited political space for radical black women within either the Black Nationalist or white feminist movements. . . . We felt poised between two distinct movements that did not fully represent our unique intersectional experiences."[27] Black Nationalist men spoke out vociferously against birth control use among black women as genocidal and often argued that black women should take on a supporting role in the movement.[28]

Due to a variety of personal circumstances, Ross found her way into the City Wide Housing Coalition, fighting "for rent control and against gentrification." From there she became involved in a Marxist-Leninist study group and with anti-apartheid activism. The study group introduced her to Nkenge Touré, a member of the Black Panther Party and the executive director of the D.C. Rape Crisis Center (RCC).[29] RCC was founded in 1972 by a group of white women active with Women's Liberation in Washington, D.C., and connected to the Washington Area Women's Center.[30] Although the organization had been created by white feminists, black women became the majority of the staff. The D.C. anti-rape activists believed that black women should be at the forefront of the rape crisis center's community service work because the organization catered to a predominantly black population. Ross took over as executive director of the organization in 1979.[31]

While at the City Wide Housing Coalition, Ross also became involved with the National Black United Front by founding a women's section of the organization. The purpose of the women's section was to bridge the divide between black feminism and Black Nationalism.[32] Ross explained that the experience of educating Black Nationalist men about gender politics and sexual violence among blacks was often frustrating. She recalled,

A lot of black men said we were airing dirty laundry by talking about rape. Someone called me an agent provocateur for talking about rape and said we must be allied with COINTELPRO—Black Nationalist men also adhered to the narrative that rape happened at the hands of white men, not black men. We would get booed for talking about these issues. Black Nationalists in particular felt that we were betraying the black movement.[33]

Her attempts to bridge Black Nationalism and feminism made Ross very aware of how black women could be marginalized in both movements. Many black feminists responded to this sort of marginalization by founding their own black feminist organizations such NBFO, Combahee, or the National Black Women's Health Project (NBWHP). Some also responded by shying away from "feminism" as a term to describe their politics. Ross noted that this rejection of the term "feminist" was her response as well.[34]

In the 1980s at NOW, Ross began to call herself a feminist, although she had been working on issues of women's oppression for years, and had dedicated much of her political activism to reproductive rights politics and the prevention of violence against women. In the early 1980s, Ross struggled with the question of whether the feminist movement and its politics were "legitimate expressions of the history, concerns and aspirations of Black women specifically and Black people in general."[35] She explained that black women were involved in Women's Liberation from the beginning, but "they were often repelled by the reproduction of the racist and classist tendencies in the feminist movement inherited from the larger society." She continued, emphasizing that most white feminists were "unable or unwilling to address their own racism and classism," and thus, "Black women felt alienated from a movement that purported to want our presence."[36] Yet, despite her doubts, Ross brought her experience with both antiracism activism and Women's Liberation to the mainstream feminist movement in her work with NOW. In that work, she demanded that reproductive rights issues of importance to women of color, like sterilization abuse, lack of access to quality health care, and medical neglect, become central issues within the mainstream feminist movement.

Ross looked back at her own reproductive history and singled out a 1976 hysterectomy, which ended her reproductive capacity, as a turning point in her political perspective on racism, gender oppression, and reproductive freedom. The hysterectomy followed a bout of pelvic inflammatory infection caused by a Dalkon Shield IUD implanted in 1972.[37] Ross argued that a doctor's misdiagnosis of venereal disease rather than the infection itself ultimately led to the rupture of her fallopian tubes and the necessary removal of her reproductive organs. She contended that if her physician had diagnosed the infection in time she never would have lost her reproductive organs.[38] She sued A. H. Robins, the producer of the Dalkon Shield, after her hysterectomy and settled out of court in 1980. Her individual case helped pave the way for the national class action suit against A. H. Robins.[39]

Ross represented this tragedy as essential to her development as a woman of color reproductive rights activist who recognized race and racism as integral to gender oppression. She concluded that she had not experienced reproductive abuse as an individual or merely as a woman. Rather, her experience was also reflective of reproductive abuses lived by other women of color. I will quote extensively from a section of the 2004 interview with Ross because it is so important to her construction of her narrative of herself as a woman of color who had experienced reproductive abuse akin to the forced and coerced sterilizations of other women of color. Ross recalled,

> I'm happy to say that my case along with the other pre-suit cases blew the lid off of Dalkon Shield. Because I signed no confidentiality agreements and I was telling the world and my lawyer was telling the world and the next thing I know, there was a huge class action against AH Robins about the Dalkon Shield. So it was in that moment that I'm conscious of becoming a reproductive rights activist, 'cause I was pissed off . . . all this that has happened to me shouldn't happen to nobody else. . . . And so, I entered the movement, feeling that I'd been the victim of sterilization abuse, but not the classic sterilization abuse where you go in the hospital and you're sterilized without your consent. Well, it was without my consent. I was unconscious. But at the time, I do not believe that sterilization was avoidable. . . . It was the fact that for six months, I'd been going to this joker and his misdiagnosis and maltreatment ended in sterilization. That made me mad. But that's when I began reading more and paying more attention to how many women were sterilized. . . . I looked at my sister and

my mother. . . . [T]here were very few women who were ovulating in my family by their thirties. And so, it was really much more widespread, and that this had to happen to me for me to start paying attention. . . . I was, like, what the hell is going on here?[40]

Although Ross had experienced unwanted pregnancy and abortion—incidents reflective of her limited reproductive control—it was her involuntary sterilization and her subsequent lawsuit against A. H. Robins that she highlighted as the turning points in the development of her position as a black feminist reproductive rights activist. She emphasized that these were not merely personal experiences but catalysts for her activism within the movement for reproductive freedom and justice for women of color. Yet, as she noted in the 2004 interview, her hysterectomy as a result of an infection from an IUD was different from the forced and coerced sterilizations experienced by other women of color and popularized in the movement against sterilization abuse in the 1970s. In those cases women of color had been sterilized without their knowledge or consent or coerced to sign a consent form, often during labor by doctors who believed they should have no more children.[41] Ross's sterilization, alternatively, was linked to the disproportionately high rate of reproductive tract infections among women of color as well as their lack of access to high-quality medical care. Ross made a rhetorical link among her individual experience, the sterilization experiences of her female family members, and the sterilization experiences of other women of color as a group to situate herself personally and politically within the movement to oppose sterilization abuse.

Ross's self-described transformation into a reproductive rights activist came at the same time she was also being exposed to a proliferation of writings by black feminists. She recalled reading and being influenced by women of color publications on feminism, including *But Some of Us Are Brave*, edited by Gloria T. Hull, Patricia Bell Scott, and Barbara Smith; Cherrie Moraga's and Gloria Anzaldua's *This Bridge Called My Back*; *Sister Outsider*, by Audre Lorde; Michelle Wallace's *Black Macho and the Myth of the Superwoman*; *Color Me Flo: My Hard Life and Good Times*, by Flo Kennedy; and Shirley Chisholm's *Unbought and Unbossed*, "as well as everything published by Kitchen Table Press."[42] These writings brought attention to the simultaneous oppressions lived by women of color. For example, Barbara Smith, former member of NBFO and Combahee, explained in an interview published in 1981 in Moraga's and Anzaldua's edited anthology *This Bridge Called My Back*, "I feel it is radical to be dealing with race and sex and class and sexual identity all at one time."[43] Ross's description of her hysterectomy represented her personal connection to the black feminist and reproductive rights movement as one who both suffered from raced and gendered victimization and became an activist to prevent others from being victimized. Although Ross had already been involved in Women's Liberation and had been active in opposition to sterilization abuse before her own hysterectomy, her self-description as an explicitly feminist activist for reproductive justice came at a time when she could bring together both black feminism as articulated by many women of color activists, on the one hand, and her own experience with sterilization and medical neglect on the other. The high incidence of reproductive tract infections, medical abuse, and sterilization among women of color would continue to shape her reproductive rights politics after she left NOW.

Building a Coalition Movement: NOW, Reproductive Rights, and Antiracism

Ross helped build a reproductive rights movement in the 1980s that made the demands of women of color central. This movement was attractive to many women of color who had rejected the 1970s majority-white feminist abortion rights movement as too narrowly focused on legal abortion. Ross's work contributed to coalition building among white women and women of color that focused on expanding reproductive justice beyond legal abortion. The set of demands that women of color felt needed to be included in a comprehensive reproductive rights movement reflected some of the experiences that separated their perspectives from that of white feminists. Ross explained,

> Women of color constitute 83% of the female prison population, because she is a nonentity with no rights under America's criminal justice system. The infant mortality rate is overwhelmingly higher for women of color over their white counterparts. It is no accident that 33% of the women in Puerto Rico have been sterilized, or used as test objects during the

experimental state of the "pill." Both in America and abroad, Third World Women suffer all forms of medical/scientific/physical abuses as they are systematically sterilized, or "dumped" with unsafe American products overseas.[44]

This passage exemplifies some of the ways that women of color tried to forge a coalitional feminist politics that did not make gender oppression the singular subject of feminism. For Ross, prisoners' rights, infant mortality rates, sterilization abuse, and other medical abuses all constituted significant issues to address within a feminist reproductive rights politics. Yet, in the early 1980s, when Ross wrote this essay, protecting legal abortion still topped the list of most feminist organizational agendas.

Ross's task within NOW was to address internal racism and help the organization to better integrate racial justice into its gender politics.[45] One of the suggestions Ross made was to build a broad reproductive rights agenda that took seriously the difficulty many poor women and women of color faced having and caring for wanted children. Helping prisoners to see their children so they could retain custody, the right to reject sterilization as a primary method of reproductive control, and the right to remain free from medical tests that might jeopardize a woman's health or reproductive ability all constituted reproductive rights, but were unrecognized by many white women. Often when these topics were recognized by white feminists as important elements of a total reproductive rights movement, they were still placed on the back burner when legal abortion was threatened.

Ross pointed out that women of color organizations prioritizing reproductive rights demands important to women of color and working-class women did exist at the time. She noted that the Alliance Against Women's Oppression was one such organization that fought to restore federal funding for abortions for poor women after the 1976 Hyde Amendment excluded abortion from health services for the poor funded through the federal Medicaid program.[46] At the same time, she noted that until the late 1980s, "there wasn't any real evidence of a women of color movement. There was evidence of women of color leaders, but we were leaders without a constituency. We had a vision that a large number of people hadn't bought into."[47]

The passage of the Hyde Amendment was a revealing moment in reproductive rights organizing, because it exposed which mainstream organizations really prioritized the needs and demands of poor and minority women, those women who most often relied on federal Medicaid to access health care. Without the federal Medicaid program to fund abortions, reproductive rights activists concerned with the rights of poor women argued, women with limited resources would go without needed abortions or might resort to dangerous self-abortions instead.

Was it enough, however, for women of color to do the work to make an important feminist issue such as reproductive control more inclusive? Many women of color, including Ross, believed that more mainstream and majority-white feminist and pro-choice organizations such as NOW and RCAR needed to step up to the challenge to realize the radical feminist goal of making feminism about all women.[48] NOW and RCAR made the protection of abortion rights one of their fundamental political goals in the 1980s. Women of color activists like Ross argued that this goal failed to respond to the reproductive experiences of black women, Latinas, Native American women, and other women of color.

Responding to these criticisms, NOW and RCAR attempted to incorporate these expanded reproductive rights goals into their agenda in the 1980s. Molly Yard, at the time the political director of NOW and later in the decade president of NOW, asked Ross to help NOW improve its antiracism reputation by building coalitions with women of color organizations before the March to Save Women's Lives to be held in Washington, D.C., and in Los Angeles in March of 1986. This march was to be a massive answer to an anti-abortion movement that had made few legal gains at this point—*Roe* had been affirmed in the most recent Supreme Court decision (*Akron vs. Akron Center for Reproductive Health* in 1983)—but had made political inroads with the rise of the New Right and support from President Ronald Reagan. A vigorous right-to-life movement had been gaining momentum since the Supreme Court's 1973 *Roe v. Wade* decision legalizing abortion. The movement also received important national political backing in the late 1970s and early 1980s with congressional passage of the Hyde Amendment.[49]

Organizers at NOW did not want to stage a historic march for abortion rights that appeared racist to women of color nationwide. Women of color had been critical of both NOW's narrow focus and its organiz-

ing strategies. NOW's abortion rights strategy revolved around supporting national elected officials who publicly supported abortion, ousting
anti-abortion legislators, and defending *Roe v. Wade.*[50] If NOW leaders
wanted to increase the number of women of color in the feminist movement they needed to demonstrate that they had responded to criticisms
of racism and shifted their politics to be more inclusive.[51] Ross also
explained that coalition organizing had not been a practiced political
strategy for NOW. They needed to overcome a long-term policy of not
forming coalitions with other organizations.[52]

Ross acknowledged the challenge of integrating women of color and
their concerns into the majority-white feminist movement. She wrote,

> This is not a simple task because women of color, by and large, support
> feminist principles while distrusting feminists because of the racism and
> classism of the organized women's movement. Furthermore, the process
> of empowering women of color is often viewed as taking place at the
> expense of white women, so that resistance is by both sides. Yet the chal-
> lenge remains of building a multicultural, broad-based women's move-
> ment that accurately reflects the full diversity of American women, not
> just middle-class white women.[53]

She expressed a strong sense of skepticism about the possibility for a
successful partnership between NOW and women of color organizations given the experiences of racism recalled by many women of color
who had attempted to join mainstream feminist groups. She explained
to Molly Yard that there were subtle forms of exclusivity that turned
women of color away from the organization that might not be recognized by white women leaders. She remembered explaining to Yard, "[T]
here are some institutionalized practices . . . that may be part of the
reason why women of color don't stay. One of these practices is both
the marked and unmarked power within NOW. The marked power is
positional. The officers and all that. The unmarked power seems to be
more relationship based."[54] Ross added that "[s]hining a light on this
sort of process was decidedly uncomfortable for much of the leadership.
They would say they were not doing it to exclude women of color. The
racism was unintentional."[55] She explained that organizational power
often flowed through personal networks that excluded women of color.

She viewed one of her tasks at NOW to be the correction of this unfair and often subtly racist channeling of decision-making power.[56]

To address these sorts of subtle racist practices, Ross developed an "unlearning racism" program for white NOW members. She used small consciousness-raising groups in the workshops so that white members could discuss topics like white privilege and internalized racism. She explained that white feminists needed to understand how they had internalized racist views before they started to build coalitions with women of color. In a memo on the subject she wrote, "[L]earning about privilege and internalized racist views among the majority group requires small consciousness raising groups and experienced facilitators—internal awareness of racism among the majority group is necessary before coalition building can happen."[57]

Ross pointed out that NOW would have to reach out to women of color by adopting issues that made race and fighting racism central before they hoped to create a multiracial organization. There were already organizations run by women of color for women of color. Not all of these were focused on feminist issues, at least within a narrow definition of the term "feminist," yet they were working on political topics important to women of color. NOW could only build ties with these organizations by genuinely addressing issues of importance to women of color.[58] She explained,

It may seem that the Negro Business and Professional Women's Association, for example, is not interested in abortion rights, yet they endorsed and participated in our March for Women's Lives in 1986. Similarly, a number of Asian women's groups may not be prepared to work on reproductive rights, but issues of employment discrimination or the ERA may appeal to this sector of women of color. Or a Puerto Rican group may be largely Catholic and not actively working on abortion rights, but can relate to discussions of sterilization abuse and immigration reform.[59]

Ross suggested that feminism needed to be defined flexibly within a social and historical context that acknowledged the different needs of women in different social, cultural, and regional circumstances. To be inclusive, feminists needed to broaden their agenda to include activism that addressed women's different circumstantial and subjective liberation needs regardless of whether they called those demands feminist or not.

During her time as director of Women of Color Programs, Ross constructed a network of women of color reproductive rights activists. Her effort culminated in the national conference and the series of regional forums on reproductive issues of concern to women of color called the "Between Ourselves" forums. The national conference, titled "Women of Color and Reproductive Rights," was held in Washington, D.C., in May 1987 at Howard University. Ross organized the conference and the regional forums in a collaborative effort with her counterpart at RCAR, Judy Logan White, founder of the Women of Color Partnership Project (WOCPP). Women of color at RCAR created WOCPP "as a vehicle by which African-American, Latin American, Asian-Pacific-American, Native American, and all Women of Color . . . [could] become actively involved, as decision makers, in the reproductive choice movement." They believed that WOCPP might become a "foundation on which to build a united multi-cultural coalition."[60] They organized in churches to involve women of color in reproductive rights campaigns.[61] Lynn Paltrow of the ACLU Reproductive Freedom Project, and Byllye Avery, founder of NBWHP, and women of color at Planned Parenthood and NARAL also helped organize the national and regional conferences.[62] Regional forums were held in Atlanta, Hartford, Chicago, Oakland, and on a reservation near Sioux Falls, South Dakota, mostly incorporating African American, Latina, and Native American reproductive rights activists.[63] The national conference theme was "Being Oppressed Is the Absence of Choices." Financial contributors to the conference included NARAL, NOW, the Ms. Foundation, and Planned Parenthood.[64]

According to Dázon Dixon Diallo, cofounder of SisterLove and longtime women's health activist, the national conference organizers met their goal of creating an inclusive and racially diverse meeting. She attended as a representative of the Atlanta Feminist Women's Health Center to demonstrate self-help cervical exams. She recalled that there were considerable numbers of Latina and Native American women present, although black women were still the majority. She also remembered a significant international presence at the conference that reflected increasing attention to a global women's health movement.[65]

Coalitions were also forged at the regional "Between Ourselves" forums although each one tended to be more racially homogenous than the national conference. Ross recalled that among the smaller regional forums, the Atlanta forum, at about seventy-five to eighty attendants, was mostly African American. The Latina Health Project, however, primarily organized the Hartford forum, so drew largely from a Latina activist core. The South Dakota forum was dominated by Native American activists and focused on such issues as sterilization abuse among Native women.[66] Other topics covered at the regional forums included teen pregnancy, AIDS, sexually transmitted infections, medical abuses against women of color, infertility solutions, new reproductive technologies, and violence against women.[67] Asian/Pacific Islander women were also involved in "Between Ourselves" reproductive rights coalition work at this time, chiefly organized by the National Network of Asian/Pacific American Women, founded in 1984.[68]

Ross believed that the only way to build a massive feminist reproductive rights movement was to bring women of color into the mainstream of it. She explained, "The narrow agenda of this [abortion rights] movement alienates women of color. We cannot define our men or our church as the enemy—this equation does not work for women of color . . . because we are in a different place and have a different history."[69] Women of color and white women did not have the same historical relationship to reproduction, men, or religion because of the history of racism and the development of racial identity over time. Although some men had not been supportive of women's control of their reproductive bodies— specifically men in the Black Nationalist movement in the 1960s and early 1970s—few women of color viewed their engagement with reproductive politics as opposing men in some sort of gendered political dichotomy. Women of color knew they would need to ally with men to end racism. Thus, the positions of women of color feminists on these issues were not identical to the positions delineated by many white feminists.[70]

Byllye Avery of NBWHP agreed that a multi-issue movement that linked issues associated with race, class, and gender was essential to the success of the feminist women's health movement in the 1980s; she said,

> We told them [white women in the abortion rights movement] it was unwise to just talk about abortion. We felt that a lot of [black] children were dying from infant mortality and a lot of other things that were not being talked about. We never [focused on] a single issue at all, but they didn't

listen. It would have been a perfect way to defeat the "right" [wing] to be inclusive and be integrated. They wouldn't listen.[71]

Ross and Avery concurred that mainstream feminists had an opportunity in the 1980s to build a large, inclusive movement that joined white women and women of color in common cause to fight intensifying right-wing forces supported by the Reagan administration and opposed to women's reproductive freedom.

Participants in the "Between Ourselves" forums also discussed how white feminist organizations had failed to acknowledge the activism of women of color in the movement for reproductive rights. Too often, white women declared that women of color were not part of the pro-choice movement: "Often, pro-choice organizing by women of color is unacknowledged in our movement. Projects such as the Alliance Against Women's Oppression, the International Council of African Women, the National Black Women's Health Project, the Black Women's Self-Help Collective, the Sisterhood of Black Single Mothers, and the National Network of Black Midwives are virtually unknown and unsought by the pro-choice movement."[72] The failure to acknowledge the political activism of women of color created another barrier between white and women of color reproductive rights activists. White feminists wondered why black women and other women of color did not join their organizations without recognizing that they were already active in the movement and building alliances with each other.

Ross commented on the Religious Coalition for Abortion Rights' unique success in building alliances with other women of color organizations through their Women of Color Partnership Project. She noted in particular WOCPP's ability to work "closely with the religious community in organizing pro-choice women of color." She continued, "One of the strengths of the WOCPP is that they are effective at taking their message to communities and to church women and fostering the debate among church women on these issues." WOCPP's strategy of organizing through the church worked because many women of color still looked to the church and religion as a guide for moral decision making. Leaving religion out of the discussion alienated women of color.[73]

Between 1985 and 1988, Ross reported feeling relatively optimistic and successful in her role as director of the Women of Color Programs for

NOW. She explained that the 1986 March for Women's Lives "turned out to be a wonderful success. Eighty-seven women of color organizations ended up endorsing the march. A fairly large number showed up."[74] According to sociologist Zakiya Luna's article on the "reframing" of NOW's "choice" focus by women of color, two thousand women of color attended the 1986 march.[75] Ross explained, however, that the march itself did not inspire women of color to become active in the movement for reproductive freedom. Rather, women of color organizations were already experiencing a groundswell of membership and increased activism around reproductive rights in the mid- and late 1980s. As a result, they began to build their own movement and collaborated with mainstream feminist organizations such as NOW. Organizations such as the NBWHP and Latina Roundtable on Health and Reproductive Rights in New York had already begun to organize women of color on issues related to health, reproductive rights, and social and economic rights. In 1988 the Native American Women's Health Education Resource Center was founded on the Yankton Sioux Reservation in South Dakota.[76] Ross recalled that the 1989 follow-up March for Women's Lives involved even more women of color. She wrote that "more than 2,000 women came together, to form the largest delegation ever of women of color marching to support abortion rights."[77]

Thus, Ross believed that her efforts to build liaisons between NOW and women of color organizations began to pay off as these groups became more visible in the national reproductive rights movement in the mid-1980s. She explained that "the greatest single infusion of energy and resources [into the reproductive rights movement] is coming from women of color. . . . These groups of highly organized, highly visible women are becoming increasingly vocal on pro-choice issues and will be important in the future development of women of color within the reproductive rights movement."[78] The next question became how to sustain partnerships and the infusion of women of color into the movement over time.

To sustain the coalitions after the 1986 March for Women's Lives, Ross put significant time and energy into building goodwill between NOW and women of color organizations and individuals. She very consciously departed from methods that white NOW members had employed in the past to "recruit" minority women. Instead, Ross explained,

We wish to attract women of color to NOW by our effective work, by building bridges of trust and unity, and by demonstrating our commitment to both an anti-sexist and anti-racist American future. We dropped both recruitment efforts and the word itself, because the word recruit implies that our agenda and efforts do not convince women of color to join us; they must be "recruited," much as the military needs to recruit a few good men. This sexist, militaristic term is alienating to women of color and should offend every woman who hears it.[79]

Rather than "recruit," Ross believed that NOW could win the trust of women of color through concrete activism that legitimately addressed the problems that they faced in their lives. She continued, "By establishing an agenda and program that substantively addresses the concerns of women of color, NOW won't have to recruit them. We believe that women of color will independently join an organization that demonstrates effectiveness on their issues."[80]

Despite successes and moments when she expressed considerable optimism about building multiracial coalitions with NOW and placing women of color issues at the top of NOW's agenda, in 1989 Ross decided to leave the organization and her position as director of the Women of Color Programs to join Byllye Avery at the NBWHP in Atlanta. She explained that she came to see NOW as "inherently inimical to the empowerment of women of color." She recalled that both RCAR and NOW "continued their use of women of color to raise funds without any real commitment to the projects for women of color." She further explained, "It was hard to get the money for the programs on women of color. It was a struggle to allocate the money here."[81]

Ross explained that her decision to depart was linked to the 1987 national "Women of Color and Reproductive Rights" conference at which Smeal gave her address. Yet, she remained at NOW for two more years after that address. The years following the 1987 address failed to erase her fear that the organization would continue to marginalize women of color reproductive justice issues. Ultimately, these fears were confirmed rather than dispelled. Ross explained that other women of color had come to the same conclusion: "In the 1980s women of color were having conversations about having their own organizations. They were becoming more gender conscious but that

didn't lead them into the mainstream organizations."[82] To better build
a movement of women of color activists, Ross and Sabrae Davis,
the new director of WOCPP at RCAR, decided to establish an "independent women of color and reproductive rights organization . . .
because we find we cannot advance our work without encountering
active hostility and resistance by our respective bosses." In addition
to their work at NBWHP and WOCPP, Ross, Davis, Avery, and civil
rights lawyer Sherrilyn Ifill founded the Women of Color Title X Coalition as a move away from NOW and an expression of the doubts
Ross had about whether it was possible for a majority-white feminist
organization to effectively address the problems faced by women of
color at that point in history. Members of the Women of Color Title X
Coalition formed in direct response to restrictions to Title X Family
Planning Programs, which funded family planning services and other
preventive health measures for poor women.[83]

Conclusion

Ross's experience building interracial coalitions as part of a mainstream
feminist organization was short-lived but offers important lessons.
The first lesson is that the battle to end racism in our society and by
extension in the feminist and reproductive rights movement needed to
continue into the 1990s and beyond. While Ross's efforts were impres-
sive, just a few years of coalition building could not erase decades of
racial conflict within the contemporary feminist movement. As Ross
and many other feminists, both white and of color, have asserted, ending racism is essential if the feminist movement hopes to continue to
transform the lives of all women, not just women in relatively privileged
positions. But addressing racism in the feminist movement is a complicated and ongoing challenge. In 1990 Ross indicated that she had not
given up on this fight either, although she was no longer doing it from
within NOW. She wrote,

> We [black women] must also contend for power within the pro-choice
> movement. . . . Those of us who do are usually isolated, pained, and ex-
> hausted by having to reinterpret the debate for white women and Black
> men. And we are demoralized by having to defend these efforts to our

Black sisters who support abortion rights yet totally distrust the pro-choice movement.[84]

Yet, predicting that if women of color persisted in being alienated from the movement it would "flounder and commit the political suicide of not truly representing all women," Ross continued, "What I am talking about is building a multi-racial movement where power and resources are equitably distributed."[85]

Ross believed that there was potential for greater coalition and movement building among white women and women of color organizations, although she had essentially given up on bringing black and other women of color into mainstream majority-white feminist organizations such as NOW. She explained, "The number of Black women's organizations has more than tripled in the past 10 years. Most Black women believe in inter-racial coalitions, not inter-racial organizations."[86] She continued, asserting that "women of color will take the lead in the coalition-building effort in the 1990s because we know this is the only way to win. In order to participate in this effort, predominantly white organizations will have to change their leadership and their agendas. And white women must do intensive anti-racist work."[87]

Women of color reproductive justice organizations proliferated in the 1990s and did lead the way in shaping coalitions with majority-white feminist groups. Organizations such as the National Black Women's Health Project, the Latina Roundtable of Health and Reproductive Rights, Asian Communities for Reproductive Justice, and the Native American Women's Health Education Center all contributed to an actively engaged women of color movement for reproductive justice in the 1990s. These groups affiliated with one another in an umbrella organization called "the SisterSong Collective" to build collaborative national projects and also work locally on reproductive justice issues. Women of color groups also collaborated with mainstream feminist groups like NOW, such as for NOW's 1992 March for Women's Lives, but did not choose to integrate themselves into the majority-white feminist movement. They remained distinctly women of color organizations. All of these organizations contributed to an exciting contemporary women's health movement dedicated to bringing the broad health needs of women in diverse contexts to national political attention. Women of color activists continued to redefine reproductive rights as well, so that in the 1990s their emphasis pivoted around what they defined as reproductive justice, which hinged on linking reproductive rights to human rights.

Another lesson learned from Ross's years at NOW was that feminist abortion rights and women's health movement organizations could be guided to incorporate issues of importance to women of color into their agendas. Ross believed that the mainstream feminist movement took steps to address racism and broaden its agenda and that women of color activists in the movement were the catalyst for the changes. She wrote, "By the mid-1990s African-American and other women of color have forced the abortion rights movement to become a broader struggle for reproductive freedom."[88] Ross continued, emphasizing how her years at NOW and collaborations between women of color and white feminists helped catalyze the women of color movement for reproductive rights:

> [W]ithout . . . the teamwork between myself and NOW, we wouldn't have this burgeoning women of color reproductive rights movement. . . . And so, in a very important way, NOW was very important, despite itself, in terms of building this movement of women of color. . . . [T]he external pressure we as women of color received in having to respond to their marches also has a catalyzing effect on women of color organizing. So even though we groan and complain when they announce that they're doing this big event and we debate amongst ourselves whether or not we're going to participate, the fact that they have forced the discussion is very significant politically and historically. . . . [I]t was probably not their intention at the time they announced this march to create all of this discussion among women of color, but that's what happens. . . . [T]here's a real symbiotic relationship between what the big mainstream organizations do and what happens in the communities of color that are working on reproductive health and rights, and probably neither side really appreciates it as much as it could be.[89]

Next, in the concluding chapter, I turn to the women of color reproductive rights/justice movement, referred to by Ross in her interview, that began to take shape in the early and mid-1980s and blossomed in the 1990s. In this movement, women of color redefined women's health and women's health activism to embrace human rights and what they termed "reproductive justice." Most of the women of color activists in the next chapter, like Ross, founded or gravitated to women of color organizations rather than attempt an integration of majority-white women's health or feminist organizations. Yet, their activism on behalf of reproductive justice can also be viewed as historically linked to the earlier civil rights, New Left, and feminist movements for health and social justice.

Women of Color and the Movement for Reproductive Justice

A Human Rights Agenda

The [reproductive rights] movement is not the personal property of middle-class white women, but without a frank acknowledgement of white supremacist practices in the past and the present, women of color will not be convinced that mainstream prochoice activists and organizations are committed to empowering women of color to make decisions about our fertility, or to reorienting the movement to include the experiences of all women.
—LORETTA ROSS, 2006

After the 1989 March for Women's Lives, Loretta Ross moved to Atlanta to become director of programs for the National Black Women's Health Project (NBWHP).[1] Jael Silliman, Marlene Gerber Fried, Loretta Ross, and Elena R. Gutiérrez, the authors of *Undivided Rights: Women of Color Organize for Reproductive Justice*, characterize the NBWHP as "the first ever women of color reproductive justice organization" and the "foremother" of organizations that make up a contemporary movement for reproductive justice among women of color.[2] Silliman, Fried, Ross, and Gutiérrez, who are also activists within the movement, elaborate on the meaning of the term "reproductive justice" for contemporary women of color organizations:

> Some women of color organizations are using "reproductive justice" to recognize that the control, regulation, and stigmatization of female fertility, bodies, and sexuality are connected to the regulation of communities that are themselves based on race, class, gender, sexuality, and nationality.

This analysis emphasizes the relationship of reproductive rights to human rights and economic justice.[3]

In this final chapter, I will trace the development of the movement for reproductive justice among women of color from the 1983 Spelman College National Conference on Black Women's Health Issues—and the founding of NBWHP—through the 1990s to the present. The authors of *Undivided Rights* claim that human rights have been a fundamental framework for this movement that links "civil, political, economic, sexual and social justice rights [to bridge] the gap between having legal rights and lacking the economic resources to access those rights."[4]

Zakiya Luna, sociologist and historian of reproductive politics and social movements, adds to this analysis by explaining that there has been a tendency to see reproductive rights and reproductive justice as the same thing. Instead, she argues, the difference rests on a "focus on social justice within the context of achieving a spectrum of human rights rather than only privacy to make a decision to legally access abortion."[5] In the concluding chapter to this book, I will also show that this human rights framework, while refined by women of color as they applied it to reproductive justice, has a longer history and should be viewed as a legacy of the civil rights, New Left, and feminist women's health movements of the 1960s and 1970s; activists in these historical movements for health reform also tied social (in)justice to community health while making the broad social and economic context for ill health a primary focus. Although women of color distanced themselves from "white" feminism, the women of color movement for reproductive justice is still historically tied, in complex and at times critical ways, to the feminist women's health movement of the 1970s and 1980s. As I argued in my 2003 book, *Women of Color and the Reproductive Rights Movement*, women of color criticized the feminist mainstream and primarily white women's health movement for focusing almost exclusively on abortion rights at the expense of a broad women's health and social justice agenda. Yet, as I hope has become clear from the preceding chapters of this book, the women's health movement also had a diverse agenda that at times reached beyond abortion to include sexual autonomy, issues of gender, race, and class equality, and overall health care access grounded in community health provision.

Political frameworks do not emerge wholly formed without connections to previous movements. Certainly, NBWHP is a foremother of the contemporary women of color movement. At the same time, however, the human rights framework claimed by women of color also has roots in civil rights struggles in Mississippi, in the New Left campaigns for better health care access for the poor in New York and Boston (discussed in chapter 1), and in the feminist women's health movement that flourished in Seattle, Los Angeles, and Atlanta (discussed in chapters 2, 3, and 4), as well as in international movements as women shared human rights perspectives at global meetings associated with the United Nations.

Loretta Ross, Sarah Brownlee, Dázon Dixon Diallo, and Luz Rodriguez, all members of the SisterSong Collective, an umbrella organization that brought sixteen women of color groups together to work collectively on reproductive justice in 1997, further explain how human rights informs their health activism:

> Rather than accept the medical model of a disease-based approach, women in developing countries and women of color in the United States have led a reconceptualization of women's health as a women's human rights issues. This needs-based approach shifts the focus from service providers to the women they serve by interrogating the way women are treated within service-delivery systems, including communication and information-sharing, establishing minimum standards for procedures and examinations, and assessing whether women receive services appropriate to their needs. Services must be accessible and must be offered in an environment that enables women to use them effectively. . . . Improvement in women's health requires more than improvements in science and health care; it also requires government action to correct injustices faced by many women and to help create enabling conditions necessary to fully exercise these rights.[6]

As with the Neighborhood Health Centers in the 1960s, the SisterSong Collective organizers argued for improved access to health care, services designed for patients, not for health care providers, and economic and political reforms that addressed complex social and health problems often shared by women living in poverty. Women's health movement feminists of the 1970s also argued that access to health services designed by and for those who used them was a fundamental pre-condition for quality women's health services.

Similarly, Luz Rodriguez, one of the founders of SisterSong and exec-utive director of Latina Roundtable on Health and Reproductive Rights beginning in 1996, elaborated on the importance of integrating health care and social services in a community-based approach in her 2006 in-terview for the Voices of Feminism Oral History Project. She discussed her work as executive director of the Dominican Women's Center in the early 1990s:

> We work more holistically with the woman and the family primarily. . . .
> [O]ne member of the family is suffering . . . let's say the child is doing bad
> in school so we're tutoring, but we're not paying attention to the grand-
> parent that's helping with homework that doesn't know English because
> the mother is working because she's got to have three jobs to pay the rent
> because the daddy's addicted to drugs or away at another job. And so, a
> colleague will be working on a drug rehab program three blocks away
> with the dad, we're over here tutoring the kid, and the grandparent is
> going to the senior citizen center for free lunch that's led by somebody
> else. And so, both public and private funding has come down in such
> compartmentalized fashion that it has diffused the manner in which we
> would, I believe, create solutions in our communities.[7]

Rather than compartmentalize services, Rodriguez advocated that health and social services be integrated and linked to a community in a manner that was similar to health service delivery designed by the NHCs. In both of these contexts emphasis was placed on holistically ad-dressing health needs that were linked to social and economic problems in particular communities of people.

As part of their broad approach to women's health, SisterSong and the women of color organizations that made up their coalition also focused on advocating for health care services that were culturally appropriate for different groups of women. For example, organizers at the Latina Roundtable, founded in New York City in 1989 by women of mostly Dominican and Puerto Rican ancestry, and one of the first organiza-tions to make up the SisterSong coalition, emphasized the importance of recognizing various cultural attitudes toward sexuality and reproduction in the delivery of reproductive health care.[8] They explained that they held discussion groups on "the influences of diverse religious and cultural norms on Latinas' sexuality, freedom of self-expression, reproductive freedoms, and sexual taboos such as bisexuality, homosexuality. Personal and cultural attitudes toward abortion for pro-choice women, and the prevailing social trends to limit access to abortion and family planning services, and other religious and cultural trends to demonize the medical procedure."[9] This focus on culturally appropriate health provision resonated with understandings of health care advocated by health reformers in the 1960s and 1970s who had focused on integrating patients into neighborhood health services tailored for those who lived in the neighborhoods. For groups in the women of color movement of the 1980s and 1990s, like the Latina Roundtable, there was a greater emphasis on recognition of racial and ethnic differences among women and how those impacted health provision and access.

The founding of the NBWHP and other women of color organizations, including SisterSong, which has fostered collaboration among many of these organizations since 1997, has been detailed elsewhere, particularly in *Undivided Rights*. But I will briefly reiterate a portion of this history here in order to provide a context for understanding the development of a human rights agenda by women of color reproductive justice activists.

The NBWHP, the oldest national black women's health organization, was created in 1983 by Byllye Avery and Lillie Allen after the June National Conference on Black Women's Health Issues held in Atlanta on the Spelman campus and sponsored by the feminist health advocacy organization National Women's Health Network. The great success of the Spelman conference, and unexpectedly explosive turnout (approximately seventeen hundred to two thousand attendees), was a testament to black women's desire for a forum that addressed their specific health issues after years spent pressing mainstream majority-white feminist organizations to respond to their activist demands related to health. Avery and Lilly Allen's "Black and Female: What Is the Reality?" workshops, which evolved into the self-help process adopted by local NBWHP chapters across the country, were particularly popular, with hundreds of women crowding into workshops. These workshops addressed "issues of racism, poverty, low self-esteem, and extreme stress that lay at the root of black women's health problems."[10] Avery had discovered while talking to African American women as she was organizing NBWHP that black women often had a lot of information about health, but they also confronted many interconnected problems related to racism, economics, and a lack of psychological empowerment and self-esteem that would be necessary to address if they were to transform both their health and their lives.[11]

NBWHP was founded during a period in the history of reproductive politics when the defense of abortion legality often took precedence in mainstream feminist organizations (like NOW) as feminists battled mounting challenges to abortion rights from the strengthening New Right and anti-abortion movements. By founding NBWHP, African American women's health activists demonstrated that there was a huge demand for autonomous women of color organizations focused pointedly on the complex and dire health problems—and social and economic contexts for those problems—experienced by large numbers of women not well-served by white feminists focused on keeping abortion legal.

Thus, although NBWHP founders were pro-abortion, they did not make abortion legality their only or primary agenda item. Byllye Avery, cofounder of NBWHP, cut her feminist and activist teeth as a cofounder of the Gainesville (Florida) Feminist Women's Health Center (FWHC), which provided abortions in a feminist context. (Avery also helped found a birth center, called Birthplace, in Gainesville.)[12] When the Hyde Amendment restricted federal Medicaid from paying for abortion, Avery noted an increasing number of African American women coming to the Gainesville FWHC for their lower-cost abortions. This instance opened her eyes to the different contexts surrounding black and white women's reproductive experiences.[13] She was also on the board of the National Women's Health Network, which helped sponsor the Spelman Black Women's Health Issues conference. Despite these strong connections to the feminist movement, Avery recognized that problems not prioritized by white feminists could not be solved without a separate movement.[14]

NBWHP's approach to self-help distinguished it from other majority-white feminist health centers. Feminist self-help focused on generating knowledge among women about their mostly healthy physical bodies. NBWHP, alternatively, focused on how "the psychological scars of racism and sexism had left black women with a deeply negative self-image." Allen also employed techniques she had learned when she had been involved in Reevaluation Counseling to help black women understand and heal self-images deeply affected by a racist society. After they addressed the internalized psychological damages caused by racism, they could address physical health, which for most women of color was also implicitly related to economic and racial inequalities.[15] NBWHP defined health holistically, or as "not merely the absence of disease; rather, health was the promotion of wellness in all areas," a definition that resonated with the 1948 World Health Organization definition as well as definitions of health used by H. Jack Geiger and other health reform activists in the 1960s.[16]

Women of color activists, like Avery, Loretta Ross, and Luz Rodriguez, believed that mainstream white feminist organizations did not make health care issues defined by women of color, and associated with their experiences of both racism and classism, priority political issues in the 1980s. So they gravitated to separate women of color organizations and generated a vibrant women of color movement. African American women, Native American women, Latinas, and Asian/Pacific Islander women all entered the movement for reproductive justice and created autonomous organizations to address reproductive justice demands; some demands were shared by women of color whereas other issues were particularly pertinent to specific racial and ethnic groups. African American women, Native American women, and Latinas shared activist roots in the movement to oppose sterilization abuse that had been in existence since the early 1970s. They also shared an emphasis on combating culturally insensitive health provision and disproportionate poverty causing ill health in their communities. But at times their issues also diverged. For Native women, "cultural survival, land rights and reproductive justice" were strongly linked.[17]

In 1988 Charon Asetoyer founded the Native American Women's Health Education Resource Center (NAWHERC) on the Yankton Sioux reservation "to raise awareness of Native women's rights over their bodies and their lives."[18] A Native Women's Reproductive Rights Coalition was created in 1990 during a conference held in Pierre, South Dakota, sponsored by NAWHERC with attendees from eleven different tribes. The coalition helped delineate a list of reproductive rights demands for Native American women. This list of demands resonated strongly with the human rights framework constructed by other women of color groups, although it also included demands particularly relevant to Native women. The coalition demanded

> [t]he right to knowledge and education for all family members concerning sexuality and reproduction that is age, culture, and gender appropriate; [t]he right to all reproductive alternatives and the right to choose the size of our families; [t]he right to access safe, free, and/or affordable abortions, regardless of age, with confidentiality and free pre and post counseling; [t]he right to active involvement in the development and implementation of policies concerning reproductive issues, to include, but not limited to pharmaceuticals and technology; [t]he right to include domestic violence, sexual assault, and AIDS as reproductive rights issues; [t]he right to programs which meet the nutritional needs of women and families.

Additionally, they demanded reduction of infant mortality rates; culturally specific chemical dependency programs; an end to coerced sterilization; culturally oriented health care; informed consent for medical treatment; the right to determine members of nations; the right to quality health care; reproductive rights for women with disabilities; and the right to parent children in nonracist and nonsexist environments.[19] Although many of these agenda items were common to women of color groups—issues like reducing infant and maternal mortality rates, which were disproportionately high among all women of color groups; ending forced and coerced sterilization and other medical abuses; gaining access to culturally appropriate health care; and improving access to reproductive health care, including abortion, but also to pre- and postnatal care and fertility treatment—other issues, such as cultural survival for Indigenous peoples, land rights, and environmental degradation on reservation lands were important to Native women.[20]

The NAWHERC sustained a consistently broad agenda with appeal across the community, indicating that it did not separate women's issues from community issues. These included

> the Child Development Program which provides tutoring to predominantly Native American children having difficulty in school; the Adult

Learning Program which teaches basic computer, word processing, Desk Top publishing, and GED tutoring; Alcohol Education, Fetal Alcohol Syndrome (FAS) Education, and Alcoholics Anonymous (AA) Meetings; Women's Reproductive Health Information; Nutrition Classes for special needs such as diabetes, hypertension, and weight loss; AIDS Prevention and Education; and Domestic Violence Safe House System, transportation and counseling.[21]

For Indigenous feminists, it did not make sense to separate women's issues from larger community issues. Although issues of importance to a mainstream feminist movement were also taken up by NAWHERC, so were issues like adult learning and substance abuse that affected the entire community.

Like Native American and African American women, Latinas have experienced disproportionately severe health problems due to lack of access to quality health care, poverty, and racism. Elena Gutiérrez explains that Latinas consistently experience poor health "with disproportionately high rates of cervical cancer, sexually transmitted diseases, HIV/AIDS, teenage pregnancy, obesity, diabetes, domestic violence, and unintentional injuries compared to other women." She emphasizes that health problems are made worse by "financial, institutional, and cultural barriers."[22] At their founding in 1989, Latina Roundtable brought attention to these sorts of broad health topics and inequalities, emphasizing that "whites had dominated the reproductive rights agenda with emphasis on choice but for Latinas, choice was not the driving force; even though the Roundtable was/is pro choice, there are other issues." Instead of abortion rights, they shifted to a reproductive justice framework that included programming "around the concept of Latina sexuality in the context of culture and religion"; sexuality and health education would target young Latinas and include mentoring for young women.[23]

Much of the work done by Latina Roundtable concentrated on the delivery of "culturally competent" sexuality and health education. La Nueva Onda series, targeting young women between the ages of eighteen and thirty, focused on "health and social issues that impact Latinas" and provided "a culturally and linguistically relevant context for dialogue and consensus building." Women involved in La Nueva Onda were encouraged to also become involved with Las Hermanitas, a men-

202 | A HUMAN RIGHTS AGENDA

toring program for adolescent Latinas.[24] In a 2006 interview with the
Voices of Feminism Oral History Project, Luz Rodriguez explained the
importance of community education and involvement in health delivery
to the goals of Latina Roundtable:

> People need to be empowered from the ground up; goes back to the idea
> of self help; women need to understand their bodies and participate in
> their own health delivery. And if we can just make a shift in the apathy
> that most people have about their lives and the lack of agency that they
> have in their lives, that good things are going to happen, there will be
> social change. . . . It has to come from the base. Social change has to occur
> within the grassroots.[25]

For Rodriguez, empowerment began with "culturally competent"
education, which fostered participation in health delivery systems. As
in the earlier community health movements and the feminist women's
health movement, Rodriguez emphasized community involvement and
self-help as pivotal to improvements in health outcomes. A medicalized
imposition of health reform from outside of the community would be
less successful, in her opinion.

In the late 1990s Latina Roundtable continued to develop culturally appropriate sexuality and health education programs. Community
Health Education forums sponsored by the group focused on breast, cervical, and ovarian cancer detection in adult Latinas and HIV screening
and sexual health education among teenagers in the public high schools.
The roundtable tied HIV screening to combating fear and shame associated with sexual topics.[26] Roundtable members argued that culturally
appropriate health provision could help Latinas better access preventive
measures and treatment for cancer, HIV/AIDS, and other health challenges related to sexuality and reproduction. To this end, they created a
Roundtable Series on Sexuality, Religion, and Culture. They explained
the purpose of the forum: "The need for age, language and culturally
appropriate public health education in the Latino community remains
unmet and despairing. The definition of 'culturally competent' . . . education must also include dialogue pertaining to the strong hold of religion
and traditional gender . . . to dispel the myths of shame that haunt even
the most progressive Latina women."[27] At the same time, the roundtable

recognized that Latinas were a diverse group. They explained, "The Latina Roundtable has become a source for community health education,
advocacy and leadership development for Latinas who represent a Dias-
pora of Latino cultures encompassing Puerto Rican, Mexican, Dominican, South American and Indigenous descent. Many of the Roundtable's
target populations are from under-served and linguistically isolated
communities."[28] Thus, they needed to produce health education materials and programs that appealed broadly to women from a variety of
cultural backgrounds. They hoped that women who participated in the
roundtable discussions would "continue dialogues on sexuality, religion
and culture within their own faith communities, families, and other
public forums coordinated by the Latina Roundtable and other identified organizations creating similar dialogues." These dialogues would
"cover areas such as sexuality messages in childhood, virginity, menstruation, homosexuality, contraception, abortion, and reproductive health
in the context of religious and cultural belief systems."[29]

Sterilization abuse was notably present in the activist literature produced by women of color reproductive justice activists during the 1980s
and 1990s. Latina Roundtable literature referenced "the mass sterilization
of Puerto Rican women in the 1950s and the subsequent use of Puerto
Rican women in medical trials for the contraceptive pill" in their discussion of "Sexual and Reproductive Health and the Latina Woman."[30] Yet,
although issues of coerced and forced sterilization often motivated women
of color activists to become active in the movement for reproductive justice, these were not the primary reproductive rights violations addressed
by reproductive justice activists in the 1980s and 1990s. Stories of reproductive violation, however, were often catalysts for involvement in the
movement. Like Loretta Ross, Luz Rodriguez was motivated to join the
movement after she became aware of the numbers of women who were
sterilized involuntarily. Unlike Ross, she did not experience sterilization
or medical malpractice personally; as a woman of Puerto Rican ancestry,
however, she felt deeply that Puerto Rican women had too often been victims of reproductive coercion and were prohibited from freely choosing to
have wanted children. Rodriguez recalled in her 2006 interview,

[T]here was all this talk among Puerto Rican women in my community
about la operacion . . . and the whole history of sterilization abuse of

Puerto Rican women. . . . As I . . . learned how to do research in college and how to process political information, I began really finding out
for myself what the hell that really meant, that it really was a systematic
population-control strategy, sterilizing tens of thousands of Puerto Rican
women. . . . I learned about the human experimentation of Puerto Rican
women to develop . . . the appropriate dose of the contraceptive pill. That
totally infuriated me. . . . To me, how I personally gained consciousness
about . . . reproductive rights was being exposed to that history of Puerto
Rican women.[31]

As with Ross's interview for the Voices of Feminism Project, I quote
extensively from Rodriguez's interview to demonstrate the extent to
which sterilization abuse figured as a central historical injustice for the
reproductive justice movement led by women of color. Women of color
activists continued to make issues of coercion and medical neglect central to their activism and often linked these issues to the historically high
incidence of coerced and forced sterilization. For example, after referring to problems of sterilization abuse in Puerto Rico, Latino Roundtable activists detailed that "[t]hreats to sexual and reproductive health of
Latinas persist to the present day with alarming statistics indicating this
population as the fastest growing in the areas of HIV infection, cancer in
the reproductive organs and teen pregnancy."[32] In a public forum sponsored by the Latino Commission on AIDS, Latina Roundtable members
participated on a panel about "Mandatory HIV Testing of Childbearing
Women and Newborns, with an emphasis on the history of reproductive rights violations of Latina women."[33] Although sterilization abuse
as it had occurred in previous decades might have been less of a problem in the 1980s and 1990s, women of color asserted that coercion for
the purposes of reproductive control was still a problem and connected
contemporary coercions to historical abuses.[34]

The involuntary use of long-acting hormonal contraceptives like
Depo-Provera and Norplant, both of which had associated risks and
side effects that were not always explained in clinics, was of particular
concern to Native women. Native women's health activists brought attention to the Indian Health Service (IHS) provision of Depo-Provera
to Native American women to prevent Fetal Alcohol Syndrome (FAS).[35]
Charon Asetoyer of NAWHERC made the link between historic forms

of sterilization abuse among women of color and coerced reproductive control by IHS using Depo-Provera:

> [E]ven though there had been all of the sterilization abuses that occurred in the '60s . . . and the process being changed for the better, in terms of waiting periods and informed consent . . . but when it came to other forms of sterilization, other than surgical sterilization or tubal ligation, there were other ways of continuing to coerce Indian women into steriliza-tion . . . meaning the use of Depo-Provera. And doctors were feeling very comfortable with using Depo on chemically dependent women, coerc-ing them. We were very uncomfortable with that, because they were not dealing with the root causes of alcohol[ism]. They were not dealing with the chemical dependency. They were just saying, we will prevent these women from having children. . . . That's a reproductive justice issue.[36]

Asetoyer recalled discussing Depo-Provera as a preventive measure for FAS with a physician at IHS. She explained that he was quite ada-mant in his belief that Depo-Provera should be prescribed to alcoholic women to prevent FAS despite any medical contraindications against using the contraceptive. Asetoyer explained, "The issue was how to stop a pregnancy from occurring. And again, no talk in this interview of try-ing to help a woman with her chemical dependency. So we could see where this whole thing was going, and so we really needed to get out into the community and talk to women about it, and to educate our tribal leadership as well."[37] Asetoyer explained that she viewed FAS as a reproductive justice issue because Native women should have the right to bear healthy children. The best way to prevent FAS was not through coercive prescriptions for Depo-Provera; rather, the root causes of alco-hol abuse needed to be addressed. Thus, alcoholism, its prevention, and the connections between alcohol abuse and reproductive coercion were all important reproductive justice issue for Native American women.

Since mainstream feminist organizations were unlikely to make FAS and coerced Depo-Provera use a priority, Asetoyer, like other women of color, explained the importance of forming separate women of color organizations to address linked reproductive justice issues of particu-lar concern to different groups of women of color. She said, "Some of the motivation for starting our own groups is because there were these mainstream issues, but the agenda was just very narrow and was not broad enough to include our issues. And so, we became very aware during that time period that we needed our own organizations, so that we *could* broaden the agenda."[38] Asetoyer continued, emphasizing that "fetal alcohol syndrome is a reproductive rights issue." She explained that mainstream white women's health organizations didn't always have the same priorities:

> [I]t just really supported my concern about the need for our own orga-
> nizations to really expand and to address our issues and to look at what
> our issues are: domestic violence . . . the right to parent your children in
> a nonviolent home; the right to live as a woman in a nonviolent environ-
> ment; the right to food, to be able to feed your family, to be able to feed
> yourself; the right to health care; the right to be able to have as many chil-
> dren as you wanted—*or not*. It isn't always about the right to terminate
> a pregnancy. In our communities, it's about the right to be able to *have*
> children, because of all the targeting in government policy in the years of
> oppression, sterilization abuses. . . .[39]

Asetoyer's broad focus on linked economic, social, and reproductive health problems that were "connected to the regulation of communities[, which is itself] based on race, class, gender, sexuality, and national-ity,"[40] reflected a human rights perspective claimed by many women of color. Yet, Asetoyer's emphasis was also on Indigenous women and their particular experiences as members of sovereign nations within U.S. bor-ders. Many reproductive justice issues were shared by women of color, but Asetoyer recalled that some issues of concern to Indigenous women were not shared: "[A] lot of women of color don't understand that whole concept of sovereignty and self-determination. We are sovereign na-tions." She continued, pointing out that sovereignty shaped Indigenous women's approach to reproductive justice: "[W]e have a whole 'nother layer of issues because of that situation that we have to address. And that's the protection of our natural resources, our land, our land base."[41] Asetoyer emphasized that women of color share economic, health, and reproductive rights concerns, but because they are a diverse population of women, their concerns are not always identical. She explained, "[W] e have different backgrounds and different historical experiences. And those need to be documented as well, because that's what makes our issues so diverse."[42]

By the 1980s and early 1990s, HIV/AIDS transmission had become a central concern and pivotal to the organizing of many women of color reproductive justice activists. Although HIV/AIDS was initially popularly conceived as a "gay male disease," reproductive justice activists quickly noticed that HIV infection rates were disproportionately high among women of color. HIV/AIDS prevention among women of color required that activists address a nexus of linked concerns, including comprehensive sexuality education, attention to economic factors that made women of color more vulnerable to sexually transmitted infections, consideration of cultural differences around open discussion of sexuality and sexuality education, informed consent for HIV testing, particularly among pregnant women, and fear that women with HIV/AIDS would be targets for medical abuses as they had been in the past in other contexts. Women of color activists often integrated HIV-positive women into the process of building a health care agenda that incorporated their demands.[43]

Consistent with their human rights framework, HIV/AIDS prevention work with women of color was not disconnected from other economic and health problems or broad social justice issues related to racism, classism, and sexism. For example, Latina Roundtable, in its summary of "Sexual and Reproductive Health and the Latina Woman," prepared as part of a 1997 grant application, detailed that "AIDS is the leading cause of death for Latinas ages 25–44 in NYC and Puerto Rico. Latinas represent 33% of the cases among women. Adolescents and young adults constitute the fastest growing groups of new AIDS cases in NYC. Breast cancer, cervical and ovarian cancer are on the rise in the Latina population." Latinas also had particularly low rates of mammogram testing for breast cancer because health care workers often did not address cultural and gender barriers to discussing health issues that dovetailed with sexual matters. Latina Roundtable and other women of color organizations also linked HIV/AIDS to the high incidence of reproductive tract infections among women color. Reproductive tract infections were epidemic due to the same nexus of cultural, class, and gender barriers to accessing high-quality health care among women of color.[44]

Founded in 1989 by Dázon Dixon Diallo, formerly of the Atlanta FWHC, SisterLove also addressed the connections between the high incidence of reproductive tract infections and the high incidence of HIV/AIDS among African American women. Furthermore, SisterLove, like Latina Roundtable and other women of color organizations focused on reproductive justice, linked HIV/AIDS to overall poor health among black women. Under the heading "Critical Issues for Consideration," SisterLove organizers detailed black women's dire health problems:

> Black women's reproductive health is most certainly in a state of crisis. Consequently, where women are in crisis, so are their families and communities. Black women live fewer years than White women, they are the majority of HIV/AIDS cases in women, are more likely to smoke and less likely to quit than White women, and have higher rates of sexually transmitted infections and pelvic inflammatory disease. More than half of Black women are overweight and have twice as many cases of high blood pressure as White women. . . .

They added that in addition to disproportionately poor health, African American women also experience high rates of violence in their lives: "[O]ver half of Black women in America have been beaten, raped or have survived incest." They further argued that lack of education and limited access to quality health care compounded health problems: "For each of the demographic characteristics used to identify high risk birth, Black mothers were twice as likely as whites to be eighteen or nineteen years old, to have had less than twelve years [of] education, or to have had late or no prenatal care." Violence, poor health care during pregnancy, and the overall poor health of black mothers led to high rates of low-birth-weight babies in black communities, which was an issue that could not be divorced from the high incidence of reproductive tract infections among black women, also caused by an overall lack of access to quality health care. All of these issues needed to be understood as linked and compounding factors in the poor health of women and children.[45]

According to Dixon Diallo, poor health, economic distress, and lack of quality health care led to the high incidence of HIV/AIDS among women of color. Solving these problems required a broad human rights/reproductive justice perspective to connect the dots and identify HIV/

AIDS as a problem as important as abortion rights to women's reproductive freedom. In her 2009 Voices of Feminism Oral History Project interview with Loretta Ross, Dixon Diallo explained why she believed mainstream feminist organizations did not identify HIV as a priority reproductive rights or women's health issue early in the epidemic:

> I think the women's health community was slow off the mark in HIV and AIDS because they had already been behind on so many other intersecting issues that had a lot to do with HIV and AIDS, such as poverty, such as some of the other oppressions affecting women of color that weren't necessarily immediately evident to the leadership of . . . the feminist health movement. . . . I just think that that had to do with that very, very narrow focus on abortion as a reproductive rights issue versus the larger framework of all of the potential factors that impact women's reproductive outcomes.[46]

A human rights focus illuminated that health care was not strictly a medical issue. Healthy and unhealthy bodies were produced by social inequalities linked to race, class, gender, sexuality, and nationality.

Dixon Diallo pointed out that SisterLove's conscious adoption of a human rights framework helped expand its work beyond U.S. borders in collaboration with organizations with a transnational human rights perspective such as the National Center for Human Rights Education, the People's Decade of Human Rights Education, Amnesty International, and Human Rights Watch. She told Loretta Ross in her interview that SisterLove "is much more engaged in looking at HIV and AIDS domestically in the US. By connecting our issues with some of these larger human rights organizations . . . we've been able to target their unique and creative ways to intervene in HIV and AIDS activism, because we use that broader framework."[47] In 1999, SisterLove increased its transnational focus on human rights and the fight against HIV/AIDS with the establishment of a trust cooperative called Thembuhlelo in Emalahleni, South Africa. The cooperative worked collectively with local grassroots organizations and individual volunteers to run a 700-acre dairy farm. She explained,

> And that happened because we bridged the notion of women's empowerment, right, with HIV—and AIDS—service delivery with the land-reform

policies that are going on to help restore the land that originally belonged to local people from the hands of the white farmers and the white government regime under apartheid. . . . We have been a part of a much larger human rights movement with regard to that, and at the same time are doing our HIV work.

Dixon Diallo emphasized that many of the problems encountered by women in South Africa were similar to those lived by black and poor women in the American South: "[I]n the South, where we are, we have a lot of the same issues, even if it's a different set of economies, right? We have a lot of poverty and violence and lack of access and opportunity that increase women's risks for HIV and AIDS." Thus, the human rights framework fostered a transnational analysis that allowed SisterLove to apply lessons from South Africa to the United States and the reverse. She concluded that the community building taking place in South Africa needed to be applied at home: "[W]e need to learn how to do that community-development bridge building between service delivery, advocacy, and growing and developing communities so that individuals, families, and whole neighborhoods are able to do what they need to do to solve their own problems."[48] Of course, Dixon Diallo and others involved in the women of color movement were not the first activists to make the connection between international efforts to link health care provision to community empowerment and efforts to address the broad social context that exacerbated poor health in the United States. Dr. Jack Geiger had learned similar lessons in South Africa that he imported to the American South in Mound Bayou, Mississippi, at the beginning of the National Health Center movement in the mid-1960s.

As Silliman, Fried, Ross, and Gutiérrez point out in *Undivided Rights*, efforts at expansive coalition building among women of color organizations around human rights and reproductive justice occurred before the creation of SisterSong. SisterSong, formed in 1997, is both the most recent collaboration and the most successful—having sustained itself for fourteen years at this writing. Preceding SisterSong, in 1992, women of color activists created the Women of Color Coalition for Reproductive Health Rights (WOCCRHR), which included some of the groups eventually gathered under the SisterSong umbrella in 1997. According to the *Undivided Rights* authors, members of WOCCRHR were "Asians and Pacific Islanders for Choice, National Black Women's Health Project, National Latina Health Organization, Latina Roundtable on Health and Reproductive Rights, National Coalition of 100 Black Women, and Native American Women's Health and Education Resource Center."[49] WOCCRHR supported NOW's 1992 March for Women's Lives, but were not included in the organizational planning for the march, reflecting NOW's tendency to reward significant donors with planning input. WOCCRHR protested this policy.[50]

In 1994 WOCCRHR became part of the U.S. delegation to the United Nations International Conference on Population and Development (ICPD) in Cairo, Egypt.[51] The activists in WOCCRHR argued that emphasis needed to be placed on reproductive freedom, human rights, and development rather than on population control.[52] Their argument was reflected in the consensus document of the ICPD, which affirmed that "countries should ensure the reproductive rights of all individuals; should provide the information and means to decide the number, spacing and timing of children; should uphold the right to have the highest standard of sexual and reproductive health, and the right to make sexual and reproductive decisions free of discrimination, coercion, and violence."[53]

Upon their return to the United States, "women of color [who] witnessed how women in other countries were successfully using a human rights framework in their advocacy for reproductive health and sexual rights . . . coined the term 'reproductive justice.'" A group of African American women formed the Black Women's Caucus to attend a national pro-choice conference sponsored by the Illinois Pro-Choice Alliance in Chicago. They wanted to "Bring Cairo Home" by creating a forum for conversations about the relationship between poverty and human rights abuses among women of color in the United States. The same group of women placed an advertisement in the *Washington Post* with six hundred signatures from African American women defining reproductive justice as "reproductive health integrated into social justice."[54]

Some members of the Cairo delegation subsequently traveled to Beijing, China, in September 1995 for the United Nations Fourth World Conference on Women. The *Undivided Rights* authors argue that "[b]y attending the conference, they connected their local and national struggles to the global movements against poverty and for women's rights. They returned home determined to forge ahead in building a national

movement for women of color for reproductive health that would . . .
incorporate the global human rights framework into their activism."[55]
These international conversations among feminists working in transnational contexts paved the way for the SisterSong Collective and a collaborative national articulation of the connection between a reproductive
justice movement and the establishment of a human rights agenda in
the United States.

SisterSong was founded as a collective to "strengthen each other's organizations, partnering more established organizations with emerging
groups. A collective structure would also enable us to have a greater
impact in our communities and within the broader reproductive rights
movement. Thus, SisterSong was born as . . . a national movement of
women of color working on reproductive health issues."[56] In her 2006
interview, in what Kimala Price would call SisterSong's "origin story,"[57]
Luz Rodriguez described herself as the midwife to SisterSong while she
was at Latina Roundtable in 1997. Rodriguez recalled that Reena Marcelo, program officer at the Ford Foundation, called her and "explained
that she was trying to create a funding strategy that would fund grassroots organizations that normally would not be funded by such a huge
foundation as Ford."[58] The focus of the new organization was going to
be reproductive tract infections in order to encompass a broad range of
reproductive health problems experienced by women of color, including higher-than-average incidences of HIV infection and cervical cancer
and also sociocultural and economic barriers to accessing health care
that would help prevent infection.[59] Marcelo and Rodriguez decided
that the organization should represent African American, Latina, Asian/
Pacific Islander, and Indigenous women. Each of these groups would be
represented by a "mini-community" of grassroots activist organizations
for a total of sixteen organizations in the collective. Women representing
the organizations would be convened—first in New York City and then
in Savannah, Georgia—to discuss their goals before and after the Fourth
International Congress on HIV/AIDS in Manila, Philippines. Participants would also attend the HIV/AIDS conference between the two collective meetings. Those in attendance in New York were Reena Marcelo,
Luz Rodriguez, Dázon Dixon Diallo, Alice Skenandore, and Luz Alvarez
Martinez.[60] Delegates to the Manila conference included Dixon Diallo,
Mary Chung of the National Asian Women's Health Organization, Ro-.

driguez, and Skytears Moore of the Moon Lodge Native Women's Outreach Project based in Riverside, California. In Manila they discussed the sex slave trade, high rates of HIV infection in Africa, and high rates of HPV infection among girls. They reported that they returned from the conference with a new perspective on how "human rights are intertwined with reproductive health and sexual rights of women of color, and how the grassroots sisterhood of activists in the United States is forever connected to the plight of women and girls of color throughout the world."[61]

Rodriguez recalled that at the second roundtable discussion in Savannah, among the women representing the sixteen women of color reproductive rights and health organizations, the common thread in their histories as activists was sterilization and other medical abuses. She remembered that as they discussed their "common histories,"

> when you looked at the history of indigenous women, African American women, Asian and Latina women, it was very striking and profound for me . . . that the common history we had was sterilization abuse and human experimentation. . . . It wasn't just Puerto Rican women. All of us had that in our histories. . . .[62]

Thus, just as Ross and Rodriguez had pointed to the history of sterilization and medical abuses among women of color as motivation for their entrance into a movement for reproductive justice, other women of color also connected their histories—either their own or their community's—to this collective history of population control. This collective history of abuse and coercion was at the center of the creation of a reproductive justice/human rights movement that could not make abortion and contraception the singular focus. Instead, women of color reproductive justice activists argued that the history of reproductive abuses necessitated an emphasis on securing fundamental human rights that would provide the political, social, and economic context for women to choose to bear and raise healthy children. As Silliman, Fried, Ross, and Gutiérrez explained, "For women of color, resisting population control while simultaneously claiming the right to bodily self-determination, including the right to contraception and abortion or the right to have children, is at the heart of their struggle for reproductive control."[63]

The original structure of SisterSong hinged on four national "anchor" organizations—one for each of the four ethnic groups—African American, Latina, Asian/Pacific Islander, and Native American/Indigenous women. Anchor organizations were tasked with coordination and administration of the other groups clustered in four mini-communities, each associated with an ethnic group. Inclusion of local and grassroots organizations within the ethnic cohorts of mini-communities was meant to maximize diversity within the organization.[64] Although certain common health problems united the groups, such as high incidences of HIV/AIDS and low screening rates for cervical cancer, the groups also charted different priorities. SisterSong attempted to address their diversity through the mini-communities.[65] For example, while Native women were more focused on what they considered to be coerced "temporary sterilization" through Depo-Provera and Norplant, as well as the preservation of their culture and health practices, the Asian/Pacific Islander community was more focused on language and cultural barriers to health care access. The Latina community shared these concerns but also emphasized poverty, lack of health insurance, and problems of documentation and deportation, among other issues. African American women also identified lack of access to quality health care, poverty, and high rates of HIV/AIDS among women as problems; they also noted that many African Americans distrusted and avoided the medical establishment because of a history of medical experimentation, most notoriously the Tuskegee syphilis study.[66]

In 2001 SisterSong members decided to transform the anchor structure into a Management Circle that broadly represented women across ethnic identifications with a national coordinator. Ross, who became national coordinator of SisterSong in 2005, noted that the anchor system made all of the groups too dependent on the lead anchor organizations; if one failed, the other groups in the mini-community suffered as well.[67] Rodriguez added that the anchor structure was too narrow because it limited SisterSong to four ethnic groupings. She noted that SisterSong outgrew the structure "as a consequence of women from other ethnic backgrounds feeling not part of it and asking for us to be more inclusive, which was a no-brainer. So now it includes North African and Middle Eastern women. There's enrichment and then there's challenges in that." She continued, explaining, "We're looking to include other voices in the leadership, to be more inclusive of other ethnic communities, to be more inclusive of younger generations of women, to be more inclusive of lesbian and gay and transgendered women." Rodriguez pointed out that increasing diversity brought challenges. She said, "[W]e have to have the capacity to deal with the issues that they're going to bring to the fore as well, and to the protocols that would allow them to feel comfortable."[68]

In 2003, at the SisterSong Women of Color Reproductive Health and Sexual Rights Conference at Spelman College in Atlanta, it appeared that SisterSong had successfully nurtured a national women of color movement for reproductive justice and human rights. Ross announced that she believed a self-sustaining women of color movement existed.[69] SisterSong's organizational success and strength was a testament to that success. Women of color had built an inclusive agenda around reproductive justice and rights to health and social welfare. And they had linked this agenda to an international movement for human rights. In her 2004 interview for the Sophia Smith Collection, Ross reported that SisterSong included seventy organizations, an increase from sixteen core organizations at its founding.[70]

Mainstream abortion rights and majority-white feminist organizations also recognized the successes of the women of color movement. As a result, they placed renewed importance on including women of color in their ongoing fight for abortion and reproductive rights. As in the 1980s, their motives for including women of color hinged, at least in part, on demonstrating that women of color supported abortion rights and reproductive choice. Yet, negotiations with mainstream abortion rights and feminist organizations about collaborative efforts revealed that some of the same fault lines still existed that had complicated alliances between women of color and majority-white organizations in the past.

Loretta Ross encountered these fault lines (again) as codirector of the 2004 national march defending abortion and reproductive rights held in Washington, D.C. After leaving NBWHP in 1990 (after just a year with NBWHP), Ross worked for the Center for Democratic Renewal (formerly called the National Anti-Klan Network) until 1995. In 1996 she founded the National Center for Human Rights Education (NCHRE), which was one of the original founding organizations that made up SisterSong. Ross remained involved with NCHRE until 2005, when she became national coordinator for SisterSong. While helping to plan the 2003 SisterSong Conference at Spelman in Atlanta, Ross turned down invitations from four groups—NARAL, Planned Parenthood, NOW, and the Feminist Majority Foundation—to discuss planning for the 2004 national abortion rights march, at the time titled "The March for Freedom of Choice."[71] Unsurprisingly given her earlier experiences at NOW, Ross recalled that she first responded, "No. I'm really tired of the white girls and their making plans and not telling us about them until they want us to participate. . . . Let's stay focused on our own agenda." Later, she relented and organized a plenary session at the Spelman SisterSong Conference to discuss women of color's participation in the march. She reported that six hundred women attended this plenary session, which allowed women of color activists to raise issues of concern about the march. She asked the four organizations planning the event—NARAL, Planned Parenthood, NOW, and Feminist Majority—to send representatives to the session.[72] Women who attended the plenary session at the conference discussed their "dissatisfaction with the fact that there were no women of color involved in the decision making about the march."[73] They also complained that the mainstream organizations expected women of color activists to drop what they were doing "to participate in their agenda."[74] Reflecting the agenda of many women of color who attended the plenary, Ross wanted to change the name of the march to the "March for Women's Human Rights," but during negotiations with Alice Cohan from Feminist Majority Foundation, they settled on the "March for Women's Lives," the same name that had been used for the two previous marches in the 1980s. Ross explained that many women at the plenary "felt that the abortion framework, the choice framework, was just too narrow a vessel to talk about the threat to women's lives. We're dealing with the Bush administration, an immoral and illegal war in Iraq, the Patriot Act, poverty . . . [I]f we made abortion totally available, totally accessible, totally legal, totally affordable, women would still have other problems."[75] Those attending the plenary also pushed for an agreement to include women of color organizations on the steering committee planning the march. The organizations they wanted to be included were the Black Women's Health Imperative, formerly the NBWHP, the Asian Pacific Islanders for Reproductive Health, and the National Latina Institute for Reproductive Health. Only Black Women's Health Imperative and the National Latina

Institute joined the march committee, however, because the march organizers thought it was too costly to add a third organization. They had
agreed to pay the women of color staff who helped organize the march.
Finally, the march organizers requested that Ross become codirector of
the march with Alice Cohan of the Feminist Majority Foundation as
the director.[76]

Ross's experience in her position as codirector of the march was
mixed. In part, it revealed that the biggest and most influential pro-
choice and feminist organizations in the United States recognized that
they could not organize a successful march without integrating women
of color and women of color reproductive justice organizations at the
planning stage. Additionally, the involvement of women of color organizations in the planning brought other women of color to endorse the
march; 140 women of color and people of color organizations publicly
endorsed the march, including the NAACP, the first time that organization endorsed a reproductive rights march.[77] At the same time, mainstream organizations still marginalized women of color and only asked
for their participation sporadically. Ross recalled that "once they had
decided that they had gotten women of color, they really weren't prepared to make any other commitments beyond what they had already
made."[78] She explained that the major funders for the march—NARAL
and Planned Parenthood—were not prepared to provide scholarships
for women of color to travel to Washington, D.C., until the very last
minute even though Ross had requested free buses. Then, suddenly,
after SisterSong announced that it would fund buses for women to
travel to D.C., just two weeks before the march, NARAL and Planned
Parenthood put up the money for free buses. Ross also recalled that
there were turf battles over who would address the march audience. In
order to increase the visible representation of women of color, she decided to call all the women of color organizers onto the stage rather than
use her time to individually address the crowd; this would demonstrate
that women of color were fundamentally involved in the planning even
if they were not well represented among featured speakers.[79] Confusion about the march name also persisted all the way up to the date of
the march. And, finally, NARAL created its own march office in Washington, D.C., indicating that the big funding organizations, particularly
NARAL, did not fully appreciate what it meant to collaborate equally

with grassroots organizations. According to Ross, they tended to put themselves in the spotlight.[80]

In the end, Ross asserted that their involvement in the march strengthened SisterSong and was an indication of the positive influence women of color had had on the movement in recent years. She explained that the march increased SisterSong's visibility and, more importantly, "[W]e were able to impose our will on this huge process and get the march name changed and women of color added to the steering committee."[81] She continued, explaining that women of color helped the march succeed by pressing for an inclusive political agenda that made it relevant to more women: "[W]hen they were just organizing under the banner of freedom of choice, they couldn't get traction for the march, they couldn't get it off the ground. The minute they adopted the broader SisterSong framework, then the march just exploded."[82] Ross believed that SisterSong's participation also helped expand the political rhetoric of the mainstream groups. She explained, "[W]e hear a lot of the people who participated in the march using the phrase 'reproductive justice' that they'd never used before. It's becoming the connective framework that ties economic justice, human rights, reproductive rights, immigration rights, those kinds of things, together."[83] In her study of SisterSong's involvement in the organization of the march, Luna also found that "after SisterSong joined the coalition, the frame eventually emphasized broader concepts related to human rights, which has increased its usage among organizations."[84] Over a million people came to the march, so it was successful on multiple levels, although conflicts in the planning and ongoing battles over the agenda indicated that coalition work with mainstream organizations was still complicated. Ross reported that after the march NARAL, NOW, Planned Parenthood, and Feminist Majority abandoned much of the human rights language they had adopted: "[I]mmediately after the March, they went back to business as usual. Which is, you know, something SisterSong could have predicted that they'd do. They figured [it] out but they didn't. And . . . they somewhat lost the potential for using the women's human rights framework as a way of building the new movement."[85]

In 2005 Loretta Ross became the National Coordinator for Sister-Song. She continued in that capacity until 2012. SisterSong has continued to provide a networking forum for women of color organizations working on reproductive justice and human rights. In her interview for the Voices of Feminism Project, Ross emphasized the importance of the networking functions of SisterSong. "First of all, we need to create the spaces for women of color to meet, network, and organize, because there aren't that many spaces for us to do that on a national level."[86] Regional and national conferences sponsored by SisterSong provided women of color these spaces to network and collaborate. This had been one of SisterSong's original goals. Founders of the group, including Luz Rodriguez, had articulated that they would "focus on collaboration and coalition-building with nation-wide reproductive health community-based orgs and advocacy groups; create a network for resource sharing, research and development for culturally competent service delivery and community health education."[87] According to Ross, another associated role played by SisterSong has been to "strengthen the existing women of color organizations. . . . They're underfunded, understaffed, and yet they have huge missions: trying to service the community in which they're embedded, represent the voice of marginalized or silenced women, have an impact on even local or national politics, and sustain themselves."[88] As a self-sustaining national organization, SisterSong currently provides that support for eighty local grassroots organizations around the country.[89]

Thus, SisterSong and the women of color movement for reproductive freedom sustains a grassroots commitment to community-based and accessible health care linked to the specific social and economic contexts of the diverse groups of women involved in the coalition. Their activism is part of a women of color political movement now approaching its fourth decade that also finds important historical roots in the earlier movements for community-based health care.

Historians don't like to make predictions, but looking forward, I will hazard a prediction that this broad movement for health and social justice—now well over a half-century old—will continue to be necessary even as President Obama's Affordable Care Act is implemented over the next few years. Without groups committed to ensuring that those with the least can access quality health care, without groups pressing for health care provision that attends to social inequalities grounded in race, gender, nationality, sexuality, and class, and without groups listening to what those who suffer from discrimination need to live healthy, fulfilled lives, we risk continuing to make health care a commodity available to those with means, to those with social advantage, even as our entire society pays for the suffering of those without means and without social advantage. Health care needs to be a human right, not a commodity to be bought and sold in a marketplace. Nor should it be a political football subject to the ups and downs of electoral politics. The right to health and quality health care needs to be fundamental to our social fabric, a commitment we make to building and sustaining healthy communities and futures for the people who live in our global community.

NOTES

INTRODUCTION

1. "Constitution of the World Health Organization," available at http://www.who.int/
governance/eb/who_constitution_en.pdf; this statement was reaffirmed by the
WHO Alma-Ata Declaration made at the International Conference on Primary
Health Care, Alma-Ata, USSR, September 6–12, 1978.

2. H. Jack Geiger, "The Unsteady March," *Perspectives in Biology and Medicine* 48.1
(Winter 2005): 7–8.

3. Sheryl Burt Ruzek, *The Women's Health Movement: Feminist Alternatives to
Medical Control* (New York: Praeger, 1978); Sandra Morgan, *Into Our Own Hands:
The Women's Health Movement in the United States, 1969–1990* (New Brunswick,
NJ: Rutgers University Press, 2002); Anne Enke, *Finding the Movement: Sexuality,
Contested Space, and Feminist Activism* (Durham, NC: Duke University Press,
2007); Wendy Kline, *Bodies of Knowledge: Sexuality, Reproduction, and Women's
Health in the Second Wave* (Chicago: University of Chicago Press, 2010).

4. Sara Evans, *Personal Politics: The Roots of Women's Liberation in the Civil Rights
Movement and the New Left* (New York: Vintage, 1980).

5. Dorothy Roberts, *Killing the Black Body: Race, Reproduction, and the Meaning of
Liberty* (New York: Pantheon, 1997); Benita Roth, *Separate Roads to Feminism:
Black, Chicana, and White Feminist Movements in America's Second Wave* (New
York: Cambridge University Press, 2004); Jael Silliman et al., *Undivided Rights:
Women of Color Organize for Reproductive Justice* (Cambridge, MA: South End
Press, 2004); Kimberly Springer, *Living for the Revolution: Black Feminist
Organizations, 1968–1980* (Durham, NC: Duke University Press, 2005); Premilla
Nadasen, *Welfare Warriors: The Welfare Rights Movement in the United States*
(New York: Routledge, 2005); Johanna Schoen, *Choice and Coercion: Birth Control,
Sterilization, and Abortion in Public Health and Welfare* (Chapel Hill: University of
North Carolina Press, 2005); Rickie Solinger, *Pregnancy and Power: A Short
History of Reproductive Politics in America* (New York: New York University Press,
2007); Elena R. Gutierrez, *Fertile Matters: The Politics of Mexican-Origin Women's
Reproduction* (Austin: University of Texas Press, 2008); Rebecca M. Kluchin, *Fit to
Be Tied: Sterilization and Reproductive Rights in America, 1950–1980* (New
Brunswick, NJ: Rutgers University Press, 2009); Kimala Price, "What Is
Reproductive Justice? How Women of Color Activists Are Redefining the
Pro-Choice Paradigm," *Meridians: Feminism, Race, Transnationalism* 10.2 (2010);

Michelle Murphy, *Seizing the Means of Reproduction: Entanglements of Feminism, Health, and Technoscience* (Durham, NC: Duke University Press, 2013).

6. Judith Ezekiel, *Feminism in the Heartland* (Columbus: Ohio State University Press, 2002); Jack E. Davis and Kari Frederickson, eds., *Making Waves: Female Activists in Twentieth-Century Florida* (Gainesville: University Press of Florida, 2003); Anne Enke, *Finding the Movement: Sexuality, Contested Space, and Feminist Activism* (Durham, NC: Duke University Press, 2007); Anne M. Valk, *Radical Sisters: Second-Wave Feminism and Black Liberation in Washington, D.C.* (Chicago: University of Illinois Press, 2008); Gutierrez, *Fertile Matters*.

7. Murphy, *Seizing the Means of Reproduction*, 65.

8. Movements to reform health care have both domestic and international roots. United States feminists have been involved in transnational conversations about redefinitions of health care for decades. For example, long-time feminist and reproductive justice activist Dr. Helen Rodriguez-Trías looked to the Beijing Declaration and Platform for Action, forged at the Fourth World Conference on Women and associated Non-Governmental Organizations Forum in Beijing, China, in September 1995, as an illustration of feminist public health promotion. This document was written within a framework that brought together international human rights and feminist discourses first made popular at the 1975 World Conference of the International Women's Year, held in Mexico City, and developed at subsequent World Conferences on Women in Copenhagen, Nairobi, and, most recently, Beijing. The Beijing Platform for Action announces a "commitment to address poverty, educational opportunity, health care, violence, access to resources and inequalities in power, in opportunities for advancement, in management of natural resources, and in protection of human rights from the perspective of women." Furthermore, Rodriguez-Trías pointed out that the platform identifies barriers to health as "inequality, both between men and women and among women in different geographical regions, social classes and indigenous and ethnic groups and urges increased primary health care and social services for women throughout their lives." She explained that a focus on "inequalities in income, rights, resources, and power as the basis of inequalities in health" helped define an international "public health agenda for women." Quotations are from Helen Rodriguez-Trias, "Topics for Our Times: From Cairo to Beijing—Women's Agenda for Equality," *American Journal of Public Health* 86.3 (March 1996): 305–6.

9. John Dittmer, *Local People: The Struggle for Civil Rights in Mississippi* (Chicago: University of Illinois Press, 1995), 255–65; John Dittmer, *The Good Doctors: The Medical Committee for Human Rights and the Struggle for Social Justice in Health Care* (New York: Bloomsbury Press, 2009), 36–37; Alondra Nelson, *Body and Soul: The Black Panther Party and the Fight against Medical Discrimination* (Minneapolis: University of Minnesota Press, 2011), 34–35.

10. Nelson, *Body and Soul*, 10.

11. Geiger, "The Unsteady March."

12. H. Jack Geiger, "Community-Oriented Primary Care: A Path to Community Development," *American Journal of Public Health* 92.11 (2002): 1716.

13. Eli Y. Adashi, H. Jack Geiger, and Michael D. Fine, "Health Care Reform and Primary Care: The Growing Importance of the Community Health Center," *New England Journal of Medicine*, June 3, 2010, 2049.

14. Barbara Ehrenreich and Deirdre English, *Complaints and Disorders: The Sexual Politics of Sickness*, 2nd ed. (New York: Feminist Press, 2011), 35–36.

15. Ibid., 32, 120.

16. Judith A. Houck, "The Best Prescription for Women's Health: Feminist Approaches to Well Woman Care." In Jeremy A. Greene and Elizabeth Siegel Watkins, eds., *Prescribed: Writing, Filling, Using, and Abusing the Prescription in Modern America* (Baltimore, MD: Johns Hopkins University Press, 2012), 135.

17. See Ricki Solinger, *Reproductive Politics: What Everyone Needs to Know* (New York: Oxford University Press, 2013) for a concise summary of the history of illegal abortion and the movements for abortion reform in the United States.

18. Ehrenreich and English, *Complaints and Disorders*, 142.

19. Jennifer Nelson, *Women of Color and the Reproductive Rights Movement* (New York: New York University Press, 2003), 34–37, 42–45.

20. See Jeanne Flavin, *Our Bodies, Our Crimes: The Policing of Women's Reproduction in America* (New York: New York University Press, 2009).

21. Murphy, *Seizing the Means of Reproduction*, 42.

22. Ibid., chapters 2 and 3.

23. Beatrix Hoffman, *Health Care for Some: Rights and Rationing in the United States since 1930* (Chicago: University of Chicago Press, 2012), 147–48.

24. Loretta Ross, "The Color of Choice: White Supremacy and Reproductive Justice." In INCITE! Women of Color against Violence, ed., *The Color of Violence: The Incite! Anthology* (Cambridge, MA: South End Press, 2006).

25. Loretta Ross, Sarah J. Brownlee, Dazon Dixon Diallo, and Luz Rodriguez, "The 'SisterSong Collective': Women of Color, Reproductive Health, and Human Rights," *American Journal of Health Studies* 17.2 (2001): 86.

26. Ibid., 85–86.

27. Ibid., 86.

28. Price, "What Is Reproductive Justice?"56.

29. Ibid., 62.

30. Andrea Smith, "Beyond Pro-Choice versus Pro-Life: Women of Color and Reproductive Justice," *NWSA Journal* 17.1 (Spring 2005): 119–40.

CHAPTER 1

1. "Medical News: Can Community Centers Cure Health Problems of the Poor?" *JAMA*, March 23, 1970, 1943–55, quotation on 1954.

2. H. Jack Geiger, "The New Doctor." In Ronald Gross and Paul Osterman, eds., *The New Professionals* (New York: Simon & Schuster, 1972), 97–98.

3. David Farber, *The Age of Great Dreams: America in the 1960s* (New York: Hill & Wang, 1994), 77; see Barbara Ransby, *Ella Baker and the Black Freedom Movement: A Radical Democratic Vision* (Chapel Hill: University of North Carolina Press, 2003).

4. Farber, *Age of Great Dreams*, 192–93.

5. Michael Harrington's *Other America* (1962) was one of the key popular texts that raised awareness about the persistence of poverty in the United States.

6. Nicholas Lemann, *The Promised Land: The Great Migration and How It Changed America* (New York: Knopf, 1991), 119–22.

7. Alice O'Connor, *Poverty Knowledge: Social Science, Social Policy, and the Poor in Twentieth-Century U.S. History* (Princeton, NJ: Princeton University Press, 2001), 140; Lemann, *The Promised Land*, 121–33.

8. O'Connor, *Poverty Knowledge*, 159.

9. Ibid., 163.

10. Lemann, *Promised Land*, 151–52.

11. Although it is beyond the scope of this book to do so, it is also possible to trace the roots of OEO public health programs to the New Deal, particularly programs administered by the Farm Security Administration. See Michael R. Grey, *New Deal Medicine: The Rural Health Programs of the Farm Security Administration* (Baltimore, MD: Johns Hopkins University Press, 1999).

12. A coalition of government interests in the Department of Labor, the Department of Health, Education, and Welfare, the Council of Economic Advisors, the Bureau of the Budget, and Congress comprised OEO.

13. Joseph T. English, "Is the OEO Concept—the Neighborhood Health Center—the Answer?" In John C. Norman, ed., *Medicine in the Ghetto* (Meredith Corp., 1969), 261.

14. David Barton Smith, *Health Care Divided: Race and Healing a Nation* (Ann Arbor: University of Michigan Press, 1999), 46–47, 100–101.

15. Ibid., 96.

16. Ibid., 119–20.

17. Beatrix Hoffman, *Health Care for Some: Rights and Rationing in the United States since 1930* (Chicago: University of Chicago Press, 2012), 127.

18. John Dittmer, *Local People: The Struggle for Civil Rights in Mississippi* (Chicago: University of Illinois Press, 1995), 244.

19. Ibid.

20. Dittmer, *Local People*, 255–65; John Dittmer, *The Good Doctors: The Medical Committee for Human Rights and the Struggle for Social Justice in Health Care* (New York: Bloomsbury, 2009), 36–37.

21. Dittmer, *Local People*, 242–49; Constance Curry, *Silver Rights* (New York: Harvest Books, 1996), 58–65.

22. Ibid.

23. Dittmer, *The Good Doctors*, 61–62.

24. John W. Hatch and Eugenia Eng, "Community Participation and Control: Or Control of Community Participation." In *Reforming Medicine: Lessons of the Last Quarter-Century* (New York: Pantheon, 1984), 231–32.

25. H. Jack Geiger, interview with author, 2003.

26. H. Jack Geiger, "Community Health Centers: Health Care as an Instrument of Social Change." In Sidel and Sidel, eds., *Reforming Medicine*, 12–14.

27. Dittmer, *The Good Doctors*, 64–65; Bonnie Lefkowitz, *Community Health Centers: A Movement and the People Who Made It Happen* (New Brunswick, NJ: Rutgers University Press, 2007), see chapter 1.

28. Geiger, "Community Health Centers," 17; Dittmer, *The Good Doctors*, 8; quotation in Geiger.

29. H. Jack Geiger, "A Life in Social Medicine." In Ellen L. Bassuk, ed., *The Doctor-Activist: Physicians Fighting for Social Change* (New York: Plenum, 1996), 15.

30. Dittmer, *The Good Doctors*, 61; Lefkowitz, *Community Health Centers*, chapter 1.

31. Dittmer, *The Good Doctors*, 67, 70–71.

32. Ibid., 80–84.

33. Geiger interview, 2003.

34. John Hatch, interview with author, 2003.

35. Dittmer, *The Good Doctors*, 82; Richard Hall, "A Stir of Hope in Mound Bayou," *Life Magazine*, 1969. Delta Health Center Records, Box 12, Folder: "Articles on Mound Bayou/Bolivar County Health Needs." Southern Historical Collection, University of North Carolina, Chapel Hill.

36. Dittmer, *The Good Doctors*, 82–84.

37. Herbert E. Klarman, "Major Public Initiatives in Health Care." In Eli Ginzberg and Robert M. Solow, eds., *The Great Society: Lessons for the Future* (New York: Basic Books, 1974), 108.

38. Sar A. Levitan, "Healing the Poor in Their Back Yard." In Robert Holister, Bernard Kramer, and Seymour Bellin, eds., *Neighborhood Health Centers* (Lexington, MA: Lexington Books, 1975), 51–64; H. Jack Geiger, "Community Control—or Community Conflict." In *Neighborhood Health Centers*, 133–42; Hatch and Eng, "Community Participation and Control: Or Control of Community Participation," 226–27.

39. Geiger, "Community Health Centers," 18–19; Lisbeth Bamberger Schorr and Joseph T. English, "Background, Context, and Significant Issues in Neighborhood Health Center Programs." In *Neighborhood Health Centers*, 45–50.

40. Gerald Sparer and Joyce Johnson, "Evaluation of OEO Neighborhood Health Centers," *American Journal of Public Health* 61.5 (May 1971): 931–42; quotation on 931.

41. Robert Holister, "Neighborhood Health Centers as Demonstrations." In *Neighborhood Health Centers*, 1–12.

42. Levitan, "Healing the Poor," 57.

43. Rashi Fein, "An Economist's View of the Neighborhood Health Center as a New Social Institution." In *Neighborhood Health Centers*, 189–93.

44. Sparer, "Evaluation of OEO Neighborhood Health Centers," 934–35; Levitan, "Healing the Poor," 56.

45. Sparer, "Evaluation of OEO Neighborhood Health Centers," 936.

46. Ibid., 931.

47. Gerald Sparer, "Consumer Participation in OEO-Assisted Neighborhood Health Centers," *American Journal of Public Health* 60.6 (June 1970): 1091–1102.

48. "Medical News," 1945.

49. English, "Background, Context, and Significant Issues," 262.

50. Daniel Zwick, "Some Accomplishments and Findings of Neighborhood Health Centers." In *Neighborhood Health Centers*, 75.

51. Alondra Nelson, *Body and Soul: The Black Panther Party and the Fight against Medical Discrimination* (Minneapolis: University of Minnesota Press, 2011), 56–60.

52. "Medical News," 1946.

53. Lefkowitz, *Community Health Centers*, chapter 1.

54. Sparer, "Evaluation of OEO Neighborhood Health Centers," 938.

55. Robert Hollister, "Introduction." In *Neighborhood Health Centers*, 109.

56. "Medical News," 1945, 1955; Sparer, "Consumer Participation in OEO-Assisted Neighborhood Health Centers," 1100–1101.

57. Zwick, "Some Accomplishments," 78–79.

58. "Medical News," 1946–47.

59. H. Jack Geiger, "Community Health Centers," 21.

60. Geiger, "Community Control—or Community Conflict?" 133–42.

61. Hatch and Eng, "Community Participation and Control," 231.

62. Lefkowitz, *Community Health Centers*, chapter 3.

63. Geiger, "Community Control—or Community Conflict?" 139.

64. Dittmer, *Local People*, 42.

65. Dittmer, *The Good Doctors*, 230; Geiger interview, 2003; Geiger, "Community Health Centers," 25; Geiger, "Community Control—or Community Conflict?" 134, 139.

66. H. Jack Geiger, "Community-Oriented Primary Care: A Path to Community Development," *American Journal of Public Health* 92.11 (November 2002): 1714.

67. Dittmer, *The Good Doctors*, 230–31; Lefkowitz, *Community Health Centers*, chapter 2.

68. Lefkowitz, *Community Health Centers*, chapter 2.

69. Geiger, "Community Control—or Community Conflict," 139–40.

70. Dittmer, *The Good Doctors*, 232.

71. Geiger, "A Life in Social Medicine," 16; Geiger, "Community Control—or Community Conflict," 139.

72. Geiger, "Community Control—or Community Conflict," 139.

73. Geiger interview, 2003.

74. Geiger, "Community Control—or Community Conflict," 141–42.
75. Dittmer, *The Good Doctors*, 232–33.
76. H. Jack Geiger, "The Unsteady March," *Perspectives in Biology and Medicine* 48.1 (Winter 2005): 6–7.
77. "'To be, or not to be': Mound Bayou," *Medical World News*, March 16, 1973, 55. Delta Health Center Records, Box 12, Folder: "Articles on Mound Bayou/Bolivar County Health Needs." Southern Historical Collection, University of North Carolina, Chapel Hill; "Mound Bayou's Crisis," *Time Magazine*, November 25, 1974. Delta Health Center Records, Box 12, Folder: "Articles on Mound Bayou/ Bolivar County Health Needs." Southern Historical Collection, University of North Carolina, Chapel Hill.
78. Jennifer Nelson, "'Hold your head up and stick out your chin': Community Health and Women's Health in Mound Bayou, Mississippi," *NWSA Journal* 17.1 (Spring 2005): 103; Keith Wailoo, *Dying in the City of the Blues: Sickle Cell Anemia and the Politics of Race and Health* (Chapel Hill: University of North Carolina Press, 2001), 100.
79. L. C. Dorsey, interview with author, 2003.
80. Hall, "A Stir of Hope in Mound Bayou."
81. Nelson, "Hold your head up," 102–3; Susan L. Smith, *Sick and Tired of Being Sick and Tired: Black Women's Health Activism in America, 1890–1950* (Philadelphia: University of Pennsylvania Press, 1995), 118–48.
82. Dorsey interview, 2003.
83. Dittmer, *The Good Doctors*, 234; Geiger, "Community-Oriented Primary Care," 1715.
84. "Medical News," 1947, 1951; quotation on 1951.
85. Ibid., 1954.
86. Ibid., 1953.
87. Ibid., 1954.
88. Dorsey interview, 2003; Dittmer, *The Good Doctors*, 234.
89. Geiger interview, 2003. Women dominated the community boards, staff, and patient populations at other NHCs as well. A few NHCs tried to change the ratio of men to women to empower more men in the community. For example, the NHC in South Central Los Angeles sponsored by the University of Southern California argued that encouraging men to take a leadership role at the NHC could combat a "matriarchal family structure," which some considered harmful.
90. Efforts to provide family planning in the United States were also closely linked to Johnson's War on Poverty. Unlike other contraceptive programs abroad, there was no single government agency in charge of the promotion of birth control or family planning in the United States. Instead, services for the poor were distributed through nonprofit organizations that received government subsidization. By the early 1960s, the U.S. federal government had committed significant funding to population research as well. With the rise in concern about overpopulation and "urban" poverty (which was often a code word for poverty among African

Americans), the creation of Medicaid, increase in Aid to Families with Dependent Children, and President Johnson's establishment of a War on Poverty channeled in part through the OEO, federal and state welfare programs increased their funding and development of family planning programs. In the year 1965, 1.5 million birth control pills were distributed to poor women in the United States through these programs. The population establishment in the United States led by the Population Council and Planned Parenthood Federation of America pushed for this funding increase through lobbying efforts and a cultural campaign to raise public concern about overpopulation. See Jennifer Nelson, "'Breaking the Chain of Poverty': Family Planning, Community Involvement, and the Population Council/Office of Economic Opportunity Alliance," *Journal of the History of Medicine and Allied Sciences* 69.1 (2012); Matthew Connelly, *Fatal Misconceptions: The Struggle to Control World Population* (Cambridge, MA: Harvard University Press, 2008), 199; Johanna Schoen, *Choice and Control: Birth Control, Sterilization, and Abortion in Public Health and Welfare* (Chapel Hill: University of North Carolina Press, 2005), 22.

91. Helen Barnes, interview with author, 2003.

92. Ibid.

93. Cynthia Kelly, "Health Care in the Mississippi Delta," *American Journal of Nursing* 69.4 (April 1969): 758–63.

94. Barnes interview, 2003; Jessie Rodrique, "The Black Community and the Birth Control Movement." In Judith Walzer Leavitt, ed., *Women and Health in America*, 2nd ed. (Madison: University of Wisconsin Press, 1999), 293–305.

95. Jennifer Nelson, *Women of Color and the Reproductive Rights Movement* (New York: New York University Press, 2003), 55–84.

96. Barnes interview, 2003.

97. Ibid.

98. Mary Stella Simpson, *Sister Stella's Babies: Days in the Practice of a Nurse Midwife* (New York: American Journal of Nursing Company, 1978), 5.

99. Ibid., 20.

100. Ibid., 39.

101. Ibid., 20.

102. Ibid., 19, 82.

103. Lefkowitz, *Community Health Centers*, chapter 2.

104. Wanda Barfield, "Infant Mortality in the US: Where We Stand," *Centers for Disease Control and Prevention*, Oct. 16, 2011, available at www.cdc.gov/about/grand-rounds/archives/2012/pdfs/GR_Infant_Mortality_Final_Oct16.pdf, 5.

105. Gopal K. Singh and Peter C. van Dyck, *Infant Mortality in the United States, 1935–2007: Over Seven Decades of Progress and Disparities* (Rockville, MD: U.S. Department of Health and Human Services, 2010), 2, available at www.hrsa.gov/healthit/images/mchb_infantmortality_pub.pdf.

106. Rebecca W. Tardy, "'But I Am a Good Mom': The Social Construction of Motherhood through Health Care Conversations." In *Journal of Contemporary*

Ethnography 29.4: 433–73; Boston Women's Health Book Collective, *Our Bodies, Ourselves for the New Century* (New York: Simon & Schuster, 1998), 507.

107. Simpson, *Sister Stella's Babies*, 82.

108. Ibid., 40.

109. Ibid., 32.

110. Ibid., 29.

111. Barnes interview, 2003.

112. Kelly, "Health Care in the Mississippi Delta."

113. Dorsey interview, 2003.

114. Kelly, "Health Care in the Mississippi Delta."

115. English, "Background, Context, and Significant Issues," 262.

116. Ibid., 263–64.

117. Sparer, "Evaluation of OEO Neighborhood Health Centers," 934.

118. Ibid., 940.

119. Ibid., 938–39.

120. Eugene Feingold, "A Political Scientist's View of the Neighborhood Health Center as a New Social Institution." In *Neighborhood Health Centers*, 97.

121. Fitzhugh Mullan, *White Coat, Clenched Fist* (New York: Macmillan, 1976), 50.

122. Dittmer, *The Good Doctors*, 205–8.

123. Ibid., 209.

124. Howard Levy, "Counter Geiger," *Social Policy*, May/June 1971, 50–57; quotation on 56.

125. Ibid.

126. "From Our Readers," *Social Policy*, November/December 1971, 60–61.

127. Ibid., 64.

128. H. Jack Geiger, "Hidden Professional Roles: The Physician as Reactionary," *Social Policy*, March/April 1971, 24–33.

129. Dittmer, *The Good Doctors*, 213–14, 226–28; Naomi Rogers, "Caution: The AMA May Be Dangerous to Your Health: The Student Health Organizations (SHO) and American Medicine, 1965–1970," *Radical History Review* 80 (Spring 2001): 5–34.

130. "From Our Readers," 64.

131. Ibid., 235.

132. Geiger, "Community Health Centers," 23; Hatch and Eng, "Community Participation and Control," 234–37.

133. In subsequent chapters, I will further consider the alternative posed by Levy, that autonomous health centers created by locals for locals (in this case by feminists for women within a defined community) offered many advantages.

134. Geiger, "Hidden Professional Roles," 31–32.

135. Dittmer, *The Good Doctors*, 219–20; Mullan, *White Coat*, 125–27.

136. Cleo Silvers, interview with author, 1997; Mullan, *White Coat*, 139.

137. Dittmer, *The Good Doctors*, 220; Mullan, *White Coat*, 139–42.

138. Mullan, *White Coat*, 141–42.

139. Mullan, *White Coat*, 104–9, 143.

140. Carl Pastor (Ministry of Health), "T.B. Truck Liberated," *Palante*, July 3, 1970.
141. Dittmer, *The Good Doctors*, 220; Mullan, *White Coat*, 145.
142. Mullan, *White Coat*, 144.
143. Dittmer, *The Good Doctors*, 220; Mullan, *White Coat*, 147.
144. Mullen, *White Coat*, 147–48.
145. Harold Osborne, interview with author, 1997.
146. Mullen, *White Coat*, 149–50.
147. Ibid., 180–84.
148. Osborne interview, 1997.
149. Geiger, "Community Health Centers," 28–30.
150. Geiger, "Community-Oriented Primary Care," 1716.
151. Ibid.

CHAPTER 2

1. In addition to these states, twelve others had reformed their abortion laws. Most states, including Washington, had a residence requirement of thirty to ninety days. Carole Joffe, *Doctors of Conscience: The Struggle to Provide Abortion before and after Roe v. Wade* (Boston: Beacon, 1994), 6; James Mohr, *Abortion in America: The Origins and Evolution of National Policy* (New York: Oxford University Press, 1978); Rosalind Petchetsky, *Abortion and Woman's Choice: The State, Sexuality, and Reproductive Freedom* (New York: Longman, 1984); Linda Gordon, *Woman's Body, Woman's Right: Birth Control in America* (New York: Penguin, 1990).
2. "July 13, 1972, note on discussion with Ray Lee, attorney for Koome, responding to call from I. Levine re: Legality of ABCRS operations," Young Women's Christian Association (University of Washington) Records (hereafter YWCA Records), Box 18, Folder: "Minutes—Emergency Meetings re: Legality of ABCRS operations 1972."
3. Jan Krause (Knutsen), interview with author, April 21, 2011.
4. Joffe, *Doctors of Conscience*, 47–49, 51–52, 137–38, 147–48.
5. Patricia Valdez, interview with author, April 15, 2011.
6. Ibid.
7. Joffe, *Doctors of Conscience*, 10.
8. "Reproductive Center," *Pandora* 1.1 (1970): 3, YWCA Records, Box 4, Folder: "Periodicals—Pandora 1970–71"; "Continuing the Struggle," *Pandora*, Nov. 16, 1970, 5, YWCA Records, Box 4, Folder: "Periodicals—Pandora 1970–71."
9. "Abortion Reform," *Pandora* 1.4, YWCA Records, Box 4, Folder: "Periodicals—Pandora 1970–71."
10. YWCA Records, Box 19, Folder 12: "Abortion Feedback Forms, 1970–74."
11. Ann McGettigan, interview with author, May 16, 2011.
12. "Abortion–Birth Control Referral Service," YWCA Records, Box 19, Folder 2: "Abortion Referral Service."

13. Valdez interview, 2011.
14. Leslie Reagan, "Crossing the Border for Abortions: California Activists, Mexican Clinics, and the Creation of a Feminist Health Agency in the 1960s," *Feminist Studies* 26.2 (Summer 2000): 323–48.
15. Lawrence Lader, *Abortion II: Making the Revolution* (Boston: Beacon, 1973), 27, 42–45.
16. Joffe, *Doctors of Conscience*, 29–32, 36–37.
17. Laura Kaplan, *The Story of Jane: The Legendary Underground Feminist Abortion Service* (New York: Pantheon, 1995), 15–30.
18. Kaplan, *Story of Jane*, 114–16, 175–77; Pauline Bart, "Seizing the Means of Reproduction: An Illegal Feminist Abortion Collective—How and Why It Worked," *Qualitative Sociology* 10 (Winter 1987): 339–57; Wendy Kline, *Bodies of Knowledge: Sexuality, Reproduction, and Women's Health in the Second Wave* (Chicago: University of Chicago Press, 2010), 70–76.
19. Lorraine Rothman, "Menstrual Extraction," *Quest* 4.3 (Summer 1978): 45.
20. Sheryl Burt Ruzek, *The Women's Health Movement: Feminist Alternatives to Medical Control* (New York: Praeger, 1978), 26.
21. Valdez interview, 2011.
22. McGettigan interview, 2011.
23. "Bad Feedback on Doctors," YWCA Records, Box 19, Folder 12: "Feedback Forms, 1970–74."
24. YWCA Records, Box 19, Folder 11: "Feedback Forms, 1970–74."
25. YWCA Records, Box 19, Folder 9: "Forms—Feedback, 1971–73".
26. Sandra Morgen, *Into Our Own Hands: The Women's Health Movement in the United States, 1969–1990* (New Brunswick, NJ: Rutgers University Press, 2002), 70–79.
27. Barbara Ehrenreich and Deirdre English, *Complaints and Disorders: The Sexual Politics of Sickness*, 2nd ed. (New York: Feminist Press, 2011), chapter 4; Ruzek, *Women's Health Movement*, 9–19.
28. "Abortion Reform."
29. Letter from Jeanne Mangold, Abortion–Birth Control Referral Service, dated June 28, 1971, YWCA Records, Box 18, Folder: "Outgoing Letters, 1970–1972."
30. "Abortion Referral Service Enters Second Year," *Pandora*, January 11, 1972, 1, YWCA Records, Box 4, Folder: "Periodicals—Pandora 1971–72."
31. Letter sent out to friends of the ABC Referral Service, dated July 17, 1973, YWCA Records, Box 18, Folder: "Outgoing Letters 1972–1973."
32. Valdez interview, 2011.
33. Krause interview, 2011.
34. "Abortion Referral Service Enters Second Year."
35. "Abortion Service Planned," *Pandora*, December 14, 1970, YWCA Seattle University collection, Box 4, Folder: "Periodicals—Pandora 1970–71";

"Contraceptive Counseling," *Pandora*, December 27, 1970, YWCA Records, Box 4, Folder: "Periodicals—Pandora 1970–71."

36. Valdez interview, 2011.

37. "Contraceptive Counseling."

38. "Family Planning: Abortion Referral Information," n.d., YWCA Records, Box 12, Folder: "Birth Control 1969."

39. Ibid.

40. "Referral Sources for Pregnancy Termination," March 1974, YWCA Records, Box 23, Folder: "Lists—Medical Facilities for Pregnancy Termination."

41. Roz Kramer, "Erosion of Abortion Rights: 1973–1981," *Village Voice*, March 11–17, 1981.

42. "Minutes, Monthly Meeting October 12 & 13, 1971," YWCA Records, Box 18, Folder: "Minutes and Agenda Misc. 1971–73."

43. Kaplan, *Story of Jane*, 135, 145, 175.

44. Jennifer Nelson, *Women of Color and the Reproductive Rights Movement* (New York: New York University Press, 2003), 56–57.

45. Valdez interview, 2011.

46. Susan Paynter, "Women Help Women after Referendum 20," YWCA Records, Box 22, Folder: "Clippings 1970–75."

47. Ibid.

48. Valdez interview, 2011.

49. Letter from Jeanne Mangold to Abortion Counselor, Outside-In, Portland, OR, dated July 20, 1971, YWCA Records, Box 18, Folder: "Outgoing Letters, 1970–1972."

50. Susan Paynter, "Women Voice Protest of Koome Conviction," *Seattle Post-Intelligencer*, December 3, 1972, G5, YWCA Records, Box 22, Folder: "Clippings 1968–72."

51. Neil Modie, "Dr. Koome Placed on Probation," *Seattle Post-Intelligencer*, December 5, 1972, A5, YWCA Records, Box 22, Folder: "Clippings 1968–72"; "Dr. Koome Appeals Conviction," *People's Health: A Voice of Seattle's Health Movement*, January–February 1973, 2.

52. "UW Department Honors Doctor Who Led Abortion-Law Reform," *Seattle Times*, October 6, 1996; *Seattle Post-Intelligencer*, December 4, 1969; also see Cassandra Tate, "Koome, Dr. Adriaan Frans (1929–1978)," HistoryLink.org, essay 2642.

53. Mary Ellen Walker, interview with author, April 5, 2011.

54. Elaine Schroeder, interview with author, May 18, 2011; Joffe, *Doctors of Conscience*, 133–35.

55. Letter from woman from Nevada, dated August 23, 1971, YWCA Records, Box 17, Folder: "Incoming Letters, 1971–1973."

56. Sharon Gold-Steinberg and Abigail J. Stewart, "Psychologies of Abortion: Implications of a Changing Context." In Rickie Solinger, ed., *Abortion Wars: A*

Half-Century of Struggle, 1950–2000 (Berkeley: University of California Press, 1998), 356–73.

57. YWCA Records, Box 12, Folder: "Abortion Feedback Forms 1977–79."

58. YWCA Records, Box 19, Folder 9: "Forms—feedback 1971–73."

59. Feedback forms in the collection are from 1971 to 1979.

60. YWCA Records, Box 12, Folder: "Abortion Feedback Forms 1977–79"; for more on abortion in the pre-*Roe* era, see Leslie Reagan, *When Abortion Was a Crime: Women, Medicine, and the Law in the United States, 1867–1973* (Berkeley: University of California Press, 1997) and Rickie Solinger, *The Abortionist: A Woman against the Law* (Berkeley: University of California Press, 1994).

61. YWCA Records, Box 19, Folder 9: "Forms—feedback 1971–73."

62. YWCA Records, Box 19, Folder 11: "Feedback Forms 1972–1974."

63. YWCA Records, Box 19, Folder 12: "Feedback Forms, 1972–74."

64. While feminists and others campaigning for legal abortion played up the dangers of illegal abortion, Leslie Reagan and other historians show that safe abortions were performed by "professional abortionists" before *Roe*. Reagan, *When Abortion Was a Crime*, 133.

65. YWCA Records, Box 19, Folder 12: "Feedback Forms, 1972–74."

66. YWCA Records, Box 12, Folder: "Abortion Feedback Forms 1977–79."

67. Ibid.

68. YWCA Records, Box 19, Folder 9: "Forms—feedback 1971–73."

69. YWCA Records, Box 12, Folder: "Abortion Feedback Forms 1977–79."

70. YWCA Records, Box 19, Folder 12: "Feedback Forms, 1972–74."

71. Gold-Steinberg and Stewart, "Psychologies of Abortion," 358.

72. Rosalind Petchetsky, *Abortion and Woman's Choice: The State, Sexuality, and Reproductive Freedom* (New York: Longman, 1984), 103.

73. Gold-Steinberg and Stewart, "Psychologies of Abortion," 368.

74. YWCA Records, Box 19, Folder 12: "Feedback Forms, 1972–74."

75. Ibid.

76. Ibid.

77. YWCA Records, Box 19, Folder 11: "Feedback Forms 1972–1974."

78. Gold-Steinberg and Stewart, "Psychologies of Abortion," 358.

79. "Minutes, Monthly Meeting October 10, 1972: Discussion of Negative Feedback on Doctors," YWCA Records, Box 18, Folder: "Minutes and Agenda Misc. 1971–73"; "Minutes from ABCRS meeting, April 10, 1973," YWCA Records, Box 18, Folder: "Minutes and Agenda Misc. 1971–73."

80. YWCA Records, Box 19, Folder 9: "Forms—feedback 1971–73."

81. YWCA Records, Box 12, Folder: "Abortion Feedback Forms 1977–79."

82. YWCA Records, Box 19, Folder 9: "Forms—feedback 1971–73."

83. Ibid.

84. YWCA Records, Box 19, Folder 12: "Feedback Forms, 1972–74."

85. Sara Dubow, *Ourselves Unborn: A History of the Fetus in Modern America* (New York: Oxford University Press, 2011), 55, 67–111.

86. YWCA Records, Box 12, Folder: "Abortion Feedback Forms 77–79."
87. Ibid.
88. Ibid.
89. Ibid.
90. YWCA Records, Box 19, Folder 9: "Forms—feedback 1971–73."
91. Ibid.
92. Ibid.
93. Ibid.
94. YWCA Records, Box 12, Folder: "Abortion Feedback Forms 1977–79."
95. Ibid.
96. Ibid.
97. Ibid.
98. Ibid.
99. Ibid.
100. YWCA Records, Box 19, Folder 11: "Feedback Forms, 1972–1974."
101. Ibid.
102. Ibid.
103. YWCA Records, Box 19, Folder 9: "Forms—feedback 1971–73."
104. YWCA Records, Box 19, Folder 11: "Feedback Forms, 1972–1974."
105. Ibid.
106. Kathryn Draper, interview with author, May 16, 2011.
107. YWCA Records, Box 19, Folder 11: "Feedback Forms 1972–1974."
108. YWCA Records, Box 19, Folder 12: "Feedback Forms, 1972–74."
109. McGettigan interview, 2011.

CHAPTER 3

1. Leslie Reagan, "Editor's Note: Reproduction, Sex, and Power," *Journal of Women's History* 22.3: 7–12.
2. Wendy Kline, *Bodies of Knowledge: Sexuality, Reproduction, and Women's Health in the Second Wave* (Chicago: University of Chicago Press, 2010); Anne Valk, "Fighting Abortion as a 'Health Right' in Washington D.C." In Stephanie Gilmore, ed., *Feminist Coalitions: Historical Perspectives on Second Wave Feminism in the United States* (Chicago: University of Illinois Press, 2008); Anne Enke, *Finding the Movement: Sexuality, Contested Space, and Feminist Activism* (Durham, NC: Duke University Press, 2007); Judith A. Houck, "The Best Prescription for Women's Health: Feminist Approaches to Well Woman Care." In Jeremy A. Greene and Elizabeth Siegel Watkins, eds., *Prescribed: Writing, Filling, Using, and Abusing the Prescription in Modern America* (Baltimore, MD: Johns Hopkins University Press, 2012).
3. "The Feminist Health and Abortion Coalition," YWCA Records, Box 17, Folder: 12.
4. Barbara Ehrenreich and Deirdre English, *For Her Own Good: Two Centuries of the Experts' Advice to Women*, rev. ed. (New York: Random House, 2005), 117–27;

Valk, "Fighting Abortion as a 'Health Right' in Washington D.C."; Jennifer Nelson, *Women of Color and the Reproductive Rights Movement* (New York: New York University Press, 2003), chapter 5; Sheryl Burt Ruzek, *The Women's Health Movement: Feminist Alternatives to Medical Control* (New York: Praeger, 1978), 8.

5. Becky Ludwig, "Women Act to Meet Health Needs," *People's Health: A Voice of Seattle's Health Movement*, June–July 1973, 3.

6. Carol Isaac, email communication with author, August 27, 2013.

7. "Four Women's Clinics Newsletter," YWCA Records, Box 9, Folder: "Women's Clinics Newsletters and Correspondence 1973–74."

8. Carol Isaac, "Health Notes: Groups Join in New Health Coalition," *Pandora*, October 5, 1971, 3, YWCA Records, Box 4, Folder: "Periodicals—Pandora 1970–71."

9. University of Washington YWCA, Press Release, n.d., YWCA Records, Box 15, Folder: "Sex and Sexuality 1971."

10. Carol Isaac, email communication, September 27, 2013.

11. Kline, *Bodies of Knowledge*, 77–82.

12. "Proposal for Restructuring the Coven," YWCA Records, Box 23, Folder: "Restructuring the Coven 1973."

13. Carol Isaac, interview with author, March 15, 2011.

14. "Proposal for Restructuring the Coven."

15. Kline, *Bodies of Knowledge*, 78.

16. "Aradia Clinic," YWCA Records, Box 23, Folder: "Organizational Materials 1971–73."

17. JoAnn Keenan, interview with author, March 15, 2011.

18. "Seattle's Free Clinics and the PHCC," *People's Health: A Voice of Seattle's Health Movement*, January–March 1972, 10.

19. "Family Planning Grant Proposal to HEW," YWCA Records, Box 23, Folder: "Outgoing Letters 1971–74."

20. Linda McVeigh, interview with author, July 7, 2011.

21. Open Door was founded in 1967 as a general health clinic.

22. "Some New Beginnings," *Open Door Clinic Newsletter*, n.d., private collection of Nancy Stokley.

23. Nancy Stokley, interview with author, April 7, 2011.

24. Judith A. Houck, "The Best Prescription for Women's Health: Feminist Approaches to Well Woman Care." In Greene and Watkins, eds., *Prescribed*, 136.

25. "Educationals," private collection of Nancy Stokley; "Women's Health Movement," private collection of Nancy Stokley.

26. "Meet the Fremont Women's Clinic," n.d., YWCA Records, Box 16, Folder: "Women and Medicine—Related Papers 1971–72."

27. "Fremont Free Women's Health Clinic, Program Description, 1971," YWCA Records, Box 16, Folder: "Women and Medicine—Related Papers 1971–72"; Lois Thetford, interview with the author, April 6, 2011.

28. "Fremont Free Women's Health Clinic, Program Description."

29. Ibid.

30. Barbara Ehrenreich and Deirdre English, *Complaints and Disorders: The Sexual Politics of Sickness*, 2nd ed. (New York: Feminist Press, 2011), 137.

31. Sarah Kaiser (aka Moosh Graber), author's interview, March 15, 2011; "Four Women's Clinics Newsletter," YWCA Records, Box 9, Folder: "Women's Clinics Newsletters and Correspondence 1973–74."

32. "Herstory," YWCA Records, Box 23, Folder: "Organizational Materials 1971–73."

33. "Thoughts on Aradia Clinic," private collection of Nancy Stokley.

34. Kaiser interview, 2011.

35. "Meet the Fremont Women's Clinic."

36. Dyan Edison, interview with author, March 15, 2011.

37. Houck, "Best Prescription for Women's Health," 151.

38. Susan Paynter, "Paramedicas: Women Helping Women," *Seattle Post Intelligencer*, March 17, 1974.

39. Sharon Baker, interview with author, March 15, 2011.

40. Kaiser interview, 2011.

41. Michelle Murphy, "Immodest Witnessing: The Epistemology of Vaginal Self-Examination in the U.S. Feminist Self-Help Movement." In *Feminist Studies* 1 (Spring 2004): 115–47.

42. "We need . . . a women's health clinic," n.d., YWCA Records, Box 16, Folder: "Women and Medicine—Related Papers 1971–72."

43. Edison interview, 2011.

44. Kaiser interview, 2011.

45. Murphy, "Immodest Witnessing," 115–47.

46. Leslie Reagan, "Crossing the Border for Abortions: California Activists, Mexican Clinics, and the Creation of a Feminist Health Agency in the 1960s," *Feminist Studies* 26.2 (2000): 325.

47. Sheryl Burt Ruzek, *The Women's Health Movement: Feminist Alternatives to Medical Control* (New York: Praeger, 1979), 53.

48. Sandra Morgen, *Into Our Own Hands: The Women's Health Movement in the United States, 1969–1990* (New Brunswick, NJ: Rutgers University Press, 2002), 7–8.

49. Morgen, *Into Our Own Hands*, 99–101; Anne Enke, *Finding the Movement: Sexuality, Contested Space, and Feminist Activism* (Durham, NC: Duke University Press, 2007), 179.

50. Nancy Tuana, "The Speculum of Ignorance: The Women's Health Movement and Epistemologies of Ignorance," *Hypatia* 21.3 (Summer 2006): 14.

51. Susan Reverby, "Thinking through the Body and the Body Politic: Feminism, History, and Health-Care Policy in the United States." In Georgina Feldberg, Molly Ladd-Taylor, and Kathryn McPherson, eds., *Women, Health, and Nation: Canada and the United States since 1945* (Montreal: McGill-Queen's University Press, 2003), 410–11.

52. "Aradia Clinic."

53. Marcia Schultz, "Women's Clinics Advise Persons Who Wouldn't Seek Medical Aid," *Seattle Times*, July 30, 1972, YWCA Records, Box 16, Folder: "Women and Medicine—Related Papers 1971–72."

54. "Paramedics: A Complicated Future," *People's Health: A Voice of Seattle's Health Movement*, n.d., 4, YWCA Records, Box 17, Folder 1; for a discussion of historical debates about medical and legal limits placed on lay feminist well-woman health care provision in California see Houck, "The Best Prescription for Women's Health."

55. "Political Education Committee Report," YWCA Records, Box 23, Folder: "Minutes, Meetings 1972–73."

56. "An Approach to Women's Health Care," *People's Health: A Voice of Seattle's Health Movement*, n.d., 1, YWCA Records, Box 17, Folder 1.

57. "Political Education Committee Report."

58. Larraine Rothman, interview with author, March 15, 2011.

59. "Aradia Clinic."

60. "An Approach to Women's Health Care," 2.

61. Ibid.

62. Edison interview, 2011; Kaiser interview, 2011; Larraine Volkman, interview with author, March 28, 2011.

63. "Aradia Clinic."

64. "Four Women's Clinics Newsletter," YWCA Records, Box 9, Folder: "Women's Clinics Newsletters and Correspondence 1973–74."

65. "Aradia Clinic Opens," *Pandora*, May 16, 1972, 2, YWCA Records, Box 4, Folder: "Periodicals—Pandora 1972–74."

66. Edison interview, 2011.

67. "Aradia Clinic."

68. Ibid.

69. Joe Freeman, "The Tyranny of Structurelessness." In Jane S. Jaquette, ed., *Women in Politics* (New York: Wiley, 1974).

70. Ibid.

71. Sandra Morgan, *Into Our Own Hands: The Women's Health Movement in the United States, 1969–1990* (New Brunswick, NJ: Rutgers University Press, 2002), chapter 3.

72. Volkman interview, 2011.

73. Nancy Marie Robertson, *Christian Sisterhood, Race Relations, and the YWCA, 1906–1946* (Urbana: University of Illinois Press, 2007), 121–22, 153, 158.

74. "Press Statement," December 18, 1973, YWCA Records, Box 16, Folder: "Other Funding, 1973, n.d. Third World Women Family Planning Needs Assessment Project."

75. Ehrenreich and English, *Complaints and Disorders*, 159.

76. "Catalyst Committee Proposal for a Third World Women's Resource Center," YWCA Records, Box 12, Folder: "Third World Women Clinics 1970–1973, n.d."

77. Letter to Lyn Reynolds, Executive Director, Planned Parenthood, Yakima Co, from Theresa Saludo, dated May 6, 1974, YWCA Records, Box 16, Folder: "Presentation Materials 1974, n.d. Third World Women Family Planning Needs Assessment Project."

78. Ibid.

79. "Project Proposal," YWCA Records, Box 23, Folder: "Organizational Materials 1971–73."

80. "HEW Seed Monies—Award as Supplement to Aradia," YWCA Records, Box 23, Folder: "3rd World Women 1973."

81. Ibid.

82. Rebecca Kulchin, *Fit to Be Tied: Sterilization and Reproductive Rights in America, 1950–1980* (New Brunswick, NJ: Rutgers University, 2009), 98–99.

83. "Third World Women Family Planning Needs Assessment Project, Implications," n.d., YWCA Records, Box 16, Folder: "Reports, Third World Women Family Planning Needs Assessment."

84. "HEW Seed Monies."

85. Ibid.

86. "Project Proposal."

87. Letter to Janet Krause, Co-Director, Administration, U of W YWCA, from David Hansen, Acting Director, Division of Health Services, Department of HEW, dated June 20, 1974, YWCA Records, Box 16, Folder: "Incoming Letters 1973–1974. Third World Women Family Planning Needs Assessment Project."

88. "Third World Women's Family Planning Needs Assessment Project Meeting, January 7, 1974," YWCA Records, Box 12, Folder: "Letters 1973–1974. Third World Women Family Planning Needs Assessment Project."

89. "Third World Women Family Planning Needs Assessment Project, Implications."

90. Carol Isaac, email communication, September 27, 2013; JoAnn Keenan, email communication with author, September 27, 2013.

91. Letter from Constance Miller Engelsberg, January 25, 1974, YWCA Records, Box 16, Folder: "Conference and Convention Files: Third World Women's Conference 1974 Third World Women Family Planning Needs Assessment Project 'Third World Women's Conference & Festival '74.'"

92. "Third World Women's Conference & Festival '74," YWCA Records, Box 16, Folder: "Conference and Convention Files: Third World Women's Conference 1974 Third World Women Family Planning Needs Assessment Project 'Third World Women's Conference & Festival '74.'"

93. Letter from Constance Miller Engelsberg.

94. Email communication with Marcy Bloom, September 13, 2011.

95. Marcy Bloom, interview with author, February 24, 2011.

96. Ibid.

97. Ibid.

CHAPTER 4

1. Sharon Baker and Loraine Volkman, interview with author, March 15, 2011.
2. Lynne Randall, interview by Johanna Schoen, July 24, 2012, 9–12.
3. Ibid., 11–12.
4. Ibid., 15; Wendy Simonds, *Abortion at Work: Ideology and Practice in a Feminist Clinic* (New Brunswick, NJ: Rutgers University Press, 1996), 26.
5. Ruth Rosen, *The World Split Open: How the Modern Women's Movement Changed America* (New York: Penguin, 2006), 331–32.
6. Feminist Women's Health Center flyer, "Women's Self-Help Clinic—Where Do We Go from Here?" Sallie Bingham Center for Women's History and Culture, Duke University, Feminist Women's Health Center Records (hereafter FWHC Records), Box 62, Folder: "Participatory Clinic."
7. Simonds, *Abortion at Work*, 49.
8. Judith A. Houck, "The Best Prescription for Women's Health: Feminist Approaches to Well Woman Care." In Jeremy A. Greene and Elizabeth Siegel Watkins, eds., *Prescribed: Writing, Filling, Using, and Abusing the Prescription in Modern America* (Baltimore, MD: Johns Hopkins University Press, 2012); Sheryl Burt Ruzek, *The Women's Health Movement: Feminist Alternatives to Medical Control* (New York: Praeger, 1979), 170–71; Sandra Morgan, *Into Our Own Hands: The Women's Health Movement in the United States, 1969–1990* (New Brunswick, NJ: Rutgers University Press, 2002), 24–26.
9. Randall interview, 2012, 17–18.
10. Jennifer Burgess and Carol Downer, "How to Start Your Self-Help Clinic, Level II, West Coast Sisters," 1971, revised September 1974, FWHC Records, Box 62, Folder: "Participatory Clinic."
11. Ibid.
12. "Health Education," FWHC Records, Box 10, Folder: "Administrative Files General/Clinic Guidelines/Standardized Procedures, April 1984."
13. "FWHC Health Worker Evaluation," FWHC Records, Box 10, Folder: "Administrative Files General/Orientation/Training Manual for Clinic Employees, 1984."
14. "Health Education."
15. "FWHC Health Worker Evaluation." By the early 1990s, self-help groups were no longer a part of the Atlanta FWHC. See Simonds, *Abortion at Work*, 40.
16. "Health Education."
17. Ibid.
18. "Annual Meeting/March 29, 1978: Significant Events 1977," FWHC Records, Box 17, Folder: "Annual Meeting 1978."
19. There is very little historiography on the Women's Liberation or feminist movement in southern states. It is an area that deserves further historical research and discussion. For material on the origins of women's liberation in the civil rights movement in the South, see Sara Evans, *Personal Politics: The Roots of*

Women's Liberation in the Civil Rights Movement and the New Left (New York: Vintage Press, 1980) and Carol Giardina, "Origins and Impact of Gainesville Women's Liberation, the First Women's Liberation Organization in the South." In Jack E. Davis and Kari Frederickson, eds., *Making Waves: Female Activists in Twentieth-Century Florida* (Gainesville: University of Florida Press, 2003).

20. "FWHC Health Worker Evaluation." The word "counselor" is often used in Atlanta FWHC literature. At the same time, there are assertions that the word "educator" was preferred over "counselor." See Simonds, *Abortion at Work*, 65; see Michelle Murphy, *Seizing the Means of Reproduction: Entanglements of Feminism, Health, and Technoscience* (Durham, NC: Duke University Press, 2013), 63–64, for a discussion of state restrictions on nonprofessional health workers in feminist clinics.

21. Simonds, *Abortion at Work*.

22. "Health Education."

23. "Birth Control Services and Screening," FWHC Records, Box 10, Folder: "Administrative Files General/Orientation/Training Manual for Clinic Employees, 1984."

24. "1984 Clinic Administrator's Report," FWHC Records, Box 17, Folder: "Annual Meeting Report 1984."

25. "1990 Executive Director's Report," FWHC Records, Box 18, Folder: "Monthly Meetings, 1990."

26. "Executive Director's Report for 1985," FWHC Records, Box 17, Folder: "Annual Meeting 1985 and 1st Quarter."

27. "FWHC fact sheet, The Threat to Health Care Workers and Patients: Antiabortion Violence and Harassment, January 1988," FWHC Records, Box 54, Folder: "Clinic Violence."

28. Lynne Randall, interview by Johanna Schoen, October 22, 2012, 25.

29. Dallas A. Blanchard, *The Anti-Abortion Movement and the Rise of the Religious Right: From Polite to Fiery Protest* (New York: Twayne, 1994), 35.

30. Guttmacher Institute: State Policies in Brief, "Targeted Regulation of Abortion Providers," August 1, 2013, available at http://www.guttmacher.org/statecenter/spibs/spib_TRAP.pdf.

31. Johanna Schoen, chapter 1: "Living through some Giant Change: The Establishment of Abortion Services," 16–17. In *Abortion since Legalization, 1970–2000* (Chapel Hill: University of North Carolina Press: forthcoming 2014).

32. "In Brief: Fact Sheet: Facts on Induced Abortion in the United States," May 2011, Guttmacher Institute, available at http://www.guttmacher.org/pubs/fb_induced_abortion.html. A study from the Alan Guttmacher Institute suggests that much of the decline in abortion rates since 1994 can be attributed to women's use of emergency contraception. See http://www.guttmacher.org/media/nr/nr_121702.html.

33. Tony Cooper, "Women's Pavilion Case: Girl, 15, Dies after Being in Coma since Last June," *Atlanta Journal*, Oct. 25, 1979, 2C; Dale Russakoff and Raleigh Bryans,

"Abortion Clinic Indictment Out for Now—DA," *Atlanta Journal*, July 25, 1979, 1C, 2C; Dale Russakoff, "Abortion Clinic Delayed Ambulance's Departure," *Atlanta Journal*, June 27, 1979; Dale Russakoff, "Help Delayed in Abortion Case," *Atlanta Journal*, June 25, 1979, 1A, 22A, FWHC Records, Box: 102, Folder: "News Articles."

34. Ibid.

35. The patient hemorrhaged from a perforated uterus. Fran Hesser, "Pregnancy Test Controls Urged," *Atlanta Constitution*, November 8, 1979, 4C, FWHC Records, Box 102, Folder: "News Articles."

36. "Abortion Rights Movement of Women's Liberation and Feminist Women's Health Center," June 9, 1979, FWHC Records, Box: 102, Folder: "Abortion Complications June '79 News Statement."

37. Ibid.

38. "Statement to the News Media," June 5, 1979, FWHC Records, Box: 102, Folder: "Abortion Complications June '79 News Statement."

39. "Abortion Rights Movement of Women's Liberation and Feminist Women's Health Center."

40. Ibid.

41. Dale Russakoff and Vicki Pearlman, "Rule for Abortion Clinics Is There Are No Rules," *Atlanta Journal*, n.d., 1A, 6A, FWHC Records, Box 102, Folder: "News Articles."

42. Ibid.

43. Rebecca Linn, "Abortion Study: Separate Clinic Rules Proposed," *Atlanta Constitution*, July 12, 1979, FWHC Records, Box 102, Folder: "News Articles."

44. Linn, "Abortion Study"; "State Policies in Brief: An Overview of Abortion Laws," June 2014, Guttmacher Institute, available at http://www.guttmacher.org/ statecenter/spibs/spib_OAL.pdf.

45. *Roe v. Wade*, 410 U.S. 113 (1973).

46. Michelle Green, "Abortion Rights versus Regulations," *Atlanta Constitution*, August 21, 1979, FWHC Records, Box 102, Folder: "News Articles."

47. Ibid.

48. Ibid.

49. Ibid.

50. "Commentary by Lynn Thogersen, Director, Feminist Women's Health Center," FWHC Records, Box 102, Folder: "Press Statement 7/11/79—Subcommittee to FWHC Original."

51. "Feminists Address Board on Abortion Facility Regulations," June 20, 1979, FWHC Records, Box 102, Folder: "Press Statement Original 6/20/79."

52. Michelle Green, "Abortions: Just How Safe?" *Atlanta Constitution*, August 20, 1979, FWHC Records, Box: 102, Folder: "News Articles."

53. Dale Russakoff, "Centers Won't Be Singled Out: New Abortion Clinic Rules Labeled Illegal," *Atlanta Journal*, November 8, 1979, 20D, FWHC Records, Box 102, Folder: "News Articles."

54. "Abortion Study: Separate Clinic Rules Proposed."

55. Rebecca Linn, "House Abortion-Safety Probers Will Tour Atlanta Clinics," *Atlanta Constitution*, July 11, 1979, 2C, FWHC Records, Box 102, Folder: "News Articles."

56. "McKinney Warns on Abortion Rules," July 12, 1979, FWHC Records, Box 102, Folder: "News Articles."

57. John Hanna, "Kansas Abortion Rules in Works," *Wichita Eagle*, July 4, 2011.

58. Marc Santora, "Mississippi Law Aimed at Abortion Clinic Is Blocked," *New York Times*, July 1, 2012.

59. John Schwartz, "Texas Senate Approves Strict Abortion Measure," *New York Times*, July 13, 2013.

60. "Editorial: The Courts Step In," *New York Times*, July 13, 2011.

61. "Feminists Address Board on Abortion Facility Regulations."

62. *City of Akron v. Akron Center for Reproductive Health*, 462 U.S. 416 (1983).

63. Carol J. C. Maxwell, *Pro-Life Activists in America: Meaning, Motivation, and Direct Action* (Cambridge: Cambridge University Press, 2002), 28–89.

64. Blanchard, *The Anti-Abortion Movement*, 28, 35, 52; *Webster v. Reproductive Health Services*, 492 U.S. 490 (1989); *Planned Parenthood of Southeastern Pennsylvania v. Casey* 505 U.S. 833 (1992).

65. Blanchard, *The Anti-Abortion Movement*, 53–55.

66. "Anti-Abortion Violence Drops since '94 Law: Operation Rescue Defunct in City, Dying around US," *Los Angeles Times*, December 9, 1996, FWHC Records, Box 1, Folder: "FWWHO Political Operation Rescue Correspondence."

67. Maxwell, *Pro-Life Activists*, 53–54, 62–64.

68. Ibid.

69. Marion Faux, *Crusaders: Voices from the Abortion Front* (New York: Carol, 1990), 117.

70. Ibid., 129.

71. Randall interview, October 22, 2012, pp. 13–14.

72. Blanchard, *The Anti-Abortion Movement*, 64–67.

73. "1988 Annual Meeting Report—Executive Director's Report," April 4, 1988, FWHC Records, Box 17, Folder: "Annual Meeting 1988."

74. Blanchard, *The Anti-Abortion Movement*, 65.

75. "1988 Annual Meeting Report—Executive Director's Report."

76. Morris S. Thompson, "Atlanta Police Use Tougher Tactics as Abortion Foes Return to Streets," *Washington Post*, October 5, 1988, FWHC records, Box 54, Folder: "Clinic Violence."

77. "1988 Annual Meeting Report—Executive Director's Report."

78. Simonds, *Abortion at Work*, 108.

79. Randall interview, October 22, 2012, 13.

80. Ibid., 20.

81. Simonds, *Abortion at Work*, 133.

82. AB Injunction, FWHC Records, Box 2, Folder: "AB Injunction."

83. James Risen and Judy L. Thomas, *Wrath of Angels: The American Abortion War* (New York: Basic Books, 1998), 271–78.

84. Lorri Denise Booker, "Jailed Abortion Protesters Say They're Staying Put," *Atlanta Journal-Constitution*, July 28, 1988, FWHC Records, Box 54, Folder: "Clinic Violence"; Risen and Thomas, *Wrath of Angels*, 273.

85. Risen and Thomas, *Wrath of Angels*, 274–75.

86. "Abortion Foes Suspend Week-Long Demonstrations, Leaving 282 Jailed," *Washington Post*, October 11, 1988, FWHC Records, Box 54, Folder: "Clinic Violence"; Marshall Ingwerson, "Antiabortion Protesters Try a Tougher Strategy," *Christian Science Monitor*, October 7, 1988, FWHC Records, Box 54, Folder: "Clinic Violence."

87. Risen and Thomas, *Wrath of Angels*, 276.

88. Tom Peepen, "Operation Rescue Plans Return Engagement in Courtship with Atlanta," *Atlanta Journal-Constitution*, November 21, 1989, A11, FWHC Records, Box 54, Folder: "Clinic Violence."

89. Melissa Healey, "10 More Atlanta Abortion Protesters Held," *Los Angeles Times*, October 7, 1988, FWHC Records, Box 54, Folder: "Clinic Violence."

90. "Operation Rescue—Atlanta/October 3–8, 1988" flyer, FWHC Records, Box 54, Folder: "Clinic Violence."

91. "Operation Rescue, Atlanta Continues, October 3–8," FWHC Records, Box 49, Folder: "Operation Rescue Return Engagement."

92. Letter to Edris Branch, National Black Women's Health Project Conference Report, Progress Report to Heartstrings, November 16, 1988, FWHC Records, Box 18, Folder: "Monthly Meetings—1987."

93. Peepen, "Operation Rescue Plans Return Engagement."

94. Larry Martz, "The New Pro-Life Offensive" *Newsweek*, September 12, 1988, 25, FWHC Records, Box 54, Folder: "Newspaper Clippings, July 1988–March 1989."

95. Ronald Smothers, "Abortion Protest Grows in Atlanta," *New York Times*, August 11, 1988, 1, 6, FWHC Records, Box 54, Folder: "Newspaper Clippings, July 1988–March 1989."

96. Mark Sherman, "Young Refuses to Help Free Abortion Protesters," August 18, 1988, 1B, 4B, FWHC Records, Box 54, Folder: "Newspaper Clippings, July 1988–March 1989."

97. Risen and Thomas, *Wrath of Angels*, 280.

98. Lorri Denise Booker and Gustav Neibuhr, "Abortion Foes Running Out of Steam, Police and Clinic Directors Believe," *Atlanta Journal-Constitution*, September 1, 1988, 1c, 5c, FWHC Records, Box 54, Folder: "Clinic Violence"; Risen and Thomas, *Wrath of Angels*, 275.

99. Martz, "The New Pro-Life Offensive."

100. Jerry Schwartz, "400 Are Arrested in Atlanta Abortion Protests," *New York Times*, October 5, 1988, FWHC Records, Box 54, Folder: "Clinic Violence."

101. AB Injunction, Bob Dart, "Atlanta Abortion Clinics Remain Off-Limits, Justices Tell Protesters," *Atlanta Journal-Constitution*, May 15, 1990, FWHC Records, Box 54, Folder: "Clinic Violence."

102. "1990 Executive Director's Report," FWHC Records, Box 18, Folder: "Monthly Meetings, 1990."

103. "Monthly Meeting/May 25, 1989," FWHC Records, Box 18, Folder: "Administrative Files Meetings/Monthly Meetings, 1989."

104. "1989 in Review/Annual Meeting/Executive Director's Report," FWHC Records, Box 18, Folder: "Administrative Files Meetings/Monthly Meetings, 1989."

105. "Executive Director's Report for 1985"; Randall interview, October 22, 2012.

106. "Executive Director's Report—Annual Meeting 1986," FWHC Records, Box 17, Folder: "Annual Meeting Reports 4/7/86."

107. "1992 Annual Report," FWHC Records, Box 17, Folder: "Annual Meeting 4–27–92."

108. Blanchard, *The Anti-Abortion Movement*, 115–16.

109. Risen and Thomas, *Wrath of Angels*, 193–94, 278.

110. Ibid., 287, 295.

111. Blanchard, *The Anti-Abortion Movement*, 53–54; Maxwell, *Pro-Life Activists*, 82.

112. Ingwerson, "Antiabortion Protesters Try a Tougher Strategy."

113. "Executive Director's Report 1991," FWHC Records, Box 19, Folder: "Monthly Meetings 1992."

114. "FWHC Executive Summary, 1993," FWHC Records, Box 7, Folder: "Administrative Files General/FWHC Executive Summary, 1993."

115. Dázon Dixon Diallo, interview by Loretta Ross, transcript of video recording, April 4, 2009, Voices of Feminism Oral History Project, Sophia Smith Collection, Smith College, 5. Diallo is a married name.

116. Ibid., 6.

117. Ibid., 6.

118. Ibid., 7.

119. "Women's AIDS Prevention Project—Grant Application," FWHC Records, Box 71, Folder: "Women's AIDS Prevention Project—CDC Grant."

120. Ibid.

121. Letter to Edris Branch, National Black Women's Health Project Conference Report, Progress Report to Heartstrings, from Dázon Dixon, FWHC Records, Box 18, Folder: "Monthly Meetings—1987."

122. Dixon Diallo interview, 26.

123. Letter to Edris Branch.

124. "Progress Report to Heartstrings/October/November 1988," Box 18, Folder: "Monthly Meetings—1987."

125. "Women's AIDS Prevention Project—Grant Application."

126. Ibid.

127. Dixon Diallo interview, 7.

128. "Herstory," FWHC Records, Box 3, Folder: "Sisterlove, Inc."

129. Love House flyer, FWHC Records, Box 3, Folder: "Sisterlove, Inc."

130. Dixon Diallo interview, 8.

131. Jennifer Brier, *Infectious Ideas: U.S. Political Responses to the AIDS Crisis* (Chapel Hill: University of North Carolina Press, 2009), 173.

132. Brier, *Infectious Ideas*, 171–79.

133. "AIDS Hotline for Women/Proposal/July 22, 1991," FWHC Records, Box 13, Folder: "Administrative Files General/AIDS Hotline for Women (AHW), 1993."

134. "Atlanta AIDS Fund Progress Report/AIDS Hotline for Women/August 15, 1993," FWHC Records, Box 13, Folder: "Administrative Files General/AIDS Hotline for Women (AHW), 1993."

135. Simonds, *Abortion at Work*, 141, 169–206.

136. "Atlanta AIDS Fund Progress Report/AIDS Hotline for Women/August 15, 1993."

137. Simonds, *Abortion at Work*, 172.

CHAPTER 5

1. Maryann Barakso, *Governing NOW: Grassroots Activism in the National Organization for Women* (Ithaca, NY: Cornell University Press, 2004), 70–72.

2. Loretta Ross, interview by Joyce Follet, transcript of video recording, November 3, 2004, Voices of Feminism Oral History Project, Sophia Smith Collection, Smith College, Northampton, MA (hereafter SSC), 192.

3. Ibid.

4. Ibid.

5. Barakso, *Governing NOW*, 111–19. See Benita Roth, *Separate Roads to Feminism: Black, Chicana, and White Feminist Movements in America's Second Wave* (New York: Cambridge University Press, 2004) and Kimberly Springer, *Living for the Revolution: Black Feminist Organizations, 1968–1980* (Durham, NC: Duke University Press, 2005) for more on racially homogenous organizing of the 1970s.

6. The Combahee River Collective, "A Black Feminist Statement." In Gloria T. Hull, Patricia Bell-Scott, and Barbara Smith, eds., *All the Women Are White, All the Blacks are Men, but Some of Us Are Brave: Black Women's Studies* (Old Westbury, NY: Feminist Press, 1982), 16.

7. Cherrie Moraga and Gloria Anzaldua, eds., *This Bridge Called My Back: Writings by Radical Women of Color* (New York: Kitchen Table: Women of Color Press, 1981); Hull, Bell-Scott, and Smith, eds., *All the Women Are White*; *Home Girls: A Black Feminist Anthology* (New York: Kitchen Table: Women of Color Press, 1983); Angela Davis, *Women, Race, and Class* (New York: Random House, 1981); bell hooks, *Ain't I a Woman: Black Women and Feminism* (Boston, MA: South End Press, 1981).

8. Roth, *Separate Roads to Feminism*, 100, 106–7.

9. Ibid., 111; Deborah Gray White, *Too Heavy a Load: Black Women in Defense of Themselves, 1894–1994* (New York: Norton, 1999), 243.

10. White, *Too Heavy a Load*, 223–25; Premilla Nadasen, *Welfare Warriors: The Welfare Rights Movement in the United States* (New York: Routledge, 2005), 216.

11. White, *Too Heavy a Load*, 215.

12. White, *Too Heavy a Load*, 240–43; Anne M. Valk, *Radical Sisters: Second-Wave Feminism and Black Liberation in Washington, D.C.* (Urbana: University of Illinois Press, 2008), 132.

13. Combahee River Collective, "A Black Feminist Statement," 21.

14. Johanna Schoen argues that some women, including some African American women, wanted to be sterilized and actively applied for eugenic sterilization when elective sterilization remained unavailable. See Johanna Schoen, *Choice and Coercion: Birth Control, Sterilization, and Abortion in Public Health and Welfare* (Chapel Hill: University of North Carolina Press, 2005), 5, 79.

15. Nadasen, *Welfare Warriors*, 216.

16. Dorothy Roberts, *Killing the Black Body: Race, Reproduction, and the Meaning of Liberty* (New York: Pantheon, 1997), 93.

17. Schoen, Choice and Coercion, 108–9.

18. Relf v. Weinberger, 372 F. Supp. 1196 (D.D.C 1974, vacated, 565 F.2d 722 D.C. Cir. 1977); Alexandra Minna Stern, *Eugenic Nation: Faults and Frontiers of Better Breeding in Modern America* (Berkeley: University of California Press, 2005), 200–208; Elena R. Gutierrez, *Fertile Matters: The Politics of Mexican-Origin Women's Reproduction* (Austin: University of Texas Press, 2008), 35–54; Rebecca M. Kluchin, *Fit to Be Tied: Sterilization and Reproductive Rights in America, 1950–1980* (New Brunswick, NJ: Rutgers University Press, 2009), 73–113.

19. Jennifer Nelson, *Women of Color and the Reproductive Rights Movement* (New York: New York University Press, 2003), 66–67.

20. Davis, *Women, Race, and Class*, 206.

21. Nadasen, *Welfare Warriors*, 219–22.

22. The Combahee River Collective, "A Black Feminist Statement," 13.

23. Loretta Ross, "A Personal Journey from Women's Rights to Civil Rights and Human Rights," Black Scholar 36.1 (2006): 45–72.

24. Ross, interview by Joyce Follet, 35–36.

25. Loretta Ross, interview with author, March 2, 2009.

26. Ross, interview by Joyce Follet, 71.

27. Ross, "A Personal Journey," 46.

28. Nelson, *Women of Color*, 85–94, 104.

29. Ross, "A Personal Journey," 47.

30. Valk, *Radical Sisters*, 162.

31. Ross, "A Personal Journey," 48.

32. Ibid.

33. Ross interview, 2009.

34. Ross, "A Personal Journey," 49.

35. Loretta Ross, "Black Women: Why Feminism?" Nkenge Toure Papers, Box 1, Folder: "Violence Articles, SSC."

36. Ibid.

37. Loretta Ross interview with author, June 10, 2008.

38. Ross, interview by Joyce Follet, 76–77.

39. Ross interview, 2008.

40. Ross, interview by Joyce Follet, 79–80.

41. Nelson, *Women of Color*, 65–76; Roberts, *Killing the Black Body*, 89–98; Gutierrez, *Fertile Matters*, 35–54; Stern, *Eugenic Nation*, 200–209.

42. Loretta Ross, interview with author, September 21, 2007.

43. Barbara Smith and Beverly Smith, "Across the Kitchen Table: A Sister-to-Sister Dialogue." In *This Bridge Called My Back*, 126.

44. Loretta Ross, "Third World Women and Violence," Series III Writings and Speeches, Box 2, Folder 1: "Writings Printed, 1980–81, SSC."

45. Jael Silliman et al., *Undivided Rights: Women of Color Organize for Reproductive Justice* (Cambridge, MA: South End Press, 2004), 36.

46. The Alliance Against Women's Oppression grew out of the Third World Women's Alliance (TWWA). TWWA had its origins with the Student Non-Violent Coordinating Committee and was founded by Francis Beal.

47. Ross, interview by Joyce Follet, 295.

48. RCAR was founded in 1973 in response to the commitment by the Catholic Church to overturn *Roe v. Wade*. It was a coalition of thirty Christian, Jewish, and other religious bodies. See Sabrae Jenkins, "Abortion Rights, Poor Women, and Religious Diversity." In Marlene Gerber Fried, ed., *From Abortion to Reproductive Freedom* (Cambridge, MA: South End Press, 1990), 151.

49. James Risen and Judy L. Thomas, *Wrath of Angels: The American Abortion War* (New York: Basic Books, 1998), 153.

50. Barakso, *Governing NOW*, 99.

51. Ross, interview by Joyce Follet, 32.

52. Ross interview, 2007.

53. Loretta Ross, Memo: "NOW and Women of Color" draft, August 4, 1988, Series IV, Organization Files, National Organization for Women, Box 13, Folder 17: "NOW Women of Color: Miscellaneous, 1981–83," SSC.

54. Ross, interview by Joyce Follet, 186.

55. Ross interview, 2009.

56. Ross, interview by Joyce Follet, 181.

57. Ross, "NOW and Women of Color."

58. Loretta Ross, Memo: "Combating Racism," September 23, 1988, 1–9, Series IV, Organization Files, National Organization for Women, 1979–1989, Box 13, Folder 8: "Women of Color Correspondence 1979–1989," SSC.

59. Ibid., 9.

60. "Vision Statement: Women of Color Partnership Program." In Fried, ed., *From Abortion to Reproductive Freedom*, 293–94.

61. Loretta Ross, "African-American Women and Abortion." In Rickie Solinger, ed., *Abortion Wars: A Half-Century of Struggle*, 1950–2000 (Berkeley: University of California Press, 1998), 198.

62. Silliman et al., *Undivided Rights*, 37–38.
63. "Responses to Questions in IRS Letter date 5/23/88," Series III, Writings and Speeches, Box 6, Folder 11: "International Council of African Women History and Organization info., 1986–89, n.d.," SSC.
64. "Between Ourselves: The First National Conference on Women of Color and Reproductive Rights," Series IV, Organization Files, National Organization for Women, Women of Color Correspondence 1979–1989, Box 14, Folder 2: "NOW Women of Color: Between Ourselves, Women of Color and Reproductive Rights, 1987," SSC.
65. Dázon Dixon Diallo, interview with author, June 27, 2008.
66. Ross interview, 2008.
67. "Responses to Questions in IRS Letter date 5/23/88."
68. Loretta Ross, "Women of Color: An Invisible Decade of Growth," March 25, 1987, Series III, Writings, SSC.
69. Loretta Ross, "Black Women Speak Out on Abortion: Report from 'Between Our Selves' Forum, February 8, 1986," Series III, Writings and Speeches, Box 2, Folder 6: "Writings Printed, 1986," SSC.
70. Nelson, *Women of Color*, 85–111.
71. Byllye Avery, interview with author, November 2, 2007.
72. Ross, "Black Women Speak Out on Abortion."
73. Loretta Ross, "Women of Color and the Reproductive Rights Movement/9th Annual Anti-Rape Week POWER Panel," October 17, 1987, Series III, Writings and Speeches, Box 2, Folder 6: "Writings Printed, 1986," SSC.
74. Ross, interview by Joyce Follet, 187.
75. Zakiya Luna, "Marching toward Reproductive Justice: Coalitional (Re)Framing of the March for Women's Lives," *Sociological Inquiry* 80.4 (November 2010): 554–78.
76. Silliman et al., *Undivided Rights*, 144.
77. Ross interview, 2008; Ross, "African-American Women and Abortion," 193.
78. Ross, "Women of Color and the Reproductive Rights Movement/9th Annual Anti-Rape Week POWER Panel."
79. Ross, "NOW and Women of Color."
80. Ibid.
81. Ross interview, 2009.
82. Ibid.
83. Loretta Ross to Ms. Sharon Parker, National Institute for Women of Color, Washington, DC, 27 July 1988, Series IV, Organization Files, National Organization for Women 1979–1989, Box 14, Folder 8: "NOW Title IX Women of Color Coalition, 1987–88," SSC.
84. Ross, "Raising Our Voices" in Fried, ed., *From Abortion to Reproductive Freedom*, 142–43.
85. Ibid.
86. Ibid.
87. Ibid.

88. Ross, "African-American Women and Abortion," 199.

89. Ross, interview by Joyce Follet, 223.

CHAPTER 6

1. Loretta Ross, interview by Joyce Follet, transcript of video recording, November 3, 2004, Voices of Feminism Oral History Project, Sophia Smith Collection, Smith College, Northampton, MA (hereafter SSC), 208. The epigraph for this chapter is from Loretta Ross, "The Color of Choice: White Supremacy and Reproductive Justice." In INCITE! Women of Color Against Violence, ed., *The Color of Violence: The Incite! Anthology* (Cambridge, MA: South End Press, 2006), 62.

2. Jael Silliman et al., *Undivided Rights: Women of Color Organize for Reproductive Justice* (Cambridge, MA: South End Press, 2004), 1.

3. Ibid., 4.

4. Ibid., 17.

5. Zakiya Luna, "Marching toward Reproductive Justice: Coalitional (Re)Framing of the March for Women's Lives," *Sociological Inquiry* 80.4 (November 2010): 554–78.

6. Loretta Ross et al., "The 'SisterSong Collective': Women of Color, Reproductive Health, and Human Rights," *American Journal of Health Studies* 17.2 (2001): 79.

7. Luz Rodriguez, interview by Joyce Follet, transcript of video recording, June 16, 2006, Voices of Feminism Oral History Project, SSC, 33.

8. Silliman et al., *Undivided Rights*, 229.

9. "Latina Sexuality in the Context of Culture and Religion: A Proposal to the Sister Fund, Latina Roundtable on Health and Reproductive Rights," April 1997, Luz Rodriguez Papers, Box 2, Folder: "Sister Fund," SSC.

10. Silliman et al., *Undivided Rights*, 70.

11. Evan Hart, "Building a More Inclusive Women's Health Movement: Byllye Avery and the Development of the National Black Women's Health Project, 1981–1990," Ph.D. Dissertation, University of Cincinnati, 2012, 60.

12. For more on Avery's involvement in the Gainesville birthing center, see Byllye Avery, "Bearing Witness to Birth," *Women's Studies Quarterly* 36.1/2 (2008): 221–26.

13. Ibid., 42.

14. Silliman et al., *Undivided Rights*, 66–67.

15. Hart, "Building a More Inclusive Women's Health Movement," 14–15, 104.

16. Ibid., 123.

17. Silliman et al., *Undivided Rights*, 105.

18. Ibid., 144.

19. "Native Women's Reproductive Rights Coalition Project," June 12, 1991, Native American Women's Health Education Resource Center Collection, Box 6, Folder: "Native Women's Reproductive Rights," SSC.

20. See chapter 7 in Silliman et al., *Undivided Rights* for an excellent discussion of the environmental and reproductive justice activism undertaken by Native American women in the Mother's Milk Project.

21. "Native Women's Reproductive Rights Coalition Project."

22. Silliman et al., *Undivided Rights*, 217.

23. "Latina Roundtable Board Workshop," November 21, 1997, Luz Rodriguez Papers, Box 2, Folder: "Board of Directors Development Retreat," SSC.

24. "Ms. Foundation Emergency Grant," April 24, 1998, Luz Rodriguez Papers, Box 2, Folder: "Board of Directors," SSC.

25. Luz Rodriguez, interview by Joyce Follet, transcript of video recording, June 16, 2006, Voices of Feminism Oral History Project, SSC, 34.

26. "Ms. Foundation Emergency Grant."

27. "Latina Sexuality in the Context of Culture and Religion: A Proposal to the Sister Fund," April 1997, Luz Rodriguez Papers, Box 2, Folder: "Sister Fund," SSC.

28. "Concept Paper to Ford Foundation from the Latina Roundtable on Health & Reproductive Rights," August 1997, Luz Rodriguez Papers, Box 2, Folder: untitled, SSC.

29. "Latina Sexuality in the Context of Culture and Religion."

30. "The Latina Roundtable on Health & Reproductive Rights," Concept Paper to the Ford Foundation, March 1998, Luz Rodriguez Papers, Box 2, Folder: "Board Reports," SSC.

31. Luz Rodriguez, interview by Joyce Follet, transcript of video recording, June 16, 2006, Voices of Feminism Oral History Project, SSC, 22.

32. "Latina Sexuality in the Context of Culture and Religion."

33. "Board Fundraising Letter—Draft/'97–'98," n.d., Luz Rodriguez Papers, Box 2, Folder: "Latina Roundtable," SSC.

34. NAWHERC's Charon Asetoyer reported that Native American women still experienced pressure from IHS physicians to be sterilized in the 1980s and 1990s.

35. Ross et al., "The SisterSong Collective," 84; Charon Asetoyer, interview by Joyce Follet, transcript of video recording, September 2, 2005, Voices of Feminism Oral History Project, Sophia Smith Collection, 31–33.

36. Asetoyer, interview by Joyce Follet, 2005, 34.

37. Ibid.

38. Ibid., 38.

39. Ibid., 39.

40. Silliman et al., *Undivided Rights*, 4.

41. Asetoyer, interview by Joyce Follet, 2005, 7.

42. Ibid., 82.

43. "Board Fundraising Letter—Draft/'97–'98."

44. "Latina Sexuality in the Context of Culture and Religion."

45. "SisterLove Inc., Author Concept Paper," March 24, 1998, Luz Rodriguez Papers, Box 2, Folder: "Moon Lodge," SSC.

46. Dázon Dixon Diallo, interview by Loretta Ross, transcript of video recording, April 4, 2009, SSC, 6.

47. Ibid., 9.

48. Ibid., 43–44.

49. Silliman et al., *Undivided Rights*, 40.

50. Ibid.

51. Ibid., 41.

52. Loretta Ross, interview by Joyce Follet, 2004, 274.

53. Ross et al., "The SisterSong Collective," 86.

54. Loretta Ross, "The Color of Choice: White Supremacy and Reproductive Justice." In INCITE! Women of Color against Violence, ed., *The Color of Violence: The Incite! Anthology* (Cambridge, MA: South End Press, 2006), 63.

55. Silliman et al., *Undivided Rights*, 42.

56. "The Herstory of SisterSong," November 2003, Luz Rodriguez Papers, Box 1, Folder: "SisterSong Women of Color Reproductive Health Collective," SSC.

57. Kimala Price, "What Is Reproductive Justice? How Women of Color Activists Are Redefining the Pro-Choice Paradigm," *Meridians: Feminism, Race, Transnationalism* 10.2 (2010): 52.

58. Luz Rodriguez, interview by Joyce Follet, transcript of video recording, June 16, 2006, Voices of Feminism Oral History Project, SSC, 37–38.

59. Ibid.

60. Ibid., 38, 40.

61. "The Herstory of SisterSong."

62. Rodriguez, interview by Joyce Follet, 39.

63. Silliman et al., *Undivided Rights*, 7.

64. Ross et al., "The SisterSong Collective," 81.

65. Ibid., 83.

66. Ibid., 84–85.

67. Ross, interview by Joyce Follet, 2004, 299.

68. Rodriguez, interview by Joyce Follet, 2006, 71–72.

69. Ross, interview by Joyce Follet, 2004, 295.

70. Ibid., 339.

71. Ibid., 319.

72. Ibid., 318.

73. Ibid., 319.

74. Ibid.

75. Ibid.

76. Ibid., 320–21, 326; Luna, "Marching toward Reproductive Justice," 570; Price, "What Is Reproductive Justice?" 54–55.

77. Price, "What Is Reproductive Justice?" 55.

78. Ross, interview by Joyce Follet, 2004, 326.

79. Ibid., 338.

80. Ibid., 327.

81. Ibid., 339.

82. Ibid., 352.

83. Ibid., 340.

84. Luna, "Marching toward Reproductive Justice," 562.

85. Interview with Loretta Ross, May 22, 2006, as quoted in Luna, "Marching toward Reproductive Justice," 571.
86. Ross, interview by Joyce Follet, 2004, 348.
87. "Concept Paper to Ford Foundation."
88. Ross, interview by Joyce Follet, 2004, 348.
89. *SisterSong: Women of Color Reproductive Justice Collective*, at http://www.sistersong.net/index.php.

INDEX

ABCRS (Abortion Birth Control Referral Service), 11–12, 58–75, 81–97, 116, 121

abortion: access issues and, 57–59, 61–62, 68–71, 87–88, 91, 96–97, 101, 132–34, 139–57, 198; anti-abortion activism and, 76, 120–22, 125, 132–45; counseling services and, 73–74, 80, 89, 102, 131–32; FWHCs and, 12–13, 126–27; gestation views and, 82–83, 134–35, 139–40; legalization of, 57–58, 62–63, 77, 95, 98, 107; morbidity and mortality associated with, 52–53, 77, 134–38, 140–43, 181; patients' feelings about, 12, 66–67, 74–82, 84–89; reproductive autonomy and, 57, 61, 71–72, 78, 154; restrictions on, 72, 85–86, 124–25, 137, 139–45, 155–57, 181–82; *Roe v. Wade* and, 7; Seattle YWCA and, 11; techniques of, 63–65, 68, 103, 131; Women's Liberation movement and, 2, 94, 98, 168, 171, 179, 191, 198. *See also* feminist movements; health; medical care; *Roe v. Wade*

ACA (Affordable Care Act), 5, 56, 219

ACLU (American Civil Liberties Union), 184

Adams, Jacob, 135–36

Adashi, Eli, 5

Ad Hoc Committee on Menopause, 96

AFDC (Aid to Families with Dependent Children), 227n90. *See also* welfare rights movement

African Americans: Black Nationalism and, 21, 28, 46–47, 175–76, 185; contraception use and, 38, 173–79; HIV/AIDS and, 160–65, 208, 214; medical education and, 19–20; sexual violence and, 74, 95–96, 107, 173–76, 208; sterilization and, 8, 34, 38, 92–93, 117, 171–72, 179, 246n14; Tufts-Delta Health Center and, 25–36; YWCA and, 115–20. *See also* feminist movements; intersectionality; National Black Women's Health Project; women of color; *specific organizations and people*

A. H. Robins, 177–78

AIDS Hotline (Atlanta FWHC/Sister-Love), 163–65

Alan Guttmacher Institute, 79, 134

Alaska, 57, 71

Allen, Lillie, 197

Allen, Susan, 157

Alliance Against Women's Oppression, 180, 186

Alvarez Martinez, Luz, 212

AMA (American Medical Association), 45–46

American Public Health Association, 44

Amnesty International, 209

anti-abortion movement: Catholic Church and, 79, 83, 145, 156–57, 183, 247n48; civil rights movement and, 146–54; emergence of, 78–79, 89; FWHCs and, 13, 56; strategies of, 125, 133–45; violence and, 122, 132, 145–57, 159

Anzaldua, Gloria, 178–79

Appley, Elizabeth, 154–56

Aradia clinic, 12, 63, 66, 73–74, 86, 92–115, 125–27

ABOUT THE AUTHOR

Jennifer Nelson is Director of the Women's and Gender Studies Program at the University of Redlands in southern California. Her first book, *Women of Color and the Reproductive Rights Movement*, also published by NYU Press, was one of the first books to emphasize the significant influence of women of color on feminist movements in the United States. Her current research focuses the history of gendered experiences of migration, immigration, reproduction, and reproductive politics across the Mexico and United States border.

Printed in the United States
By Bookmasters